PAX ETHNICA

KARL E. MEYER

SHAREEN BLAIR BRYSAC

PAX
ETHNICA

WHERE AND HOW
DIVERSITY SUCCEEDS

PublicAffairs

New York

Editorial production by Lori Hobkirk at the Book Factory
Book design by Cynthia Young at Sagecraft

The Library of Congress has cataloged the printed edition as follows:
Meyer, Karl Ernest.
    Pax ethnica : where and how diversity succeeds / Karl E. Meyer
and Shareen Blair Brysac.—1st ed.
        p. cm.
    Includes bibliographical references and index.
    ISBN 978-1-58648-829-1 (hbk.)—ISBN 978-1-61039-048-4
(electronic)   1. Cultural pluralism.   2. Multiculturalism.   3. Ethnic
relations.   4. Ethnic conflict.   5. Peace.   I. Brysac, Shareen Blair.
II. Title.
HM1271.M4152 2012
323.11—dc23
2011042959

First Edition
Printed in the United States of America.

10 9 8 7 6 5 4 3 2 1

To our two
Christian Scientist-Episcopalian-Jewish-
Lutheran-Muslim-Non-Believer-Unitarian-
Anglo-American-French Granddaughters,

Isadora and Heloise Affejee,

our heirs apparent

CONTENTS

AUTHORS' NOTE

In its admirable fertility, the English language offers a choice of words to describe similar things and theories. Our book thus concerns human diversity, heterogeneity, pluralism, hybridization, and multiculturalism. Among these terms, we prefer the first, since the last now tends to sow discord. We seek to challenge reflexive responses, as our very title suggests. *Pax* is Latin for "peace," *ethnos* is Greek for "people." This betrothal reflects the diversity of our language, its polygamous interbreeding of Saxon, Latin, Germanic, Norse, Celtic, and a dozen other mother tongues. Over the centuries, *pax* has identified many multinational groupings: Romana, Britannica, Americana, Sovietica, Siniaca, Hispanica, Ottomana, Mongolica, and even (implausibly) Syriana. High time, in our view, for a more universal aspiration: *Pax Ethnica.*

PROLOGUE

SANE OASES IN A RABID WORLD

Out of Ireland have we come.
Great hatred, little room,
Maimed us at the start.
I carry from my mother's womb
A fanatic heart.

—WILLIAM BUTLER YEATS,
"REMORSE FOR INTEMPERATE
SPEECH" (1931)

YEATS'S LINES COULD stand as shorthand for scores of civil conflicts that fester endlessly around our world. The smaller the room, often crowded with kindred peoples, the greater the hatred.

An exasperated observer once remarked that the Holy Land possessed more history than geography; its perennially angry inhabitants could readily be squeezed into Vermont. In neighboring Lebanon (little more than an overgrown city-state) strife persists among Muslims (Sunni and Shia), Christians (four major denominations), and the Druze (a secretive community whose origins defy brief summary). Sri Lanka's Sinhalese and Tamil inhabitants have for decades wrestled for dominion of a splinter of their shared island; ditto for Greek and Turkish Cypriots. For reasons opaque to most outsiders, Serbs, Croats, Bosnians, Albanians, Macedonians, and Montenegrins tirelessly strive for mastery of microsegments of former Yugoslavia. Sadly, in historically victimized Africa, domestic contention proliferates in Kenya, Ivory

Coast, Somalia, Uganda, Angola, and Zimbabwe, as well as in the out-sized and mineral-rich Sudan, Nigeria, and the Congo. The bleak roll extends from South and East Asia to the Pacific islands (large and small) and across the seas to the backlands of Central and South America. True and mercifully, Yeats's Ireland is for the moment calm, but as the retired Dublin diplomat Ted Smyth cautioned us, sectarian diehards in the British-ruled North remain forever ready to march forty miles out of their way to be insulted.

For most of us, familiarity with these disputes breeds fatigue. Whenever violence breaks out afresh, policymakers and their journalistic choir tend to reiterate familiar mantras. They caution that such quarrels arise from deep, tangled, and ancient hatreds, and hence may be beyond reach of reason. They note that the misnamed "international community" has a record of impotence in addressing localized disputes (e.g., Somalia, Gaza, and Rwanda). Inevitably, outside powers tend to meddle, either to appease domestic lobbies and secure access to critical resources or purportedly for nationalist, ideological and humanitarian reasons—exacerbated by the rivalry of politicians anxious to pose as martial saviors. When it becomes apparent that little can be done to resolve civil disputes, would-be mediators plead for cease-fires, UN Security Council resolutions, multiparty talks, United Nations sanctions, or a new "road map"—staple formulas for buying time, removing a crisis from the overnight news cycle, and (importantly) limiting blame. When all else fails, op-ed pundits are likely to invoke the grim existential specter of a "clash of civilizations," especially regarding conflicts that embroil Christians, Muslims, Jews, Confucians, Hindus, and/or Buddhists.

––––––

OUR BOOK CONSTITUTES a forthright dissent. Succinctly phrased, we believe it is not the clash *between* but *within* civilizations that most often sows civil discord. Typically, in the struggles listed above, secular power seekers have magnified dormant if genuine historical and social grievances to aggrandize their own faith, tribe, and (not accidentally) themselves. None of this, we hasten to acknowledge, will come as a surprise to literate students of foreign affairs. Yet remarkably and curiously, little is said in the mainstream media about the obverse phenomenon: the various instances in which human ingenuity and determined statecraft have defused potentially explosive civil conflicts. Our purpose in these pages is to describe important unsung exceptions and to identify policies that might be relevant elsewhere.

Our quest for neglected oases of civility took us from Western Europe to Russia, thence to India, returning via Australia to North America. Each of our chosen examples illuminates a commonly unexplored path to ethnic comity, or so we maintain.

We first chose Flensburg in northern Germany, because this port city was for more than a century at the epicenter of a borderlands quarrel that supposedly illustrated the intractability of "ancient hatreds" (vide today's former Yugoslavia). From Napoleonic times through two world wars, the "Schleswig-Holstein Question" embroiled Europe's royal families and its headstrong national leaders, fueling interminable press and parliamentary disputes. The Question twice provoked armed conflict between Prussia and Denmark, culminating in decades of partitions, plebiscites, and prolonged German occupation. Yet presto, following World War II a newly liberated Danish government offered to swap long-contested land for peace. The result was an innovative accord with Germany's newborn Federal Republic—an agreement so successful that the world ever since has taken little notice of the once-notorious "Duchies." In sum, peace trumped territory, and our visit to Flensburg suggested that multiple loyalties and languages can be creatively reconciled.

Similarly, after the collapse of the Soviet Union, a leader of the ethnically diverse Republic of Tatarstan stretched the meaning of the spongy word "sovereignty" in an astute bargain with Moscow that gave their republic's Muslim majority and its almost as large Orthodox population an incentive to coexist peacefully (and to continue to intermarry). Tatarstan's comity contrasts with turbulent Chechnya's unending strife, a contrast underscored by the dedication of a great mosque next to a venerable cathedral inside the walled Kremlin that overlooks Kazan, the republic's inviting capital. Here the critical role has been human agency, in the guise of a canny politician who effectively made the case for sovereignty, sans independence.

We turned as well to Marseille, France's second city and home to Europe's largest Muslim community (around 240,000 of 839,000 inhabitants) along with its sizable Jewish and Orthodox Christian minorities (roughly 80,000 each, all statistics being estimates since France does not enumerate by religion or ethnicity). In the tumultuous autumn of 2005, as riots and car burnings raged through France, the contrasting calm in Marseille attracted little media attention; it was un-news. As we found, Marseille's civility derived in part from civic branding; that is, its residents conspicuously and proudly identified themselves as citizens of their city and its neighborhoods, unlike the alienated youths rioting in the soulless *banlieues* encircling Paris. This was abetted by policies crafted by three strong mayors who skillfully promoted dialogue, while also catering separately to Marseille's ethnic communities (*clientism,* in the useful French phrase).

In South Asia, we explored the Indian State of Kerala, also known as "God's Own Country," a compact sliver of land flanking the Arabian Sea, whose population of 32 million exceeds that of super-sized Australia and Canada. Not only do Kerala's diverse residents (Hindu, Muslim, Christian) flourish peacefully, but they have led the way in literacy, life expectancy, and health care within the world's most populous democracy. Their success confirms the vital roles of empowering women, mobilizing the underclass, encouraging intercommunal professional associations, and promoting skills that enable Kerala to harvest remittances from a skilled migrant workforce. Against odds and stereotypes, Kerala's voters regularly gravitate from indigenous Marxist-led coalitions to centrist Congress-led coalitions, relegating to the fringe extremist religious, communal and ultraleftist factions that have spread terror and tears elsewhere in India.

Our fifth example is Queens, New York, arguably the world's most diverse political unit, in which 2.3 million people speak 138 languages. Yet after some rough passages in past decades, the leaders of this remarkable borough have embraced diversity, turning hyphenated citizenship into a civic asset. Here we discovered an exemplary library system that provides newcomers with polyglot books, job counseling, and computer skills that together throw a lifeline to the uprooted. And here school and community boards offer a meaningful political foothold to hyphenated politicians—such as Borough President Helen Marshall, an Afro-Caribbean-American and a former librarian, whose mantra is "Visit Queens—See the World."

Finally, weighing the experience of the world's three biggest and essentially immigrant nations—Canada, Australia, and the United States—we found reassuring evidence that diversity works on many levels: economic, educational, political, and cultural (not least in the form of teenage rap, the universal language of outsiders in a changing world). The relevant wisdom of a forgotten American sage (Washington Irving) helps us to conclude with our own summary maxims on diversity.

———

YET STRANGELY AND perversely, as we were brooding on all this, the very term "multicultural" metastasized into a controversial "ism," its failings decried in early 2011 by the leaders of France, Germany, and Britain, the rhetorical sting in the tail being another contentious word, "identity." As phrased by President Nicholas Sarkozy in a television interview, "If you come to France, you accept to melt into a single community, which is the national community, and if you do not want to accept that, you are not welcome in France. We have been too concerned about the identity of the person who was arriving, and not enough about the identity of the country that was receiving him." Chancellor Angela Merkel earlier pronounced multiculturalism "an utter failure" during a nationwide debate stirred by a best-selling book written by a German central banker averring that Muslim immigrants made his country "stupider." Merkel's comments were echoed in Britain by Prime Minister David Cameron, who claimed that "under the doctrine of state multiculturalism, we have encouraged different cultures to live separate lives, apart from each other and the mainstream."

On its surface, this disillusion is paradoxical since the European Union is itself a vibrant example of multiculturalism, a mingling of twenty republics and six monarchies whose five hundred million citizens speak twenty-three official languages, three of which (English, German, and French) are working languages. The creation of the European Union formed a redeeming epilogue to a European century scarred by ruinous wars, tyranny, dispossession, and genocide; fittingly, the

Union's anthem is Beethoven's "Ode to Joy." Any possessor of a member-state passport can settle and work in any other member state, with culinary benefits visible (and edible) in all EU capitals. The ubiquitous "Polish plumber" has long since become a familiar target of mostly good-natured jibes (west of the River Elbe).

No, it is not the Slavs or the Celts or the Hellenes that provoke lamentations about "multiculturalism." It is a specific minority: the predominantly Muslim, non-European migrants who began arriving in Europe in large numbers after World War II. These newest arrivals and their offspring today comprise around 7.5 percent of France's population, 5 percent of Germany's, and 4.6 percent of Great Britain's. So reckons the respected Pew Research Center (as of January 2011), though all such figures are estimates since definitions are plastic as to what beliefs and which genes identify a Muslim. Incontestably, as Islamic subcultures have multiplied so has European concern about a possibly hostile incubus.

A quasi-populist backlash has spread from the Baltic to the Adriatic, abetting avowedly anti-immigrant political parties whose leaders claim that secretive and sullen Islamic interlopers are responsible for rising crime, juvenile delinquency, and the abuse of women through forced marriages and honor killings. At the movement's apocalyptic fringe, some discern a Muslim conspiracy to overwhelm Europe through sheer fertility, the goal being to impose Islamic law, avenge centuries of colonial exploitation, and give birth to a baleful "Eurabia." Played down by alarmists is the soft factual base for their worst-case scenarios. Discounted or ignored are repeated surveys indicating that the most Muslim newcomers are either secularist or minimally observant, and that most aspire to a normal life within their host countries. Minimized is the hard fact that Islam, like Christianity, revels in diversity, and that its adherents are of many quarrelsome minds.

The great youthful tsunami that swept through the Middle East in 2011 offered a test of the bleak forebodings about political Islam. No sooner had a Tunisian fruit vendor drenched himself in gasoline and lit the match that ignited a rebellion in nearby Egypt than pessimists foresaw the hidden hand of the Muslim Brotherhood. In the event, the popular revolt that deposed President Hosni Mubarak was notable for its ecumenical breadth. As reported in *The Economist,* thousands of protesters in Cairo defied both brutal police and the outspoken disapproval of the aging clerisy of the Muslim Brotherhood: "Only after impatient younger members went ahead, joining secular groups that launched the demonstrations, did the [Brotherhood's] leaders throw their weight into the struggle."

Not only did Muslims and Coptic Christians mingle joyfully at that time (as the British weekly commented) but they found a unifying imagery in the rap ballads in Arabic circulating on the Internet that spoke of honor and freedom, as for example: "From every street in my country/ The sound of freedom calls/ We broke all boundaries/ Our weapon was our dreams." As we also discovered in our travels, the border-penetrating potency of rhyming rap, along with social networks and text messaging, has fostered a parallel global counterculture that unites the young against their generally baffled, often disapproving, and surreptitiously envious elders.

Still, even if rap, YouTube and Facebook are quintessential American exports, this linkage offers no assurance that the emerging leaders of a new Middle East will look kindly on Washington, given its decades of coddling Arab autocrats and ritually defending Israel. Not only are the region's youthful victors untested and democratic institutions weak, but persistent joblessness in failing economies can turn springtime optimism into winter despair. And for better or worse, the predominantly Muslim Arab heartland, given its resources and geography, is indissolubly linked to the non-Muslim West. Hence the perceived ill-treatment of Muslim minorities in Europe and America would risk reciprocal countermoves in the Middle East and heighten threats to an already isolated Israel. The more reason, in our view, for Westerners to study some of the creative, civilized, and noncondescending examples of peaceful diversity portrayed in our book.

———

GOING FURTHER, promoting multiethnic civility is not just a high–minded human rights issue or a coldly self-serving geopolitical policy. At its most basic level, what happens to ethnic minorities on disputed frontiers and the related proliferation of formally sovereign states has become a familiar source of strife in the postcolonial and post-Soviet world in which we all live. At its formation in 1945, the United Nations had 51 charter members. As of 2011, the total was 193, with Palestine, Kosovo, and two breakaway states in Georgia among the supplicants knocking at the door. Every UN member, be it large or a flyspeck, has but one vote in the General Assembly—the flyspecks including Nauru (8.1 square miles, population 9,267), Palau (177 square miles, population 20,879), Tuvalu (26 square miles, population 10,472), and Vanuatu (4,710 square miles, population 243,304). The proliferation of these flags constitutes a victory for nationalism and its linked doctrine of self-determination, the twin pillars of a supposedly globalized world that teeters unsteadily on some two hundred sovereign states.

The danger that the weak, poor, and failed states pose to global peace became evident long ago. An unlikely pair of witnesses can be summoned: the exiled Russian anarchist Mikhail Bakunin (1814–1876) and America's longtime doyen of foreign affairs commentary Walter Lippmann (1889–1974). At the twilight of his revolutionary career Bakunin in 1870 warned a younger comrade "Beware of small states." He cautioned that weaker states were invariably vulnerable to being manipulated by bigger neighbors, but that they could also strike back and wound their tormentors, his examples being Belgium and Latvia. For a more recent example, we might recall Fidel Castro's Cuba during the 1962 missile crisis. In an epilogue Bakunin could not have imagined, successive crises in small or weak states, each involving great power manipulations, led directly to World War I. Imperial Germany cheered Boer guerrillas and Irish rebels against Great Britain; imperial Russia conspired with Britain to carve Persia into zones of influence; Germany dueled with France and Britain over the Third Republic's annexation of Morocco—and fatefully, in the wake of two Balkan wars, Russia sided with its ally Serbia when a Belgrade-trained assassin killed Archduke Ferdinand in Sarajevo; this was the spark igniting the Great War. (Fortunately for humanity, President John F. Kennedy in 1962 had just read Barbara Tuchman's *Guns of August*, narrating this sequence, and during the Cuban crisis, kept asking his hawkish military advisers what might follow if US warplanes actually bombed Soviet-installed missile bases.)

It chanced that Walter Lippmann, recently graduated from Harvard, was present in London as Prime Minister Herbert Asquith's Liberal Government declared war on the Central Powers in August 1914, the casus belli being Germany's invasion of neutral Belgium. Commenting in *The Stakes of Diplomacy,* published the following year, Lippmann remarked on a reality he feared might seem a paradox to many readers:

> that the anarchy of the world is due to the backwardness of weak states; that the modern nations have lived in an armed peace and collapsed into hideous warfare because in Asia, Africa, the Balkans, Central and South America there are rich territories in which weakness invites exploitation, in which inefficiency and corruption invite imperial expansion, in which the prizes are so great that the competition for them is to the knife. This is the world problem upon which all schemes for arbitration, leagues of peace, reduction of armaments, must prove themselves.

Welcome to 2012! Of all peoples, Americans have the most reason to ponder the earth's multiplying weak states, since most owe their nationhood to doctrines made in the USA. In 1918, President Woodrow Wilson told a cheering joint session of Congress that "National aspirations must be respected; peoples may now be dominated and governed only by their own consent. 'Self-determination' is not a mere phrase. It is an imperative principle of action, which statesmen will henceforth ignore at their own peril." His words caught fire, his "mere phrase" which Lenin had earlier endorsed became official Bolshevik policy articulated by Joseph Stalin, the first Soviet commissar of nationalities, and author in 1913 of *Marxism and the National and Colonial Question.* There was a catch: Wilson really meant it, while in Soviet times self-determination was in truth a mere phrase, until taken literally by the collapsing USSR's many ethnic republics in the 1990s. As we learned while visiting Tatarstan, arguments over the phrase still resonate. Indeed, by an historic irony, if measured by his imprint on global maps, Wilson proved a more successful revolutionary than Lenin. This was in part because in the consensual interpretation, "self-determination" has been continually linked to "nationalism," the true tiger in our sovereign world's forest.

———

NO IDEOLOGY HAS borne stranger fruits than nationalism. It has liberated and enslaved, enriched and impoverished, and spawned unifying songs and pernicious theories that incite genocide. Yet its roots, by historical measure, are shallow. According to the *Oxford English Dictionary*, the term first surfaced in an 1844 magazine article claiming that "nationalism is another word for egotism." Tellingly, the OED's third citation is from an 1853 book by John Henry Newman, in which he declared that the Muslim religion is "essentially the consecration of the principle of nationalism." The principle remained so novel that the magisterial eleventh edition of the *Encyclopedia Britannica* (1910) contains only a one-paragraph entry entitled "Nationality," defined as "a somewhat vague term, used strictly in international law." (The brief entry added prophetically that "nationality" also refers to "an aggregation of persons claiming to represent a racial, territorial or some other bond of unity, though not necessarily recognized as an independent political entity. In this latter sense, the word has often been applied to such peoples as the Irish, the Armenians and the Czechs.")

Astonishingly, this novel term within a few decades "developed into the greatest emotional-political force of the age." So reflected George F. Kennan, looking back during the 1990s at his long career, initially as a young diplomat who in 1934 helped open America's first embassy in the Soviet Union, and who served in Hitler's Berlin, Stalin's Moscow, and Tito's Yugoslavia. Kennan drew a careful distinction between patriotic love of country and "morbid nationalism," marked by pseudoreligious incantations, truculent intolerance, and warlike posturing. This "diseased form of nationalism" in his view was a fundamental cause of World War I, "the great formative catastrophe of European civilization."

What gestated nationalism in all its forms was the concept's association with the American and French Revolutions, both rooted in the radical belief that ordinary people were the ultimate source and judge of sovereign rule. Its rise coincided with industrialization, increasing literacy, and the spread of urban culture, so writes the Johns Hopkins

University scholar Michael Mandelbaum, who adds that nationalism, like the modern state, began in the West but spread to every corner of the globe. He expresses a consensual academic view:

> The national principle for determining borders is also a liberal one. It stands in contrast to the traditional method, whereby hereditary rulers drew lines arbitrarily, heedless of the wishes of the people affected. The national principle responds to what are, in most cases, popular wishes, since people ordinarily prefer to be grouped with others like themselves. National self-determination may be seen as democracy applied to the task of allocating sovereignty.

Well, yes. But Mandelbaum also acknowledges that self-determination has a serious flaw "since there is no clear definition of a nation, no universally accepted way of deciding which group deserves its own state, and which does not. . . . It would scarcely be possible to honor all such claims. The result would be international chaos, the specter of which offered a powerful argument in favor of keeping existing borders intact." Yes, again, but in any case the result is just short of chaos.

Few public figures dwelled more thoughtfully on the resulting conundrum than Daniel Patrick Moynihan, a onetime professor of government at Harvard, later ambassador to the United Nations and to India, and then New York's Democratic senator (1977–2001). To learn more about the doctrine's origins, senator Moynihan asked the Library of Congress to excavate the unpublished diaries of Robert Lansing (1864–1928), President Wilson's Secretary of State. A New York attorney and a moderate Democrat, Lansing was a founder of the American Society for International Law, whose journal he edited for twenty years.

Lansing listened as Wilson informed the world that self-determination was "not a mere phrase." He confided to his diary on December 30, 1918, that the president's phrase was "simply loaded with dynamite." Since he did not specify what unit he had in mind, the words "will raise hopes that can never be realized. It will, I fear, cost thousands of lives. . . . What a calamity that the phrase was ever uttered! What misery it will cause!" A year later at the Paris Peace Conference, Wilson himself grappled with the perplexities of his doctrine. Egyptian reformers appealed directly to him for permission to address the conferees, as did Persian and Irish nationalists (all requests blocked by the British). When an Irish-American delegation appeared in Paris to protest the British veto, Wilson's response was recorded by Francis Patrick Welsh, a lawyer who had served in the wartime labor relations board: "When I gave utterance to those words, I said them without knowledge that nationalities existed that are coming to us day after day. . . . You do not know, and cannot appreciate the anxieties I have experienced of these many millions of people having their hopes raised by what I said."

Moynihan's researches culminated in a slim, impassioned volume: *Pandaemonium: Ethnicity in International Politics* (1993), named after the capital of hell in Milton's *Paradise Lost.* In its pages, the senator cited a scholar's finding that only seven states evidently had no border problems: Denmark, Iceland, Japan, Luxembourg, the Netherlands, Norway, and Portugal. Yet if Danes made the list, it was only because a decent end was finally written to a notorious quarrel with Germany concerning the political and language rights of ethnic minorities straddling a shared frontier. This was the Schleswig-Holstein dispute, involving a splinter of land (7,338 square miles) on the Jutland peninsula. It anticipated many of the issues that sow discord in today's world, most especially demagogic assertions of alleged harassment of minorities. Not only did it precipitate two wars in the nineteenth century, but no fewer than ten European powers and their hereditary rulers were entangled in the dispute (Great Britain, Denmark, Prussia, Russia, France, Austria, Spain, Belgium, Portugal, and Italy). So convoluted was "The Schleswig-Holstein Question" that its history consumed six oversize pages in tiny agate print in the monumental 11th edition of the *Encyclopedia Britannica* (1910).

An informed American assessment of "The Question" is afforded by the eminent educator and diplomat, Andrew Dickson White, the founding president of Cornell University and (among his attainments) Washington's first ambassador (1897–1902) to a newly united, and rising, German Empire. Of the myriad subjects that tormented statesmen of his era, White recalled in 1910, Schleswig-Holstein proved "the most vexatious":

Its intricacies were proverbial. . . . There were rights to sovereignty under Danish Law and estoppels under Salic Law; rights under German Law and extinguishments by treaty or purchase; claims to the Schleswig Duchy as adjoining Denmark and containing a considerable admixture of Danish blood; claims to the Holstein Duchy as adjoining Germany and thoroughly of German blood. . . . Throughout Denmark it was fanatically held that control of the duchies should be Danish; throughout Germany, it was no less passionately asserted that it should be German. Learned lawyers wrote convincing opinions on either side; on both sides orators moved men to desperation with the wrongs of "our Schleswig-Holstein brothers"; poets wrote songs, both in Germany and Denmark, which "got themselves sung" with fervor, with rage—even with tears.

Moreover, the conflict's initial resolution had an enduring significance. In the words of Oxford's A. J. P. Taylor, writing in *The Struggle for Mastery of Europe 1848–1918*, it was Prussian Chancellor Otto von Bismarck's conquest of Schleswig-Holstein that "announced the rise of Germany nationalism, which was to eclipse all others." German nationalism attained its crescendo during Hitler's Third Reich, whose death throes, by uncanny symmetry, occurred in Flensburg, the cultural center of Schleswig. And yet, since 1945 peace has prevailed in the duchies. How and why? What tamed the passions that for centuries sowed discord between Denmark and Germany?

We decided early on to visit Flensburg, and we came upon an unexpected answer to our questions.

1

FLENSBURG: LAND OR PEACE?

Only three people have really ever understood the Schleswig-Holstein business—the Prince Consort, who is dead—a German professor who has gone mad—and I, who have forgotten all about it.

—ATTRIBUTED TO LORD PALMERSTON,
AS QUOTED IN LYTTON STRACHEY,
QUEEN VICTORIA (1921)

SAY "FLENSBURG" to even the well-traveled American, and you are likely to get a blank look. Nautical-minded Germans know the South Jutland city for its picture-book harbor and fjord; its fine ship museum; and not least, its seafood restaurants. Like many visitors, we dined at Piet Henningsen, established in 1886, its gleaming tables evoking the well-scrubbed galleys of the port's once-formidable mercantile fleet. Giant stuffed turtles and crocodiles hang from the restaurant's ceiling; the walls are adorned with African leopard skins and Polynesian weaponry, attesting to the global reach of the city's sailors. Flensburg's past prosperity owed much to an annual harvest of herrings, and even more to the sale of rum distilled from sugarcane imported from the Danish Virgin Islands. A tourist exploring this tranquil town of some 90,000 inhabitants, with its cobbled byways, seven museums, and seasonal street musicians would hardly guess that Flensburg lay at the heart of northern Europe's oldest established dynastic duel, a contest generating invasions and occupations, sieges and riots, repression and plebiscites and begetting a landfill of mostly unread books.

The dispute over the Duchies is not merely dusty history. To a surprising degree, most of the elements inflaming today's angry clash over "identity" propelled this forgotten dispute: demagogic politicians, press rivalry, quarrels over language rights, and cold-eyed or misguided diplomatic realpolitik—a major difference then being the complicating role of royalty.

This is what truly brought us to Flensburg: to learn more of the Schleswig-Holstein dispute and its stirring, forgotten, and significant postscript. The story can be briefly told. Having long coveted the "Duchies" (as everybody called Schleswig and Holstein), Prussia seized these lands in two nineteenth-century wars that signaled the rise of united Germany and its Iron Chancellor, Otto von Bismarck. Then, in plebiscites conducted after the Allied victory in the Great War, German speakers in picture-book South Schleswig voted to remain part of a new Weimar Republic, a decision consistent with the doctrine of self-determination promoted by Woodrow Wilson. However, this obliged democratic-minded Danish speakers to submit to Nazi rule following Hitler's 1933 seizure of power. The pivotal moment occurred after V-E Day, when the British offered liberated Danes the choice of annexing the contested, predominantly German-speaking borderlands, and Copenhagen's leaders said no—on condition that the newborn Bonn Republic provided guarantees that the cultural and civil rights of Danish speakers would be respected. Did this peace-for-land swap succeed? We wanted to find out.

We first came upon a discreet reminder of Flensburg's tumultuous past in walking along the city's bustling waterfront. A small brass doorplate at Schiffbrücke 12 identified its enclosing stone-and-tile seventeenth–century building as the home of the European Centre for Minority Issues (ECMI), our initial port of call. Established on December 4, 1996, on the initiative of Germany and Denmark, the ECMI pays explicit homage to the rare act of reconciliation just described, since minority communities were stranded on both sides of Jutland's long-disputed frontiers. And in the 1990s, as Europe was shaken by the Balkan wars and by ethnic-based confrontations elsewhere, these half-forgotten accords "suddenly became relevant," in the words of Ewa Chylinski, the ECMI's deputy director.

We met with Ms. Chylinski and her colleagues in their offices, walled with books and filing cabinets, which overlook the Flensburg waterfront. Among our questions: Just what brought about those accords? Had reconciliation succeeded? If so, what were its lessons? A woman of middle years with focused eyes, Deputy Director Chylinski, a Danish national, spoke with an authority honed by her own background as a human rights officer and field researcher in the Caucasus and Central Asia as well as Eastern Europe. "If you start your book with Schleswig-Holstein, you are making the right choice," she told us. "The situation we have here is interesting. It could be called nonterritorial or functional autonomy." As she amplified, this autonomy was not promised in a binding treaty but derived from declarations of intent signed by West Germany and Denmark, generating legislation that affirmed the rights of respective minorities to their own languages, schools, and organizations.

An aide produced a book, *Living Together: The Minorities in the German-Danish Border Regions,* published by the ECMI in 2001. The appendix reprints the full text of the Bonn-Copenhagen Declarations of April 1, 1955, these being the key clauses relating to the Danish minority inhabiting the German state of Schleswig-Holstein:

> It shall be possible to freely profess one's loyalty to the Danish people and Danish Culture and such profession of loyalty shall not be contested or verified by an official authority. Members of the Danish minority and their organizations may not be hindered from speaking and writing in the language of their choice. The use of the Danish language in courts and administrative agencies shall be governed by the relevant legal provisions.
>
> In respect of financial assistance and other benefits from public funds on which discretionary decision is taken, members of the Danish minority may not be treated differently from other citizens. The special interest of the Danish minority in fostering contacts with Denmark in the religious and cultural as well as in specialist fields shall be acknowledged.

Were the pledges honored? Yes, so we were told, in both letter and spirit. If so, did this success offer lessons to other troubled societies? On the tactical level, certainly. Most important, what could explain the turn-about over Schleswig-Holstein? Surely this was the overriding question.

––––––

WE TURNED FIRST to two legislators belonging to the Danish minority's political party—the South Schleswig Voters' Association (SSW)—Lars Erik Bethge and Anke Spoorendonk. Yes, they said, SSW is fully represented at the local and state level, even though the Danish community numbers at most 50,000 persons, a fraction of Schleswig-Holstein's 2.83 million population. According to Bethge, one of four SSW members in the Landtag (the state legislature), his party has also reached out to win votes from non-Danish minorities and from the dis-gruntled in the German majority. Success ignited a controversy in 2005. "The Landtag was closely divided," Bethge said, "and the SSW decided to support a new minority [left of center] coalition. Elsewhere in Ger-many, conservative politicians began demanding, 'How is it possible that a Danish person can decide a German government?' I even had to get a bodyguard. Well, there was a secret ballot, and it turned out that our vote was not really decisive." The dispute faded, and in the 2009 general election, the SSW held its own, winning 69,000 votes. (The German minority in Denmark, numbering about 15,000, also has its own regional Schleswig Party. When in the late 1970s it lost its sole seat in the Folketing, or national parliament, a special office was created in 1983 and a senior official appointed, tasked with speaking for the Germans.)

How then about the cultural promises? "First of all," said Bethge, "ours has always been a multicultural society. You never had a pure Dan-ish, nor a pure German society, even when we were part of Denmark. My grandfather, for example, was from North Jutland, and was defi-nitely Danish. Yet he became German during Prussian times in North Schleswig. He joined the Young German movement after the First World War—yet after the Second War, he said, 'I'm going back to my roots—now I'm Danish.' So you have this mobility. . . . What we can teach people here is that you can change, and that's important. It applies to newer migrants as well; it's no longer a novelty to have two passports."

At this point in our interview, Bethge was joined by his legislative partner, Anke Spoorendonk. "My own history is similar," she said. "My family comes from [the city of] Schleswig, and had some connection with the Danish minority during the 1920s, but not much. But after 1945, my parents said, 'We want to be part of the Danish community,' and they learned Danish as grownups. I always spoke Danish with my mother, and German with my father."

Bethge added: "Somebody used the image of an onion to describe the Danish minority, because you have some people who only watch Danish television and live a pure Danish life, and maybe they don't even speak German well. Our older generation married within the minority, but today you marry whom you like. So you peel through different layers, one in which you are Danish, and another when you become part of the majority. And," he added, "at the onion's core, we tell Danish jokes."

Spoorendonk elaborates: "Then you also make translating jokes and sit together changing your language as much as you like, and everyone understands what you are saying. Yes, it's okay. We like it."

We asked about Danish-language schools and history texts. Spoorendonk, a former schoolteacher, said that in 2009 there were fifty-five Danish kindergartens, forty-eight primary schools, and two high schools with a grand total of 5,655 students. Concerning textbooks Spoorendonk said, "I've taught history for many years, but naturally we have German textbooks for German history." How does one deal with conflicts past? It hasn't been easy, she said. A committee was formed, and it produced a small book on how to handle German-Danish history: "It was about a hundred pages long, and it dealt not with conflicts but with harmony; it was too neat. You can laugh about it, but the problem remains."

What is inarguable is that the 1955 declarations proved a precedent for extending recognition to other minorities in Schleswig-Holstein, initially to upwards of 11,000 Frisians, the hardy descendants of North Sea seafarers who continue to speak what is deemed the closest thing to Anglo-Saxon English (e.g., Frisian for "cow," "lamb," "goose," "boat," and "dung" is *ko, lam, goes, boat,* and *dong*). Now Frisian is recognized as a legal language in law courts and is beginning to appear on multilingual street signs. Other recognized minorities include the nomadic

Roma and Sinti, and recently arrived migrant workers, many of them Muslims. (According to Ms. Chylinski, "Our shipyards in Flensburg have more Turkish and Balkan employees than Germans.")

———

NEXT, WE WONDERED, What role has Denmark played in assisting its kinfolk in Schleswig? To learn more, we proceeded to the Danish Consulate, housed in an imposing stone building cresting a hill overlooking the Flensburg harbor. A seasoned career diplomat, Consul Henrik Becker-Christiansen proved to be a historian by temper and training, with a special interest in borderland disputes. Gracious in manner, elegant in dress, he first showed us maps of South Jutland, some dating to the early Middle Ages (Flensburg's charter is dated 1284), indicating that Schleswig was part of Denmark, while Holstein was a fief of the Germano-Roman Empire.

In the fifteenth century, the two duchies were joined under feudal law into a single union linked to the Danish crown, a claim fiercely and persistently contested by Germans. The argument reopened during the Napoleonic wars. When the victors convened in Vienna in 1815 to redefine Europe's frontiers, the duchies were divorced: Schleswig going to Denmark and Holstein to a newborn German Confederation. "In the 1830s," the consul told us, "nationalism reared its head, and Germany began to insist that Schleswig and Holstein were both German, while Danes held that their border should be at the Eider River, which would incorporate all of Schleswig." The dispute provoked a war in 1848, and a second, bloodier invasion in 1864 that ended with the forcible Prussian annexation of both duchies. Nationalism was the pretext, but the subtext was Chancellor Otto von Bismarck's determination to turn a newly united Germany into a global rival of Great Britain, France, and Russia. In 1890, the Iron Chancellor was forced to resign by Kaiser Wilhelm II, who proved even more eager to challenge his grandmother Victoria's huge empire, most especially its naval mastery. By absorbing Schleswig-Holstein and its key ports at Kiel and Flensburg, the German navy in a stroke became the overlord of the Baltic Sea. The duchy's strategic value was then tripled by the completion in

1895 of a sixty-mile canal linking Kiel, along with its budding naval base and shipyards, to the North Sea.

"Until World War I, the Germans did their best to suppress their Danish minority and turn its members into good German citizens," Consul Becker-Christiansen continued. "All schools were in German; you could not fly the Danish flag; Danish journalists who were nationalists were jailed." At war's end, Danish grievances resonated empathetically among Allied leaders at the 1919 Paris Peace Conference. A provision of the Versailles Treaty called for conducting two plebiscites, a month apart, the first in northern Schleswig and the second in the southern zone. Clamorous demonstrations broke out as voting took place in February and March 1921, yielding a split verdict. In the north, 75 percent favored reunification with Denmark while in the south, 80 percent voted to remain within Germany. Even in Flensburg, a Danish stronghold in South Schleswig, only one in four voters chose Denmark. Schleswig's division thus was sealed, and its south solidly welded into Germany years before the National Socialists overthrew the liberal Weimar Republic in 1933. Out of prudence rather than principle, the Nazis in succeeding years resisted the clamor among Germans in Schleswig, north and south, to revise the border and annex the rest of the duchy. Denmark was Germany's larder, a vital source of meat and milk, and Hitler was wary of gratuitous actions during the 1930s that might fuel anger among Swedes, Norwegians, and Finns.

When World War II broke out in 1939, "We were living in the shadow of the Third Reich. They could take Denmark like this," the consul told us as he snapped his fingers. On April 9, 1940, the Nazis devoured Denmark in an undeclared assault launched through North Schleswig, abetted by a Germanic Fifth Column. Armed resistance was minimal, but most of Denmark's overseas shipping fleet, comprising 230 ships and 100 fishing vessels, made for British ports and thereafter served under the Allied flag. Initially Denmark was permitted a degree of autonomy under velvet-gloved rule, but as Hitler's war widened, the gloves came off. By 1943, the covert Danish Freedom Council mobilized a resistance of 43,000 fighters who waged an effective sabotage campaign and rescued nearly the entire Danish Jewish community. By war's end, an estimated 20,000 Danish fugitives from the Gestapo had reached neutral Sweden. But not all Danes joined the Allies. Postwar, liberation tribunals jailed some 3,000 Danes on charges of criminal collaboration with the Nazis. German property was seized and suspect institutions were closed. It constituted a substantial, if not complete, reckoning.

By a bizarre twist, Hitler's Thousand-Year Reich breathed its last in Flensburg. Here, for two weeks the Führer's chosen successor, Admiral Karl Doenitz, headed the remnants of the collapsing Nazi empire until Germany's unconditional surrender on May 7, 1945. Such was the context in September 1946 when British officials asked a newly and freely elected Danish government if it wished to repossess all Schleswig, with its key ports and Germanic inhabitants. Fearing a future of continuous trouble with an aggrieved and violence-prone minority, the Danes responded (in the consul's words), "No, we do not want to change the border." At that time, wartime bad blood still persisted between Danes and Germans, but passions cooled as Denmark unilaterally guaranteed minority rights, later to be reaffirmed in the aforementioned joint Bonn-Copenhagen Declarations.

Moreover, Copenhagen has honored its promises with cash; Denmark currently provides the equivalent of $80 million annually to assist Danish-language schools in German Schleswig-Holstein. "Relations are now better than ever," Consul Becker-Christiansen said, "with occasional flare-ups over national memorial days and battle monuments—and of course, the famous lion." What lion? He explained that an outsize stone lion commemorating the Danish victory in the Battle of Isted on July 25, 1850, once presided at Flensburg's military cemetery until it was taken as a trophy to Berlin after the Prussian victory in 1864. Eighty-one years later, US occupation authorities presented the lion as a gift to the Danish king. The huge beast and its heraldic arms were eventually replanted before a royal library in Copenhagen. In June 2009, the Flensburg city council by majority vote requested the lion's repatriation, and negotiations for its return were under way during our visit. Finally, the Danish government agreed in 2011 to repatriate the Isted Lion to its original pedestal at the Flensburg military cemetery, where its bronze eyes will once again gaze south, toward Prussia. Thus did an eight-century-long quarrel dwindle into a debate over where to locate a mostly forgotten stone memorial to a long deceased border war.

––––––

BUT HERE ONE MUST PAUSE: vital matters tend to be glazed over in this generally positive account. For one, Denmark's decision in 1946 not to follow the victor's prerogative and redraw prewar borders was not simply a rational and civilized gesture. It was a decision that ran against the grain of our modern era, beginning with the surging tides of nationalism in the nineteenth century. In effect, in today's diplomatic language, Danish politicians willingly traded land for peace—not just an unusual happening, but one rarely emulated among successive generations of even the best-intentioned statesmen and stateswomen.

A commonplace reality helps explain why embattled political leaders turn so reflexively to voluble claims for a Greater State/Nation/Kingdom/Republic incorporating disputed borderlands. Whether elected or authoritarian, politicians frequently contend with domestic grievances that resist ready solutions or even amelioration: collapsed economies, egregious inequalities, inadequate schools, lack of hospitals and highways or electricity and potable water. For embattled leaders everywhere, a time-tested diversion is to remind the disaffected that hated enemies are being punished and ancient wrongs avenged, and in any case that their own tribe is purer and better than its rivals. In Dr. Johnson's oft-quoted axiom, patriotism is the last refuge of a scoundrel (to which America's Ambrose Bierce objected, commenting that patriotism was in fact the first refuge).

A short list of disputed territories would include Romania's Transylvania; all the frontiers of Poland; the embattled armistice lines of Kashmir; the Western Sahara; all the frontiers of Syria, Lebanon, and Israel; the Himalayan boundaries separating India and China; the islands of Cyprus and Taiwan; two breakaway republics within Georgia; all the frontiers of the Congo; the jungle boundaries demarcating Venezuela, Colombia, Guyana, and Brazil; and even the frozen tundra of Antarctica. An old European diplomatic adage held that no frontier was considered entirely safe unless it made a future war inescapable, as did

Alsace-Lorraine; East Prussia; Bohemia's Sudetenland; the City of
Danzig and its problematic Corridor; the Nagorno-Karabakh enclave in
Azerbaijan; and more recently Kosovo, the Balkan successor to the once
bitterly contested seaport of Fiume (or Rijeka) on the Adriatic Coast.

Add to this equation the potent allure of a flag, notably to dispersed
kindred peoples, as attested by the Austrian-born Theodor Herzl
(1860–1904), the founder of political Zionism. In a letter unearthed by
Amos Elon, his Israeli biographer, Herzl spoke presciently in 1895
about designing a flag:

> You might ask mockingly: "A flag? What's that? A stick with a rag on
> it?" No sir, a flag is much more. With a flag you lead men . . . for a
> flag, men live and die. In fact it is the only thing for which they are
> ready to die in masses, if you train them for it. Believe me, the politics
> of an entire people—especially a people scattered all over the earth—
> can be manipulated only through imponderables that float in thin air.
> Do you know what went into the making of the German Empire?
> Dreams and songs, reveries of black, red and gold banners, all in a very
> short time. Bismarck merely shook the tree that visionaries planted.

Still, by any fair reckoning it was not just dreams and songs that
gave birth to the Second Reich. Bismarck did more than merely shake
that tree—he watered and pruned it. This leads to a second vital matter
glazed over in the consensual retelling of the Schleswig-Holstein saga.
Sectarian strife does not level cities and lead spontaneously to genocide;
it is willed by human agency. In the words of Gordon Craig, for years
the doyen of American historians of Germany, even if Bismarck "had
never risen to the top of Prussian politics, the unification of Germany
would probably have taken place anyway, but not at the same time or in
quite the same way." It was the Iron Chancellor who, more than anybody, determined the new empire's character, ignited its untrammeled
nationalism, and provided a prototype for worse despots to come. In
doing so, he used a bold and unusual political weapon: he spelled out
his goals clearly and frankly and then proceeded to carry out his program, step by determined step, while his wide-eyed compatriots and
disbelieving opponents looked on. In so doing, Bismarck was assisted

by a Europe-wide network of allies and opponents in a struggle that was to color Europe's maps. Thus by failing to stress the unbridled furies that set Danes against Germans in South Jutland, the narrative of today's reconciliation would be incomplete, a Hamlet without the Prince of Denmark.

––––––

TO GRASP THESE multiple dynamics, one needs to flash backward to 1848, a year celebrated for its contagious revolutions and remembered as the "Springtime of Peoples." Not accidentally, these upheavals coincided with the European debut of railroads and telegraphy, which enabled rebels and ideas to fly across frontiers like sparks in a hayrack. Early in 1848, friends of freedom and foes of hereditary privilege brought down a king in France; challenged Prussia's autocracy; struggled to unify Italy; and roused Poles, Czechs, and Hungarians against their Austrian and/or Russian masters. On the movement's left flank, Karl Marx and his partner Friedrich Engels published their epochal summons to the proletariat, *The Communist Manifesto,* with its opening thunderclap ("A spectre is haunting Europe—the spectre of Communism") and its primal catechism ("The history of all hitherto existing society is the history of class struggle").

In May, five hundred deputies to a self-anointed National Assembly, claiming to speak for a phantom Germanic Union, convened in Frankfurt at St. Paul's Church, the only building with space sufficient for the delegates and their swarm of aides. In the words of Andrew White, the first US ambassador to a united Germany, "Rarely has any public body contained so many men of profound thought and high ideals; rarely has any public body contained so few members of practical experience; never was there a more discouraging failure." As the year progressed, so did uncertainty in Frankfurt as to what was occurring elsewhere and how to proceed. This was notably the case regarding the Duchies. In January, Frederick VII ascended the Danish throne, becoming the last of his male line. He then honored his father's deathbed wishes and announced plans for instituting a liberal new constitution, which he proposed to extend to Schleswig, the northernmost of the disputed Duchies.

Outraged Germans assailed his plan; unilaterally proclaimed the Duchies' independence; and assembled an army of seven thousand, its ranks swelled by prisoners released from the jails in Holstein. The German-speaking insurgents then appealed to Prussia and Frankfurt for support. Danish patriots were equally furious. They called on the new king to protect his Danish kinfolk in Schleswig, and they marched through Copenhagen shouting, "Denmark to the Eider!" The Danes then turned hopefully to Britain and Russia, since both powers were known to be chary of German control of access to the Baltic.

The appeal of the German-speaking insurgents was rhapsodically greeted in Frankfurt. The National Assembly's deputies vowed to uphold the basic rights, the sacred *Grundrechte*, of their linguistic brethren in the Duchies. They found an ally in Prussia's vacillating Frederick William IV, who opportunely seized on the rebellion to justify an armed assault on Denmark, in good part to divert pressure for reforms at home. When the king's army occupied Jutland, the Danes retaliated by sealing Prussia's ports, much in the spirit of their Viking ancestors. Frederick William now had second thoughts. He had already looked to London and St. Petersburg for support, and both capitals prudently chose neutrality. When Prussian hopes for a quick and easy victory evaporated, the king abruptly reversed course and agreed to an armistice that allowed Denmark to retain provisional title, subject to adjudication, of *both* duchies. In his history of the year 1848, the British author Raymond Postgate describes the sequel:

> There was a burst of fury in the Frankfurt Parliament; after a wild debate, it voted not to accept the armistice. By that vote it showed itself and its enemies the great weakness of the revolutionary movement. Neither it nor any of the German parliaments had secured control of any armed forces. It had no troops with which to back up its angry words. . . . In a few days' time the Parliament realized this, swallowed "German honour," and unhappily reversed its vote.

It was a retreat foreshadowing the frustrations of global reformers in years to come, who after encouraging democratic uprisings (as in

Hungary in 1956, in Czechoslovakia in 1968, and in Georgia in 2008) lacked the arms or the will to intervene once autocrats struck back.

In Cologne, Karl Marx, then thirty years old, was appalled by what he viewed as a spineless surrender. His newspaper, the *Neue Rheinische Zeitung*, lashed out at the Frankfurt delegates for endlessly debating "with the washerwoman loquacity of medieval scholastics" a nonexistent Reich constitution while brave rebels in Schleswig bled to death. The paper derided the Danes as oafs and peasants who ungratefully relied on Germans for what passed as their culture.

Indeed, Marx insisted, it was the Germans who were defending civilization against barbarism, and progress against stagnation—the refrain of every apostle of colonialism.

Marx's scathing rhetoric sprang from his conviction, nurtured during his years as a student in Berlin, that he had unmasked history's immutable laws and therefore could decode the deceptive mummery of bourgeois politicians. On this, he brooked no dissent, as attested by a young German named Carl Schurz, who as a student became "a shy and silent observer" when Marx addressed a rally in Cologne. His words were indeed "full of meaning, logical and clear," but what most struck Schurz was Marx's arrogance: "Everyone who contradicted him he treated with abject contempt; every argument he did not like he answered either with biting scorn at the unfathomable ignorance that had prompted it, or with opprobrious aspersions on the motives of him who advanced it." (Schurz would become the most celebrated of the many "Forty-Eighters" who migrated to America, where he later served as a US senator and secretary of the interior.)

For all his certitude, Marx proved a problematic prophet. He could be brilliantly prescient, and/or instructively wrong. He insisted that his theory of socialism was not utopian but scientific, and indeed wished to dedicate *Das Kapital* to Charles Darwin (who politely declined). Yet, when his Bolshevik disciples finally seized power in November 1917, the long-predicted proletarian uprising took place in precapitalist, peasant-infested, icon-worshipping Russia, not in advanced, literate, and industrialized Germany. Much has been written about this paradox, but from our vantage two points seem especially relevant. Conspicuously absent in Marx's historical equation was the human variable; that is, the critical role of individuals whose shrewdness, boldness, and/or stupidity send events lurching in unexpected ways. Typically, while living as an exile in England, he pored over parliamentary blue books in the British Museum, citing their gloomy statistics on the exploitation of factory workers, yet he shrugged away as charades the debates over social legislation among the very MPs who ordered the reports.

By the same token, he grievously underestimated the potency of nationalism to disrupt proletarian solidarity. Seen from today's perspective, both human agency and the allure of the flag are essential to understanding the modern history of Germany, whose rise in the 1880s and disastrous collapse in 1945 bore the stamp of three leaders who played the nationalist card: Bismarck, Wilhelm II, and Hitler.

———

IN SEPTEMBER 1862, King Wilhelm I named Otto Leopold von Bismarck (1815–1898) as minister-president of Prussia. Count (later Prince) Bismarck presided over the dynamic expansion of a united Germany, whose rise he fostered as its founding chancellor until his resignation in March 1890. In those decades, he waged and won three wars and nurtured the growth of an industrial behemoth. To steal a march on the opposition Social Democrats, he established Europe's first modern welfare state. Yet it was an arcane quarrel over ancient rules of hereditary succession in Schleswig-Holstein that heralded Bismarck's ascent.

When Denmark's childless King Frederick VII died in 1863, a German noble boldly claimed title to both duchies, but Bismarck resisted the popular applause in the claimant's behalf. He planned instead to incorporate Schleswig-Holstein directly within Prussia, and to that end persuaded Austria to join in a war against Denmark, and then abruptly switched course to oppose Vienna to attain his coveted goal: the unification of Germany. Few foresaw his audacity.

Outwardly, Bismarck seemed a conventional Junker aristocrat. Born in Brandenburg to a landed family that had served the Prussian crown since the fourteenth century, he had loyally defended the monarchy during the upheavals of 1848. Affecting an aristocrat's disdain for money, he claimed to relish traditional bucolic pleasures. He fought the obligatory duel with a rival politician in 1852. He served dutifully as

Prussia's ambassador to Russia, and he seemed unusual only in his calculated outbursts, elliptical oratory, and linguistic gifts (he was fluent in five languages).

In truth, he was as much an original as Karl Marx. Both were physically imposing: Marx with his massive beard, Bismarck with his trademark jowls and bushy mustache; each addressed lesser mortals with the stare direct. Both despised parliamentary dithering, diplomatic cant, and conventional wisdom. Like Marx, Bismarck had no respect for "the foolish speeches delivered by amazingly childish and excited politicians." As he further elaborated in an 1862 letter to the American diplomat and historian, John Lothrop Motley, his onetime classmate at Göttingen University and thereafter his lifelong confidant: "These chatterers cannot really rule Prussia; I resist them; they have too little wit, and too much comfort; they are stupid and arrogant. . . . As far as foreign policy is concerned, they are, taken individually, children; in other matters, they become children, as soon as they meet together *in corpore.*"

Bismarck made his intentions plain in his first speech as minister-president. The great questions of his time, he accurately prophesized, "will be decided not by speeches and majorities—that was the mistake of 1848 and 1849—but by iron and blood." Thereafter it became the Iron Chancellor's habit to proclaim his intentions and then closely observe the response: a tactic ascribed to his skill at the gaming tables of Baden-Baden, where he learned to gauge shrewdly another player's nerves and cash resources. Thus while visiting England in 1862, Bismarck happened to meet Benjamin Disraeli at a diplomatic party given by the Russian ambassador. He could scarcely have been more forthright:

I shall soon be compelled to undertake the conduct of the Prussian Government. My first care will be to reorganize the army, with or without the help of the Landtag. . . . As soon as the army shall have been brought into such a condition as to inspire respect, I shall seize the first best pretext to declare war against Austria, dissolve the German Diet, subdue the minor States, and give national unity to Germany under Prussian leadership. I have come here to say this to the Queen's ministers. [Disraeli, also practiced at confounding opponents with shock tactics, whispered to a companion, "Take care of that man! He means what he says."]

In the admiring judgment of a later German-born conjuror, Henry Kissinger, Bismarck was a "white revolutionary." Schleswig-Holstein presented him with his long-sought strategic opening. In 1863, the young duke of Austenberg slipped into Schleswig and, in a speech brashly addressed "to my liege subjects," announced himself as their sole and lawful ruler. Fellow Germans were rapturous, but when his deed was discussed at the Prussian Council of State, Bismarck rose to his feet and proposed outright annexation. "But I have no rights in the duchies," said the startled Prussian king. His minister-president retorted: "Had the Great Elector, had King Frederick, any more right in Prussia and Silesia? All the Hohenzollerns have been enlargers of the State." King Wilhelm I made no answer; his eldest son raised his eyes skyward; and when Bismarck subsequently read the minutes, he was annoyed to find no reference to his proposal. On questioning the council's secretary, he was informed that His Majesty assumed that Count Bismarck had imbibed too heavily at lunch, "and would be glad to hear nothing more of what I said."

Thus in 1863, the chancellor shortly and soberly informed Count Rechberg, the Austrian ambassador, that he intended to seize the duchies single-handedly, as most Prussians ardently wished. "By this threat," writes Emil Ludwig, Bismarck's German biographer, "he compelled Rechberg to rally his side. Then, having so strong an ally, he ignored the German Federation. He now addressed the anxieties of European leaders by insinuating that the inherent hostility between the two German great powers gave security against too overwhelming a success on the part of either of them. Thus with one stroke he had made Austria his ally, and Europe neutral. The danger of a worldwide war was averted, for Prussia and Austria had jointly declared war against the Danes." It proved a *coup de maître,* and friends of Denmark looked on aghast as two armies prepared to liberate the supposedly oppressed duchies.

Yet there were complications, owing to the rise of the popular press, the politics of royalty, and the confusion arising from a phrase uttered by the wily Lord Palmerston, a populist nationalist with a free-wheeling tongue.

———

WHAT PROVED TO BE the mid-nineteenth century's most widely watched wedding took place in March 1863 when Edward, the Prince of Wales, took as his bride Princess Alexandra of Denmark. Plebeians and nobles alike rejoiced at a match that joined England's seemingly feckless heir apparent to a poised, sober, and beautiful Danish wife, yet for Victoria the match proved an interminable royal headache. Not only were the queen's own origins Germanic, but her late consort, Prince Albert, was the youngest son of Duke Ernst of Saxe-Coburg-Gotha. Worse, their oldest daughter Vicky had married Crown Prince Frederick III of Prussia in 1858, and was thus mother of the future Kaiser Wilhelm II.

At the height of the crisis, two other daughters also married German royalty: Princess Alice, the future mother of the Czarina Alexandra Feodorovna, married Ernst Ludwig, the Grand Duke Ludwig of Hesse in 1862, and Princess Helena in 1866 married Prince Frederick of Schleswig-Holstein. Tightening the dynastic web, Princess Alix of Denmark, the future Queen of England, was the older sister of Dagmar, who would later reign as Russian Czarina Maria Feodorovna.

It is difficult for today's readers to assimilate, much less care about, this ever-expanding hive, in which Victoria was unchallenged queen mother. Not so for politicians in the nineteenth century. The intermarriages yielded a swarm of relations whose affairs, marital and extramarital, were breathlessly recorded by a proliferating penny press as its members made their rounds to seasonal regattas, coronations, weddings, and funerals, with time off to visit German spas or seaside resorts in Denmark. Their encounters generated an incessant buzz of gossip, enriched by listening spies and suborned servants.

Some royals ruled with unchallenged authority, most famously in Russia, while others coped in varying degrees with nosy and annoying parliaments, increasing their resentment of populist politicians who played to the press galleries, notably Chancellor Bismarck and Lord Palmerston, Britain's forceful prime minister. At Windsor Castle, Victoria and Albert jeeringly referred in private to her first minister as "Pilgerstein," echoing the Germanized nickname, "Lord Pumice Stone," used in the Tory press. And in Potsdam, daughter Vicky and her spouse Fritz scorned Bismarck as "wicked." All this set the stage for the second Schleswig-Holstein war, which presaged greater horrors to come and underscored the perennial misjudgment among leaders of lesser powers who took too literally professions of sympathy from the ruling elite in London, Berlin, Vienna, or St. Petersburg.

————

IN SUMMER 1863, Prussia and Austria mobilized to invade Denmark, for allegedly dishonoring feudal laws and oppressing German speakers in Schleswig. British opinion favored the underdog Danes. Military experts noted that Prussian armies had not performed impressively since Waterloo. They failed to note that Bismarck, having manufactured a casus belli in collusion with Austria, had taken care to arm his forces with Alfred Krupp's newest and deadliest steel breach-loading cannons. Unsurprisingly, Queen Victoria favored Prussia, as she said her beloved Albert would have wished, notwithstanding son Edward's marital ties to Denmark. In Copenhagen's corner was the redoubtable Lord Palmerston (1784–1865), at the time still the queen's first minister. Having already held office for forty-six years as prime minister, foreign secretary, or home secretary, Palmerston had been continuously involved in the ongoing dispute over the Duchies. Physically imposing, given to vivid rhetoric, and possessing a keen ear to popular sentiment, "Pam" openly tilted to Denmark.

Speaking in July 1863, not long after the Prince of Wales's wedding, Palmerston warned that if violence were directed against the Danish nation, its perpetrators would find "that it would not be Denmark alone with which they would have to contend." His words were robustly applauded by his most influential press supporter, *The Times* of London, raising the diplomatic stakes, polarizing Parliament, and infuriating Victoria. By the time Austro-Prussian forces finally crossed the

Eider River into Schleswig, all Europe was on red alert, especially its monarchs, diplomats, generals, and—tellingly—its newspaper editors.

The second Schleswig-Holstein war confirmed the rise of a new breed of journalists who were to become wild cards in military poker.

Flash forward to January 1864. In major capitals, editors rush correspondents to the front in nervous expectation of a wider conflict. *The Times* sends a veteran troubleshooter, Antonio Gallenga, to Schleswig, where his pro-German reportage provokes a private letter of protest from then Prime Minister Lord Palmerston. Not only were Prussians excessively unreasonable, he admonished his friend, *The Times* editor William F. Delane, but "the only check we can have on them is the *indefinite notion* [our italics] that public opinion here is getting irritated against them." A chastened Delane replies: "My temporary Germanism like many other inconveniences was the direct consequence of your Lordship's gout, which shut me out from communication with yourself. Your note of today has effected a perfect cure. . . . There is no danger of relapse."

By contrast, *The Daily Telegraph's* correspondent, Edward Dicey, plainly tilted to the Danes. Very typical was his graphic firsthand account of the climactic battle in April 1864, when Prussian forces stormed the Danish redoubt at Dybol (today's Düppel), firing no fewer than ten thousand artillery shells daily at their outnumbered adversaries. Deploring the battle as "completely one-sided," Dicey likened the Prussian assault to the Anaconda strategy employed by General McClellan against the Confederates, the difference being that "the Federals had to surround in their coils a vast continent [while] the Germans only have to encircle a hill. . . . The issue cannot, I think, be doubtful; and the marvel to me is that the victim has struggled so long against the gigantic force of his destroyer." (Dicey and Gallenga recycled their dispatches into instant two-volume books, an indication of popular interest in the war.)

After Düppel, further resistance was obviously impossible, yet the Danes would not acknowledge they had lost. Why? Because, Dicey surmised, they still hoped against hope that the exorbitant character of Austro-German demands would induce neutral great powers "to interfere actively on behalf of Denmark." His elaboration anticipated the plight of future lesser powers in the postcolonial century to come. "There may be advantages in the existence of small States," he wrote, "but nothing, I think, can compensate their inhabitants for [their] dependence on foreign Powers. . . . The bare possibility that England and France might go to war for her sake has protracted and embittered the agony of this gallant country. The Danes were afraid of owning to the world, or even to themselves, that the time had come to submit to force, for fear that such an admission might extinguish the last prospect of foreign aid."

In sum, the Danes miscalculated the significance of Palmerston's words and Prince Edward's betrothal. Pam might freely utter phrases that excited Danish hopes, but in the end a divided Parliament, speaking for diverse constituencies, would be the arbiter. Backstage, the royals pulled for Germany, while a peace party in the House of Commons led by the radical Richard Cobden, opposed any military intervention. (According to Cobden's biographer, John Morley, if the House's 1864 session was to be remembered, it would be for its negative answer to the question, "Shall or shall not England take part in the struggle between Germany and Denmark?") In truth, years earlier Palmerston himself had articulated the litmus test for distinguishing substance from gas in great power diplomacy. Addressing Parliament in 1848 on whether England should intervene in support of the gallant Poles rebelling against Russia, he answered in the negative, concluding with his most-quoted axiom: "We have no eternal allies and we have no perpetual enemies. Our interests are eternal and perpetual, and these interests it is our duty to follow."

So Bismarck had his way. As foretold in his words to Disraeli, he quarreled with Austria over Prussia's deliberately vague undertakings on sharing rule of the Duchies. In 1865, he fabricated a pretext for a new war. The Iron Chancellor neutered the French, gained Italian support, and won the backing of Bavaria, Saxony, and Hanover. His Seven Weeks' War (as it was instantly named) owed its speed to a meticulously planned assault utilizing the Germanic rail network to its full capacity. Overseeing the offensive was the Prussian Chief of Staff Helmuth von Moltke, who with similar thoroughness in 1870 and 1871 orchestrated the rout of Napoleon III in the Franco-Prussian War. As Bismarck had long envisioned, Prussia then absorbed most of the lesser German kingdoms into a reborn Reich (with annexed Alsace-Lorraine as the victor's booty).

Viewed as a whole, the Second Reich with its ecumenical amalgam of ideologies and its stealth diplomacy bore the unmistakable stamp of its founding chancellor. On the progressive scale, Germany instituted universal male suffrage and pioneered social welfare legislation, but its elected Reichstag had little or no say concerning military or foreign policy. The new Reich's intricate web of diplomatic alliances owed much to Bismarck's personal relations with Europe's ruling elite, and its viability required the virtuoso genius of its architect. A telling contemporary judgment was rendered as early as 1866 by Walter Bagehot, among the sagest of Britons, writing in *The Economist*, which he edited:

> It is impossible not to see in Bismarck a sort of cynical immorality—dangerous at all times, and perhaps particularly dangerous in the present age. We do not allude to his long contest with the Assembly on the structure of the army. That army has answered so well that Prussia has pardoned, and bystanders may pardon too, his far-seeing illegality. A political philosopher will admit that for such gigantic and sudden efforts a momentary dictatorship has conclusive advantages over parliamentary government. But none of these excuses can be pleaded for the treatment of Schleswig-Holstein. It is plain that Count Bismarck wanted a spark to fire his train; he wanted a war of some sort for Germany, and he used the duchies without hesitation and without scruple to provide a war. . . . Such shameless immorality may be hidden in the blaze of success, but a grave precedent of a great crime will be marked by history, and cast a shadow over subsequent events.

The shadow deepened for the luckless inhabitants of Schleswig-Holstein following their incorporation in Germany. In Berlin-ruled Schleswig, no grievance was more infuriating to Danes than the campaign to marginalize their language. Then as now, four languages were spoken: Danish, Frisian, High German, and Low German (the latter two deemed distinct tongues). Germany devised every possible obstacle to those who would not speak High German, so attested Maurice Francis

Egan, the US minister in Copenhagen in his memoir, *Ten Years Near the German Frontier* (1919):

> Danish could not be used in courts of law. It was required that the clergy should be educated at the University of Kiel, and other officials could have no chance of advancement unless they used German constantly and fluently. Danish speech was not used in a single college. In a word, the German influence, under the eyes of a Danish king and government, was driving out all the safeguards of Danish national life in Slesvig [the preferred Danish spelling].

It is fair to add that these Danish complaints echoed those pressed by German speakers when Copenhagen ruled Schleswig. Over the decades, arguments from both sides of the linguistic barricade poured into books, pamphlets, and speeches. However, a more measured judgment was put forward in 1862 by Lord Salisbury, who as British foreign secretary and prime minister grappled for decades with the Schleswig-Holstein Question. In an 1862 essay titled "The Danish Duchies," he wrote, "The language grievance has been kept alive chiefly for popular use," thereby providing "an endless topic of declamation for platform orators and pamphleteers." Anyway, it all depended on whose tongue was being muted. He noted that Polish speakers under Austrian rule outnumbered German speakers eight to five, yet for official and educational purposes the language "was exclusively German." The same was true in Hungary, where only one-tenth of the population spoke German as a mother tongue, yet the minority prevailed.

During the arms race that preceded and helped ignite the Great War, "Prussianism" in all its presumed forms became the focus for intense criticism by politicians and the mainstream Anglo-American press. Few US officials were as opprobrious as Washington's chief representative in Copenhagen, Maurice Francis Egan. In his 1919 memoir, he described "the Rape of Slesvig" as the ineluctable prelude to the disasters that followed:

> There is no doubt that the assimilation of Slesvig by Prussia led to the Franco-Prussian war and liberated modern Germany from the

difficulties that would have hampered her intention to become the dominant power in the world. The further acquisition of Denmark would have only been a question of time, had not the march of the Despot through Belgium aroused the civilized world to the reality of German imperial aggression—until then, unhappily, not taken seriously.

Moreover, if the Wilhelm II's minions had seized Denmark, he added as a final thrust, the Danish-held Virgin Islands would have almost surely have fallen to the kaiser, giving the Prussians a threatening toehold in the Caribbean. Egan himself helped broker the 1917 treaty through which the United States acquired the Danish West Indies for $25 million, avowedly to safeguard the approaches to the Panama Canal and no less vitally, to shut out Germany.

As in much Allied wartime propaganda, the German emperor stalks through Egan's memoir like a cunning Lucifer bent on asserting diabolical mastery over the West's democracies. A less febrile judgment is rendered by the too-little-read Viennese wit and historian, Egon Friedell, who viewed Wilhelm as wholly unfit by brain and temper for his post, "which, as we know, is fairly common where thrones are concerned." The kaiser, in Friedell's eyes, was less a monster than a stunted titan who, as if possessed by a secret curse, piled mistake upon mistake: "He tried, as no Hohenzollern had done before him, to get in touch with the German working man, and was doomed to find himself more detested by the proletariat than any of his predecessors. He set German's future on the water, and the water became his grave. He wanted to create a world-empire, and what he achieved was the World War." Or, in the terse summation of George Kennan (who as a young diplomat served in Nazi Germany), by falsely portraying Wilhelm II as a virtual Hitler, his adversaries helped give birth to the genuine article. Thus does human agency affect world history.

———

KAISER WILHELM II may not have been sole author of World War I, but assuredly his subjects were the conflict's principal losers. Germany was stripped of her borderland territories and her overseas possessions, forced to pay punitive reparations, and obliged to accept moral responsibility for the war and to disavow rearmament. Almost as a footnote, the Allied victors convening in Paris in 1919 also tried to write a finale to the endless dispute over the Duchies. In the words of the Oxford historian Margaret MacMillan in her lively account of the seven-month conference, "No one wanted to reopen the old legal question, but fortunately there was the new principle of self-determination at hand."

Few principles, however, proved to be more problematic than the conviction that every ethnic, cultural, and territorial community is entitled to nationhood if its citizens so choose. The Paris peacemakers exempted British and French overseas possessions from this principle, and applied it selectively and inconsistently to the losers—namely Germany, Austria, and the Ottoman Empire. The phrase, "self-determination," which by some accounts germinated during the nineteenth century within the international Socialist movement, had been embraced by both Woodrow Wilson and V. I. Lenin. Yet in Paris, final decisions were taken impulsively by the Big Three—Wilson, Prime Minister David Lloyd George, and France's Premier Georges Clemenceau—often with an almost feckless disregard for "self-determination," as broadly and commonly construed.

Consider two snapshots. In May 1919, Harold Nicolson, then a junior official in the British delegation, confided to his wife Vita Sackville-West:

> I scribbled you a note yesterday in President Wilson's ante-room [and] just as I finished, Lloyd George burst in in his impetuous way: "Come along, Nicolson, and keep your ears open." So I went into Wilson's study and there were he and Lloyd George and Clemenceau with their armchairs drawn up close over a map on the hearth rug. I was there about half an hour. . . . But, darling, it is appalling, those three ignorant and irresponsible men [were] cutting Asia Minor to bits as if they were dividing a cake.

He reported that nobody present had any real knowledge of the region, and yet those bits of cake were to emerge as today's Iraq, Syria, and Lebanon. There was not even the pretense of consulting the region's diverse and suspicious inhabitants, breeding a sense of betrayal that persists to the present in these and other former Ottoman territories.

A comparable episode was recorded by Charles Seymour, later the president of Yale and then chief of the Austro-Hungarian division of the US delegation. In a letter home dated May 31, 1919, he described how the postwar frontiers between Italy and Austria were resolved. It was not an edifying spectacle. As an inducement to join the Allies in 1915, the Italians had been promised South Tyrol, a slice of Austria inhabited by some 200,000 German speakers, along with other territories. Prime Minister Vittorio Orlando came to Paris seeking possession of South Tyrol, which was to become the Italian provinces of Alto Adige. Here is Seymour's snapshot:

> We went into the room where the floor was clear and Wilson spread out a big map (made in our office) on the floor and got down on his knees to show us what had been done; most of us were also on our hands and knees. I was in the front row and felt somebody pushing me, and looked around angrily to find that it was Orlando, on his hands and knees crawling like a bear toward the map. I gave way and soon he was on the front row. I wish I could have had a picture of the most important men in the world on all fours over the map.

Italy did get South Tyrol, but not the Adriatic port of Fiume, which was ceded instead to newborn Yugoslavia, provoking furious Italian protests. In April 1919, Wilson addressed an unprecedented personal message to the Italian people, stressing the lavish territorial rewards already bestowed on their country. He pointed out that Fiume was the only port available to the fledgling Yugoslav nation and pleaded with Italians to display "that noblest quality of greatness, magnanimity, friendly generosity, the preference of justice over interests." To no avail; his direct appeal to common people backfired; Orlando announced in Paris that he would return to Rome, so that Italians "could choose between Wilson and me." In September 1919, the flamboyant poet and airman Gabriele d'Annunzio, aided by rogue elements of the Italian army, seized and held Fiume. It was the spark igniting the powder train that led, two years later, to Mussolini's March on Rome and the Fascist seizure of power, offering a model and precedent for the rise of National Socialism in Germany.

Italy formally annexed South Tyrol in 1920, and for the next half century the status of its German-speaking inhabitants persisted as an unhealed canker. Finally, in 1972, Italy granted a special autonomous status to the northerly region known as Alto Adige. Not only have German language rights been honored in the region, but in successive years Italy granted even more home rule rights, enabling the region to retain most of its taxes for use in schools and public services. In 1992, the Austrian Parliament declared formally that the south Tyrol/Alto Adige dispute was finally closed.

———

SO OUR QUEST BEGAN by delving into the geopolitical seedbed of today's disputes over territory and majority and minority rights that continue to reverberate around the world. In all our explorations—in India's State of Kerala, Russia's Republic of Tatarstan, France's City of Marseille, New York's Borough of Queens, and Australia's late-blooming Sydney—we discovered three keys that helped explain their comparative success in achieving a Pax Ethnica. The inhabitants of each by hard experience learned the social and economic benefits of defusing conflict between peoples of differing cultures and creeds. And always there was the human factor: the willingness of politicians to grasp the thorny nettle of nationalism, to abjure the pseudo-populist bashing of vulnerable minorities, especially with an eye to youngsters of all faiths attuned to the benefits of tolerance. As in Flensburg, we found that citizenship is not an indissoluble rock, but it can be an elastic cord reaching across the scary past to a less violent future.

2

KERALA:
GODS' OWN COUNTRY

India has 200,000 gods, and worships them all.
In religion, all other countries are paupers; India
is the only millionaire.

—MARK TWAIN, *FOLLOWING THE EQUATOR* (1897)

RARELY DOES THE INDIAN state of Kerala catch the capricious gaze of the Western media. It did so in July 2011 when a Hindu temple in its state capital was found to contain a royal ransom of solid gold statues, all piled together in a sealed vault alongside sacks of diamonds. The value of the treasure was estimated at $22 billion, which likely makes the temple the richest in South Asia, with the disposition of its wealth to be decided by India's Supreme Court. Still, having recently visited this splinter of land at India's southwestern tip, we wondered whether excited press accounts of the discovery obscured a more relevant and remarkable story.

Kerala's real treasure cannot be measured in dollars, pounds, or rupees. Its true gold is the example it sets (not just for India) of civilized coexistence among Hindus, Muslims, and Christians. Comity has been abetted by Kerala's economic progress, itself made possible in part by near-universal literacy, by the empowerment of women, and by the export of the state's most precious commodity: its people. Moreover, these feats have been accomplished by democratic means, with the crucial support of an indigenous Communist Party whose leaders have

hewed to an electoral path. Add a final twist: Kerala's progressive example owes much to past hereditary rulers and British colonial policy, yet it
currently depends—perhaps too heavily—on remittances from a
skilled, million-strong workforce in the Arab Middle East.

It chanced that we had recently met with the incumbent head of the
royal family in Kerala's capital, Thiruvananthapuram (formerly Trivandrum). At eighty-nine, Sri Marthanda Varma was still making his daily
visits to Sri Padmanabhaswami Temple, where the prodigious hidden
treasure was discovered in 2011. His forbears had ruled this princely
state from 1663 until 1948, retaining their royal titles until 1971, when
that distinction was abolished. Yet when we saw him, the ex-maharaja
expressed no regrets over his fallen majesty. He recounted with relish his
support for democratic reforms and his meetings with the state's ministers, including Communists. As to the treasure, after its discovery he
told a television interviewer that his family had been its custodian "in
the past-past tense, the present tense, and the future tense." Yes, he was
anxious to cooperate with the Supreme Court, but he urged its jurists to
heed solemn warnings by court astrologers that opening more vaults
could bring on disaster. (As we learned, in Kerala even Marxists consulted the heavens prior to major initiatives.)

Surely no ordinary imagination could invent the State of Kerala. Its
multiple improbabilities, physical and mortal, are evident in its geography, along its roadsides, and in its spoken Malayalam language: a chorus
of consonants and vowels that roll like the surf on its excellent beaches.
Consider its currently popular trademark. When New Delhi's rulers
decided in the 1990s to market their populous nation as "Incredible
India," their counterparts in Kerala gazed skyward and devised a rival
brand name, "God's Own Country," now widely imprinted on tourist
brochures. Yet for much of the past half century, the ruling coalitions in
Kerala have been led by the nominally infidel Communist Party; here
Marx and Lenin somehow coexist peacefully with more ancient deities.
Thus on Kerala's roadways, a visitor riding a wobbly auto-rickshaw
(buzzing three-wheelers resembling a tilted telephone booth astride a
lawnmower engine), adorned with decals depicting Vishnu and Shiva, is
likely to glimpse scarlet posters emblazoned with the hammer and
sickle. No less ubiquitous are polychrome images of Jesus and the

Virgin Mary, while mosques everywhere dot the skyline. Hence the apostrophe in Kerala's slogan should be moved one space: this is "Gods' Own Country."

Or so we concluded while traversing Kerala, a vertical slice of South India wedged between the Arabian Sea and a six-hundred-mile mountain range called the Western Ghats. We sought keys to a phenomenon known to political scientists and development economists, yet mostly unfamiliar to the lay public. Kerala is among India's poorest states as measured by its limp gross domestic product, yet its citizens live longer than those of other states (74 years for females, 68 for males) and lead all the others in adult literacy (91 percent). Among major Indian states, Kerala ranks first in both the Educational Development and Human Development Indexes and is deemed "least corrupt" by Transparency International. All this has occurred in a compact land (circa 15,000 square miles) smaller than West Virginia, with a population (32 million) comparable to that of Canada and one-third greater than Australia's—and with a per capita income one-seventieth that of the United States.

Within India, Kerala's reputation broadly resembles that of Massachusetts in America. Like the Bay State, Kerala is synonymous with liberal activism, outstanding schools and hospitals, a highly flavored local culture, and a seafaring past. In a nice if coincidental parallel, the hereditary grandees in Massachusetts are nicknamed Brahmins, while the Kerala originals also figure prominently in public life—and less congruently, as social reformers partnered with parliamentary Marxists. Overall, Kerala is renowned for its vibrant but nonviolent politics and for the absence of pervasive venom among its three predominant faiths: Hindu (55 percent), Muslim (24 percent), and Christian (19 percent).

So what accounts for Kerala's exceptionalism? Why is its recent history so starkly different from that of Gujarat, another notably diverse Indian state? In a few bloody weeks in early 2002, organized mobs in Gujarat claimed as many as 2,000 lives, razed some 230 mosques and shrines, and rendered homeless close to 200,000 Muslims. (Yet Gujarat's most famous son is Gandhi, the apostle of ahimsa, or nonviolence.) The only comparable pogrom in Kerala, known as the Moplah Rebellion, occurred in early 1921, when Muslim gangs murdered, raped, and forcibly converted Hindus, reversing the victim-perpetrator pattern in Gujarat. Then how, and why, does Kerala avoid communal strife?

To seek explanations, we scoured the state's major towns and questioned a spectrum of intellectuals, physicians, hotel workers, weavers, party activists, mayors, journalists, maharajas, feminists, believers, and nonbelievers, enriching their insights by trolling a multitude of specialized monographs. Put succinctly, we discovered an intricate mosaic of mutually reinforcing ingredients: geography and weather, history and culture, the rise of a knowledge society, and the surprisingly paradoxical role of a complex caste system that has fostered both repression and fundamental reform. We also added some graphic phrases to our vocabulary; for example, "love jihad" (Muslim males allegedly seeking the souls as well as the bodies of susceptible non-Muslim females) and "saffronisation" (expunging foreign words from the Hindi language and coloring history texts with a right-wing Hindu tint).

Still, what struck us most was the energy, fluency, and pungent humor of the Keralites we encountered. In the words of C. R. Neekeandam, an environmental reformer whom we met in Cochin (also called Kochi), "We jokingly say that everything we prepare has to be 'export quality.' Like cashew nuts, even our children have to be 'export quality.' We send them everywhere for jobs." This is at once Kerala's strength, and its vulnerability. More than one million Keralites (or Malayalis) toil in the Persian Gulf, most of them as technicians and construction workers, and hence when the economic fortunes of the Arab emirates fluctuate—as when Dubai nearly defaulted in 2009—so do migrant remittances. Schools, hospitals, and corporations across the globe welcome Keralites, but their gain is often Kerala's loss.

"Kerala is a consuming society, not a producing society," we were cautioned by one expatriate (who prefers to remain anonymous) before we left the United States. "People are its exports," he elaborated. "If you go to Mount Everest, you'll find a Keralite running a coffee shop."

———

NOT ON EVEREST but in the northern coastal city of Kannur (in its earlier Portuguese incarnation, Cannanore), we benefited from an informed overview of Kerala. Our tutor was a veteran environmental activist, T. Gangadharan (known universally, as with many Keralites, by his first initial). We met over kebabs on the beachside terrace of the Mascot Hotel during a long twilight when the sun, a molten orange disc, sank slowly into the deep blue of the Arabian Sea. Kannur is known to adventurous tourists as the starting point for locating the nightlong *theyyam*, a migratory forest masque in which actors in elaborate costumes become possessed by Hindu divinities and their demon adversaries. By contrast, Mr. Gangadharan was soberly clad and spoke in professorial cadences, consistent with his role as founder of the Kerala People's Science Movement, or Sasthra Sahitya Parishad (KSSP). Yet his narrative was intrinsically as dramatic as any *theyyam*.

"There are several reasons why Kerala is different," he began. "The first, I will say, is geography. On our eastern side, you see, the Western Ghats create a natural boundary, an obstruction, to people from other parts of the country, but the rest of the state is open to the sea. That is why people from the outside, especially the Arabs and later the Portuguese and then other Europeans, came first to Kerala, so you see our geographical position contributes to our multicultural aspect."

Before the Europeans arrived, the territory that comprises present-day Kerala was a maze of "tiny kingly states," mutable in every sense as borders and dynasties changed with the ebb and flow of domestic conflicts.

"Ours is a very mixed history," continued Mr. Gangadharan, "because different parts of Kerala came under different regimes." Over time, diffuse power was concentrated in regional hereditary rulers. In the south, Hindu maharajas governed in what became known as Travancore, where their heirs still live in its palaces. Kerala's sole Muslim royal dynasty reigned in Kannur, where we were sitting, and its monarchs bore the proud title of Ali Raja. Just to the south, Hindu warlords called Zamorins were masters of Malabar's Spice Coast and its thriving trading capital, Calicut (now Kozhikode). In the central area, ruled by a Hindu monarch, there flourished what was to become Kerala's biggest city, Cochin (or Kochi), where according to local tradition St. Thomas the Apostle arrived from the Holy Land to establish the oldest Christian community in Asia. Cochin is likewise home to the Pardesi Synagogue, founded in 1567 by a Jewish congregation whose origins are said to date to the destruction of the Second Temple. (Almost all its surviving members migrated to Israel in the 1940s and 1950s, commonly seeking opportunity, not asylum.)

"So my first response to your question is that geography and the administrative system helps explain the diversity of our state," pursued Mr. Gangadharan. "Number two is the climate. You know, Kerala is where the Indian monsoon enters the subcontinent, and we receive [India's] maximum rainfall, as much as 3,000 millimeters every year." The state is drenched in two rainy seasons: June to September and October to December, a total of seven months. The monsoon occurs when the seasonally heated Indian air collides with an aerial current of cooler air, pregnant with evaporated water, surging northward from the Indian Ocean. Its first landfall is near Thiruvananthapuram the capital of Kerala, where its approach is tracked by radar and satellite at the city's meteorological center. Founded in 1840 by a science-minded maharaja, the center "declares" the monsoon's arrival: the most anxiously awaited weather report on the subcontinent.

The monsoon's advent is preceded by ardent prayer, hourly news reports, and sometimes frenzied orgies. After disgorging its waters, the current moves day-by-day from the Western Ghats to northern India, and there merges with a second water-laden air stream, blowing from the Bay of Bengal. Alarmingly, during recent years, the semiannual downpour has become capricious and spiteful. Various causes have been proposed: global warming, deforestation, urban sprawl, the vagaries of El Niño (or to the devout, divine displeasure). In 2009, average rainfall dropped a record 29 percent from June to mid-August nationwide, a source of particular concern to Kerala, India's greenest state.

Thanks to the monsoon, Kerala's soil is proverbially fecund. "Kera" means coconut, and no crop is more important than this bountiful tree that yields meaty flesh, potable milk, cooking oil, and sap (used to brew the fermented alcoholic drink known as "toddy"). Dried, coconut is employed in temple offerings; its leaves thatch roofs and its husks are woven into mats and rope. It is reckoned that some 28 percent of Kerala's cultivated area is devoted to coconut trees, while the uplands provide favorable terrain for tea, rubber, and coffee plantations. Though output of rice has markedly fallen, due to a diminished area for planting, it remains the staple food grain in Kerala; fruits of every variety have long flourished, along with pepper, cinnamon, ginger, nutmeg, clove, and cardamom.

As the great Arab traveler Ibn Battuta wrote of his two-month stay in Malabar during the fourteenth century, "Not a patch of ground, be it small as a span in breadth, is left uncultivated. Every man has his own separate palm-grove, with his house in the middle." The auspicious result of this agrarian enterprise was visible to him in Calicut's harbor: thirteen Chinese junks at anchor, each with a flock of support vessels, ready to fill holds with spices. By the late Middle Ages, Malabar had become the prime source of a triangular trade whereby the Venetians purchased India's spices in Egypt or Yemen from Arab go-betweens, with every link lubricated with lucre. Absent refrigeration and the variety afforded by then-unknown tomatoes, potatoes, corn, and lemons, even royal feasts in northern Europe tended to be rancid. A pinch of pepper could mask a multitude of culinary sins; in the fifteenth century, the spice trade was to Malabar what oil today is to Saudi Arabia.

It was this race for mastery of the spice trade that initially energized the European conquest of India. Nowhere was the West's eastward thrust felt more forcibly than on the Spice Coast. Its inhabitants long ago learned the value of a united resistance and a common tongue as they contended with Portuguese, Dutch, and British intruders. And arguably, no intruder better personified the mutual bafflement arising from this collision (a better word than "clash") of civilizations than the Lisbon explorer who led the way, Vasco da Gama. To most of us, he is a vague textbook name, yet he resembled a character in a Conrad novel: a gifted Western sailor obsessed with the scorn of his infidel Eastern adversaries. His story is worth a digression; it helps explain Indian ambivalence about their former European rulers, best expressed by Mahatma Gandhi when asked what he thought of Western civilization. "I think it would be a very good idea," he replied.

———

IF ONE WERE TO SELECT a natal day for the dawn of the West's colonial ascent in the East, a plausible choice would be May 20, 1498. That Sunday, three small ships under the command of Vasco da Gama dropped anchor at an inlet on the Malabar Coast chosen by his Muslim pilot. It was the only harbor near the trading city of Calicut (as the pilot well knew) that could safely shelter the ships from the heavy swells of the oncoming monsoon (which it did). Nearly a year had passed since the flotilla embarked from Lisbon, and one can imagine the fervent hosannas of its ragged crew when they landed. Their three-masted sailing vessels, known as carracks, had rounded Africa's Cape of Good Hope (named by the Portuguese) to complete a final run of 4,500 miles and ninety days without sight of land, an unprecedented feat in Europe's age of exploration.

This feat owed much to an anonymous Moorish pilot's knowledge of the Arabian Sea's boisterous currents. Nonetheless, despite the help he and other Muslims provided, da Gama reciprocated with a holy war against their faith. His ardor mirrored European fears of an expanding Ottoman Empire, quickened by the inquisitorial zealotry then infecting Iberia. The age's crusading spirit resonates in *The Lusiads* by Luis Vaz de Camões, Portugal's national epic, as in these lines: "Great Mars will swell with envy/At the ferocity of the Portuguese,/ While the defeated Sultan, facing death,/ Will damn Mohammed with his final breath."

Having planted a marble pillar on the Malabar Coast proclaiming its conquest, da Gama, with the translating aid of multilingual Muslims, sought a meeting with Calicut's ruling Zamorin (a warrior-caste Hindu, whose title means Sea Lord),. However, as recorded by the voyage's anonymous chronicler, the newcomers were greeted by testy shouts: "To the devil with you! Who led you here? What are you seeking so far away?" Da Gama's spokesman responded: "We come seeking Christians and spices," thereby confirming what Muslim traders most feared: that their control of the spice trade was at risk. The emissaries eventually agreed to arrange a meeting with their monarch, so that the captain could offer suitable gifts and explain his mission.

At the appointed time, da Gama wore a scarlet cloak, a blue tunic, and a velvet cap as he passed through gawking onlookers in Calicut. En route to the royal palace, he noticed a Hindu temple. He stopped to inspect it. In the commonly received account, he mistook it for a church of "deviant Christians," and knelt in prayer before a carved likeness of a mother holding a child, Devaki nursing Krishna, which he mistook for the Virgin Mary and Jesus. In his eyes, this corroborated reports that a Christian kingdom ruled by Prester John existed east of Suez (Portugal's King Manuel had actually given da Gama a letter addressed to this legendary monarch).

After entering the palace gates, the Portuguese captain was led through great golden doors to the royal chamber where Zamorin Mana Vikrama was bare above his waist, lying on a green couch, and casually chewing betel nuts. From time to time, he spat in a golden cup as his servants passed around bowls of fruit. Through translators, da Gama described his arduous voyage, presented a letter from his ruler, and explained that he wished only to buy spices and depart in peace. Yet when the visitors presented their gifts—washbasins, jars of honey, strings of coral, and scarlet hoods—they were received in silence. The Arab serving as da Gama's host later admonished that "the poorest merchant from Mecca would have given more." This initial encounter foreshadowed the mutual bafflement that marked this first encounter between South India and Europe.

In a widely accepted reconstruction, the newcomers were held captive, charged with piracy, and finally released owing primarily to the Zamorin's fear of injuring Calicut's reputation as a safe harbor. As the *São Gabriel,* da Gama's flagship, departed, her cannons fired a parting broadside above the port, the first use of this terrifying weapon on the Spice Coast. Once back in Lisbon, the captain was hailed as a hero and a delighted King Manuel now styled himself "Lord of the Conquest, Navigation and Commerce of Ethiopia, Arabia, Persia, and India." It proved the prelude to Portugal's creation of a European empire that spanned great swaths of Africa, Asia, and the Americas (in fact, it was a Lisbon captain's serendipitous westward detour that led to the conquest and colonization of Brazil).

As for Vasco da Gama, by now titled an admiral, he assembled a fleet of twenty-five ships, each packed with cannons, and returned to Calicut in 1502 to avenge his prior humiliation. Rejecting overtures from the Zamorin, he ordered the capture and dismemberment of thirty-odd fishermen, sending the body parts to the ruler (so Indian chroniclers relate). By this and by less savage means, Lisbon named and established the State of India, consisting originally of coastal strongholds under the command

of a viceroy (the first being da Gama, who governed until his death in
1524). A century later, the Dutch succeeded the Portuguese as overall
masters of the Spice Coast, only to be evicted by the British.

In retrospect, India's colonial era proved as long and complex, and as
dark and bright, as the *Mahabharata*, the major epic of Hindu culture
(seven times the length of the *Iliad* and the *Odyssey* combined). Concerning the Portuguese, their presence in South India would have better
and more productive moments, but one can understand why, when
Goa, the last remnant of Lisbon's rule, was forcibly annexed by newly
sovereign New Delhi in December 1961, *The Times of India* abandoned
all pretense of objectivity and headlined its report, "Our Troops Liberate Goa."

―――――

HOW IS THIS PROBLEMATIC past relevant to present-day Kerala? Two generalizations: First, there are indeed long-established religious minorities everywhere in present-day India, but elsewhere
Muslims came in the wake of Mughal conquests, while their coreligion-
ists in Malabar settled centuries earlier as traders, along with early-day
Christians and Jews. All three faiths learned to coexist with the Hindu
majority; each became familiar with one another's rites, and crucially, all
came to speak a common language: Malayalam. Second, when Pakistan
in 1947 was hived from newborn India, precipitating both a massive
population exchange and sanguinary ethnic cleansing, few Muslims in
Kerala joined the northward exodus. Owing partly to long-standing
links among all religious communities, peace has prevailed—not a total
and unbroken peace, but by global standards, a continuous and exemplary peace.

The importance of language was elaborated in our meeting with
Professor M. N. Karassery, who described himself as a "Muslim by tradition." He is a widely read columnist who also holds the prestigious
chair in Malayalam studies at Calicut University. As he explained:

> Islam did not come to Kerala by conquest, and our Muslims are
> essentially Keralites. They are converts from different [Hindu] castes,
> mainly from lower castes, so they are Malayalis, not outsiders. The

main thing is that our Muslims don't have a separate language. Hindus, Muslims, Christians: each and every community speaks the same language, and this is very important. When you go to Bombay or Delhi, Uttar Pradesh or Hyderabad, Muslims speak their own language, Urdu. After independence, many in our own communities opened their doors and windows, and everybody came together. You don't have a special village of Hindus, Muslims, or Christians. [In Kerala] you can't bomb a Hindu or a Muslim area or a Brahmin area. When you are going to Karnataka you get a special village for a special community or caste. This is not the situation in Kerala. We have a common language; we have common villages.

Citing a tradition in North India of patronizing only establishments run by fellow Muslims or Hindus, Karassery pursued, "In Kerala, there is no Hindu water and no Muslim water." All celebrate a common ten-day new year and the autumn rice harvest holiday of Onam. Borrowed from Hindus, Onam has become a festival observed by all faiths. "It doesn't mean that I celebrate Onam here in my house," Karassery explained, "but we'll prepare vegetarian food and *payasam* [a coconut rice pudding] that is particular to Onam. We don't celebrate Christmas here, but I will go to a celebration with my Christian friends at Christmas and they will come here for Eid [the Muslim festival marking the end of Ramadan]."

Yes, he acknowledged, flare-ups erupt on occasion, owing partly to a thriving and competitive vernacular press. Keralites are voracious consumers of newsprint, and journalists tend to fan the embers of discord, as we found during our stay in Calicut, which chanced to coincide with a media-inflated controversy over "love jihad." Was it possible that as many as 4,000 impressionable Hindu and Christian women had succumbed to what one local wit impiously called the "sects appeal" of young Muslim suitors? The evening we arrived, riot police had already dispersed hundreds of demonstrators belonging to Hindu Aikya Vedi (HAV), activist sectarians who marched within a hundred yards of an Islamic social center. It was actually a "conversion center," the protestors alleged, as an ominously large crowd led by the Sunni Students Federation, known as the SKSSF, approached to protect the threatened social center. City authorities invoked a law banning provocative assemblies, a riot was averted, and the crowds dispersed. (Newspaper accounts were careful to state that during the agitation, Hindu leaders of HAV escorted a pregnant Muslim woman to a nearby hospital.) Although no substantive evidence supported claims that young Muslim males had craftily seduced thousands of Hindu and Christian females to secure their conversion, many Indians continue to believe this media-inflated assertion.

The previous day we had met with a senior and respected Muslim leader, T. Sadarikkoya, a Congress Party veteran who had taken part in Gandhi's "Quit India" campaign in 1943. He also agreed that there were communal problems. Since the 2002 killings in Gujarat, Muslim women in a display of solidarity had increasingly donned head coverings. But like his colleague Karassery, Sadarikkoya stressed the binding force of a civic culture rooted in centuries of comity. Hindus, Muslims, and Christians have traditionally worked together in a society otherwise divided by class as well as caste. His own family, for example, operated a print shop: "At our presses, we had two Muslims, one Christian, and four Hindus working for us." Moreover, Muslims in Malabar comprise 27 percent of the population: a potent electoral bloc in a state where leftist and centrist coalitions have for decades rotated in power, and where as many as 85 percent of eligible voters go to the polls. "The Muslims hold the balance of power. They never try to provoke; extremism is not our way. This is our land."

Still, this veteran freedom fighter, who as a young activist had witnessed now-unheard of ravages of famine, and who was gratified and astonished by Kerala's mass literacy and its flourishing schools, spoke cautiously about the future. He was worried about the virus of sectarian violence, and by a growing and greedy criminal class he called the "blade mafia" (as he produced a knife). "We have always realized that Kerala is a consumer society so people just want to participate. Even though they don't have money, they will borrow money from some private entrepreneur, and they will purchase a lot of things. They will construct new houses. They just want to show off." Often poor farmers sign up for usurious loans at 50 to 60 percent interest. "They won't be in a position to pay it back, so the banker will send some *goondas,* young people who get easy money to act as agents of the banker." Often this ends with the ruin of the family, and the suicide of an indebted farmer.

Muslims also predominate among Kerala's million-plus migrant workers in the Persian Gulf. Many return to buy land and build houses, and thus have a stake in the state's future. Some bring with them Saudi-style fundamentalist beliefs. Madrassas, or Islamic semi-naries, have recently proliferated in Kerala, and many teachers "have no social view" but insist on adherence to a conservative dress code for girls as young as five or six. Thus Mr. Sadarikkoya did not take lightly the uproar over "love jihad." Agreed, no substantive evidence sup-ported claims that young Muslim males had seduced thousands of Hindu and Christian females to secure their conversion, but many Indians still believed this oft-repeated, politically charged assertion. At the moment, he added, threats to Kerala's communal civility seemed less than menacing. Hindu fundamentalists had tried repeatedly but have failed to elect a single deputy to the New Delhi parliament; their vote has averaged only 6 or 7 percent. And yet Kerala has no cordon sanitaire sealing its borders against infectious outbreaks of primal fanaticism, and it would be foolish to dismiss the risks of a Gujarat-style meltdown even in Malabar.

———

ON ITS FACE, it seems unlikely, even an oxymoron, that rabid nationalism could flow from the Hindu faith. In its history and tradi-tions, Hinduism is not a proselytizing religion given to holy crusades; it possesses no Pope or Patriarch, no Grand Ayatollah or Grand Mufti, much less a College of Cardinals. It is the air of festivity rather than evangelism that impresses visitors to the houses of Hinduism's many gods, an impression enhanced by female worshippers in their colorful saris and youngsters speckled with body paint. Hindu epics indeed celebrate martial virtues, yet it is the ambivalence about spilling kindred blood that forms an underlying theme of the *Bhagavad Gita.* Moreover, Hinduism is not sexually repressive; and feminine attributes are cele-brated in sacred texts, temple sculptures, and the widespread practice of matrilineal succession. Moreover, the most universally honored modern-day Indian is Mohandas Gandhi, the apostle of "the silken cord of love" who insisted that his doctrine of nonviolent resistance derived from mainstream Hinduism.

Still, the Mahatma's pacific theology is in dispute. As Wendy Doniger (a holder of doctorates in Sanskrit from both Oxford and Harvard) writes in *The Hindus: An Alternative History* (2009), if Gandhi believed that the ancient Hindu ideal of nonviolence would succeed in postcolonial India, he was whistling in the dark:

> His method succeeded against the British but could not avert the tragedy of partition. Gandhi's non-violence failed because it did not pay sufficient attention to the other, more tenacious ancient Hindu ideal that had a deeper grip on real emotions in the twentieth century: violence. For as Krishna pointed out in the *Bhagavad Gita*, it is quite possible to adhere to the mental principles of non-violence while killing your cousins in battle.

Gandhi himself was slain by a Hindu militant in January 1948, while fasting to protest postindependence communal violence. His assassin, Nathuram Godse, impenitently cried out in court that Gandhi's "constant and consistent pandering to the Muslims" justified his crime. (After Hindu nationalists assumed power in New Delhi in 1998, Godse's name and religion were discreetly expunged from schoolbooks.)

When it comes to political violence, one may fairly remark, Indians and Americans have little reason to point reproving fingers. Each country has experienced traumatic assassinations, contagious riots, and the slaughter of innocents by armed zealots. Nonetheless some Americans speak of their country's conception as if it occurred immaculately in a City on the Hill, while their Indian counterparts likewise propagate myths about idyllic things past. The Hindu Right's ascent is consensually traced to the establishment in 1925 of Rashtriya Swayamsevak Sangh (RSS), the National Corps of Volunteers, whose recruits (beginning at age six) vow to dedicate their bodies and souls to uniting India through Hindu purity. Postindependence, the RSS spawned a political wing, the Bharatiya Janata Party (BJP), and a cluster of associated organizations known collectively as Sangh Parivar. During the 1980s, the BJP formed governments in key states and by 1998, having won a plurality of seats in the New Delhi Parliament, it cobbled a coalition headed by Prime Minister Atal Bihari Vajpayee. Defeated in the 2004 national election, BJP remains India's principal opposition party and continues to rule key states, including Gujarat and Madhya Pradesh. (However, in the 2009 parliamentary election, not one of Kerala's twenty seats went to the BJP.)

The movement's core beliefs have been summarized by the Indian scholar D. R. Goyal in an authoritative history of the RSS (to which he once belonged):

> Hindus have lived in India since time immemorial; Hindus are the nation because all culture, civilization and life is contributed by them alone; non-Hindus are invaders or guests and cannot be treated as equal unless they adopt Hindu traditions, culture, etc., the non-Hindus, particularly Muslims and Christians, have been enemies of everything Hindu and are, therefore, to be treated as threats . . . the threat continues because the power is in the hands of those who do not believe in this nation as a Hindu Nation; those who talk of national unity as the unity of all those who live in this country are motivated by the selfish desire of cornering minority votes and are therefore traitors. . . . Hindus must develop the capacity for massive retaliation and offense is the best defense.

Inarguably, many peace-loving Indians made possible the success of BJP, but the party's rise is as inarguably stained by blood. Hindu nationalists sat on their hands in 1992 when enraged rioters in the northern city of Ayodhya dismantled a mosque sacred to Muslims, the venerable Babri Masjid, claiming it rested on the remains of a Hindu temple marking the traditional birthplace of the god-hero Ram. In succeeding months, at least two thousand died in communal riots that surged like a malevolent tsunami, cresting in Bombay (now Mumbai), Ahmedabad, Hyderabad, Meerut, Aligarh, and Baroda. This was the prelude to more horrific violence in the state of Gujarat in February and March 2002. Thousands were murdered, raped, or mutilated by rampaging Hindu zealots, many supplied with addresses of Muslim homes, presumably acquired from state officials. The police stood by, and Gujarat's Chief Minister Narendra Modi all but shrugged. BJP blamed Muslims for inciting the riots by allegedly setting fire to a railroad car filled with Hindus returning from a pilgrimage to Ayodhya's shattered mosque. Fifty-eight died in the blaze. In what is now a common judgment, the evidence for arson is flimsy, and tests indicate that the fire was probably ignited within the coach when a kerosene stove accidentally burst into flames.

From our perspective, what didn't happen in Kerala during India's widespread turmoil deserves equal attention. *Pace* Gandhi, six decades of Indian nationhood have witnessed three wars with Pakistan; a border war with China; surges of terrorism and repression in disputed Kashmir (the only Indian state with a Muslim majority); recurrent outbreaks of tribal violence in northernmost Nagaland; ongoing rural insurgencies in Bengal by Naxalite (Maoist) Communists; a widespread pogrom against Sikhs to avenge the assassination of Indira Gandhi; intermittent separatist risings in Hyderabad; the kidnappings by *dacoits* (criminal warlords) in impoverished Bihar; and most recently, the seaborne terror attacks on Mumbai by Pakistani jihadists. Yet one should also note two secular miracles: first, democratic and polyglot India, with its twenty-one official languages, has not just held together, but has flourished. And secondly, successive tides of violence have conspicuously washed over Kerala, as if it were a rock pool.

Why and how did this come about?

———

THERE IS, FORTUNATELY, an extensive literature inspired by both the triumphs and tragedies of democratic India. Among scholars in the front rank in the United States is Ashutosh Varshney, formerly a political scientist at the University of Michigan and currently at Brown University, who devoted a decade to researching his compendious *Ethnic Conflict and Civic Life: Hindus and Muslims in India*. Its publication in March 2002 by grim chance coincided with the eruption in Gujarat. His fieldwork was diligent, his conclusions fortified by pages of charts and tables. A key section analyzes the communal riots that broke out in Aligarh, a university town in the northern state of Uttar Pradesh, and the absence thereof in Kerala's Calicut, both cities having sizable Muslim minorities. In Varshney's summary: "What accounts for the difference between communal peace and violence? Though not anticipated when the project began, the pre-existing local networks of civic engagement between the two communities stand out as the single most important *proximate* cause" (his italics).

Varshney distinguishes between two forms of interaction: everyday engagement, as between neighbors, and associational engagement, meaning the transcending ties nurtured within professional groups, civic organizations, and trade unions. At the village level, neighborly contacts indeed promote communal peace, but in the impersonal urban environments of Calicut or Aligarh, civic engagement, or its absence, is critical. Although Aligarh is the seat of a major Muslim university, an invisible wall has divided its religious communities. In short, crossing sectarian barricades to address shared civic and professional concerns matters far more than small talk at a corner food shop.

Yet something else was at work in Kerala. Varshney and his foundation-supported research teams discovered that nowhere in colonial times were the degrading barriers of caste more rigidly enforced than in South India, especially in Kerala where nearly 70 percent of the Hindu population was deemed not only untouchable but "unseeable," since it was once a crime for a lower caste person to come within carefully defined distances of Brahmin eyes. Yet remarkably, these immemorial traditions collapsed in a few decades. "From being the most hierarchical society in India a century ago," Varshney writes, "Kerala today is the most egalitarian in the country. The traditional rules of pollution and deference have disappeared, access to education and temples is now unrestricted, the state will soon be 100 percent literate, and feudal landlordism has been abolished. All this has been achieved in a democratic framework." (It illustrates the paranoid style prevalent in North India that when Varshney's researchers arrived in Aligarh, press reports instantly claimed US spy agencies were the paymasters, while the media in Kerala applauded their curiosity.)

Why the contrast between the two states? History suggests that the very extravagance of Kerala's caste traditions fueled a popular rebellion. Malabar alone counts two hundred castes, with as many as twenty-five coexisting in a typical village. At the summit are Brahmins (priests and landlords); followed by Upper Nairs (soldiers and administrators); next repose Kammalans (artisans and merchants); and then Lower Nairs (cultivators and servants). Below swarm Ezhavas, the most numerous caste (farmers, toddy tappers, coconut traders, weavers, and ship-builders). Finally, at the lowest depths, assigned to the most disagreeable jobs, are Pulayas and Cherumas, generically known as Untouchables or Dalits (meaning "oppressed"), or in Gandhi's term, Harijans ("Children of God"). The latter were literally pariahs, since the English word itself derives from a Keralite caste, the Paraijars.

Swami Vivekananda (1863–1902), the charismatic Hindu who captivated Americans with a memorable speech at Chicago's 1893 Columbian Exposition, spoke for his own generation of reformers in describing Malabar as "a madhouse of castes." Dalits could not enter major Hindu temples; most were bonded for life as household servants or farm laborers; they could not drink from wells reserved for their overlords. Lower castes were barred from shopping in public markets, or bathing in temple pools, and detailed dress codes were prescribed for men and women alike, lest they "pollute" the vision of their caste superiors.

Among Kerala's achievements, assuredly none ranks higher than the nonviolent abolition and/or mitigation of these codes: a reform owed to a persistent, nonviolent campaign by caste associations, political parties, trade unions, intellectuals, and religious leaders.

Two reformers stand out: Sri Narayana Guru, a devout Hindu and legendary champion of the Ezhavas, his own caste; and E. M. S. Nam-boodiripad, a Brahmin by birth, a Marxist revolutionary in theory, and a shrewd pragmatist in practice.

The son of a farmer learned in Sanskrit, Sri Narayana (1856–1928) was initially a teacher of the sacred Upanishads and the Vedas, but he later became a Parivrajaka, or a wanderer in pursuit of truth. From his meditations flowed his maxim: "One Caste, One God, One Religion for Mankind," painted everywhere on neighborhood shrines dotting Kerala, which house statues of the guru. He propagated his credo in a host of books that energized two generations of reformers, and which gained universal resonance in Swami Vivekananda's once-famous address to the Parliament of Religions that assembled in Chicago during the 1893 Columbian Exposition. "I am proud to belong to a religion which has taught the world both tolerance and universal acceptance," the swami told a rapt audience. "We believe not only in universal toleration, but we also accept all religions as true. I am proud to belong to a nation which has sheltered the persecuted and the refugees of all religions and all nations of the earth." (Vivekananda is commemorated in a monumental island shrine at Kanyakumari, located on the southernmost tip of India, where the Bay of Bengal merges with the Indian Ocean and Arabian Sea.)

By an improbable twist, as if in dialectic conjured by Marx, Sri Narayana Guru's secular counterpart is a freethinking Brahmin Marxist, E. M. S. Namboodiripad (1909–1998), known in Kerala simply as EMS (as we shall also call him). It seems fair to say that Narayana Guru signaled the wide road not taken by future Hindu nationalists, and that EMS chose a multiparty path rejected in the Soviet Union and Communist China. Standing less than five feet tall, EMS otherwise stands out as the Communist who preferred the practice that Lenin once ridiculed as "parliamentary cretinism." Yet even in his own country, EMS is normally downgraded as a "provincial" leader, despite the creative and proven originality of his politics.

EMS and his comrades adjusted otherwise orthodox Marxism to Kerala's special character. Since no single religion, or caste, or political party could realistically expect to win an electoral majority, common sense argued for coalitions based on reciprocal compromises. Having had their first elected government ousted in 1959 by New Delhi and its Congress Party leaders, EMS and his comrades turned "the Centre" into their prime target, with Kerala's Congress functionaries its servile local appendage. His chosen medium was the press. Kerala led all India in its newspaper readership, and until his death EMS contributed a weekly column to the party journal. Heading into his second term as chief minister (1967–1969), he elaborated his strategy in a book, *Kerala: Yesterday, Today and Tomorrow* (1965). The final chapter, "Towards a Non-Congress Coalition Government," conceded that yes, there might be complications in forging ties with the Muslim League, various caste associations, and with Christian factions and rival leftists, especially since Congress was assailing Communists as "anti-national" for having urged a compromise peace to end India's recent wars with Pakistan and China. And so, "Vested interests in general and Congress in particular would do their utmost to widen the differences among the constituents of the united front and of the coalition. Every constituent unit of the united front would, therefore, have to be considerate in its dealings with its partners in coalition, vigilant against the maneuvers of the vested interest." And in ignoring the precepts of Lenin, he put into effect a democratic strategy that in Kerala nurtured a bloodless revolution that respected the diverse gods of his heterogeneous state.

———

HERE ONE SHOULD pause to note a wider reality illuminated by Kerala's example. As with individual humans, bipolar tends to be more fraught than multipolar. The more numerous the aggregate influences, the less likely a schizophrenic breakdown. Allowing for exceptions (e.g., Iraq and Lebanon), domestic eruptions seem more likely in societies where two scorpions are locked in the same bottle, especially when the governing system is biased in favor the larger, more entrenched contender (e.g., Sinhalese v. Tamils in Sri Lanka). If, however, no religious, ethnic, or interest group has a dominant majority, the incentives for deal making are obvious. Or in EMS's more oblique language, "The ideal of 'unity in diversity' is the outward manifestation of a basic unity of actual life, though in diverse forms." The same thought is graphically phrased by Shashi Tharoor, the author who currently represents Kerala as Congress Party MP in Delhi: "If America is a melting pot, then to me India is a thali—a selection of sumptuous dishes in different bowls. Each tastes different, and does not necessarily mix with the next, but they belong together on the same plate, and they complement each other in making the meal a satisfying repast."

In essence, this echoes the argument advanced centuries ago by James Madison, America's "Father of the Constitution," who held that among advantages of a well-constructed union, none deserved more attention than its tendency "to break and control the violence of faction." In Federalist No. 10, published in *The New York Packet* in 1787, Madison wrote that in a diverse republic, a religious sect "may degenerate into a political faction" but that a "variety of sects dispersed over the entire face of it must secure the national councils against any danger from that source." Or as the Great Seal of the United States more simply asserts, *E pluribus unum*. In Kerala, it can be ventured, Madison trumped Lenin.

Yet it also needs stressing that special circumstances opened the path for the electoral victory of reformist regimes in Kerala: the blessings of literacy and the traumatic shock of a local sectarian meltdown. EMS was a beneficiary of the former and a witness to the latter. For nearly a century, Protestant and Catholic missionaries nurtured a thriving network of schools and colleges (including Victoria College, founded in 1866, which EMS attended). As important, the maharajas of Travancore and Cochin long promoted quality education and literacy campaigns, both from conviction and in willing response to the pressures from forward-thinking British governors. By 1931, Kerala's inhabitants were by official count India's most literate: Cochin (34 percent), Travancore (29 percent), and Malabar (14 percent), while the figure for India as a whole was 8 percent.

Simultaneously, Kerala's budding caste associations began pressing for emancipation through strikes and protests. These strands came together in the independence struggle led by the Indian National Congress, which burst forward in the 1920s, propelled by anger over Britain's failure to deliver dominion status (i.e., self-rule) in recompense for Indian sacrifices during World War I. (India not only recruited a million-plus troops for the Allies in Europe and the Middle East, but also paid their "ordinary expenses.") Out of this ferment emerged Mohandas Gandhi, the former barrister turned radical pacifist; together with his Brahmin adjutant, Jawaharlal Nehru, secular, socialist, and Cambridge educated; and Mohammad Ali Jinnah, the austere, faultlessly tailored Ismaili champion of the Muslim League. It was their shared belief that the struggle for nationhood would unite Hindus, Muslims, and Christians, an assumption jolted after World War I by the Moplah Rebellion, as it is still remembered. By ironic circumstance, this eruption occurred in literate, forward-looking Kerala.

In 1921, Congress mounted a "non-cooperation" protest in Calicut, but it was soon overwhelmed by Muslim fury over perceived British threats to humble the Ottoman Caliphate, regarded as the global voice of Islam by millions of Indian Muslims. (Three years later, the secular founders of the newborn Turkish Republic would abolish the anachronistic caliphate). In Malabar, the landless Muslims known as Moplahs, or Mapillas, vented their rage not only against the British but against their despised Brahmin landlords. In what was subsequently diagnosed as a class-based revolt not necessarily aimed at all Hindus, a hundred or more Hindu temples were sacked. Tales of murder, rape, and forced conversion abounded, along with accounts of brutal reprisals against Muslims by Hindu police. Of the rebels, 2,226 were reportedly killed, 1,615 were wounded, 5,688 were imprisoned, and 38,256 surrendered.

Nevertheless, counterintuitively, sectarian strife in Malabar thereafter ebbed. In Ashutosh Varshney's judgment, this was principally due to the gathering mobilization of lower castes: "Hindu-Muslim issues simply could not match the passions aroused by caste inequalities and injustices. A restructuring of mass politics took place. Communal bitterness increasingly disappeared from the political space. Politics, memory, and emotions were reconfigured." And in this transformation, EMS and his Marxist cadres played a vital, generally overlooked role, culminating in the 1947 victory of a Communist-led coalition.

It was the first time anywhere that Communists had come to power through elections in a populous territory. And this victory owed much to the fact that upper-caste Brahmins and Nairs had taken up the grievances of the lower castes, Muslims, and Christians. Hence our own curiosity about how and why Brahmins like EMS had become radical parliamentary Marxists. So we sought a meeting with surviving specimens of this remarkable elite.

———

PANJAL VILLAGE LIES in the former princely state of Cochin (nowadays Kochi), a mere dot on the map in the lower foothills of the Western Ghat Mountains whose local temples are favorite stops on the Hindu pilgrimage trails. As we found, its charms are amply hidden from the casual tourist. It's here that one can see the indigenous architecture—low, rambling houses with peaked tile roofs, a scattering of rice paddy fields flanked by coconut palms, and the houses of

Namboothiri Brahmin landowners, but no real town center. Yet Panjal is triply fascinating, because its five thousand or so inhabitants include all major Hindu castes, including a disproportionate number of Brahmins; because it had once been the scene of protracted conflict between the impoverished landless and their high-caste landlords; and finally, because key figures in the propertied elite took the lead in the successful campaign to end their own privileges.

We had come to meet Subramanian Namboothiri, scholar and author, the winner of the Kerala Literary Academy award to its best dramatist, and a longtime member of the Communist Party of India (CPI) and Vasudevan Namboothiri, art critic, Sanskrit scholar, former secretary of the Kerala Kalamandalam, the renowned performing arts center. He's also a patron of Kathakali, the region's classical dance drama, and a leading left-wing journalist, whose living room tables displayed an array of newspapers (delivered that morning by bus). On the walls hung glassed-fronted shelves displaying fading photographs of eminent ancestors and civic awards. All the elder Brahmin males were bare chested, save for the sacred white thread they wear denoting their priestly caste. Instead of trousers they wore the traditional dhoti or *mundu* as it is called in Kerala. Wives and daughters were ceremoniously introduced but took little part in our meetings except to offer tea and after our interviews to cook a *thali*—an assortment of vegetarian dishes served on traditional banana leaves (conveniently composted after use).

Both elders followed a similar political trajectory. Each was a Namboothiri (also spelled Nambudiri), among the most orthodox of the priestly Brahmin castes; their families once owned the greater part of the tillable land in Panjal Village, most of which was leased to upper caste Nairs but farmed by lower caste workers. In former times, when their fathers strolled through their ancestral fields, as one son recalled, they were preceded by servants shouting "Ho!" to warn untouchables to scatter immediately and avoid visual pollution of their approaching masters. Strict rules governed everything, most especially marriage. Only the eldest son was allowed a Brahmin bride; all other boys were expected to dedicate themselves to study, and if they married, it was to a Nair bride. Yet when these Brahmins became adults they began to question and eventually contest the venerable caste system.

In the 1940s, they joined the Indian National Congress, whose big tent offered space to Indians of every class, caste, and religion seeking to end alien rule. Outcaste Dalits were followers of the political activist B. R. Ambedkar, a fellow Dalit who converted many of his followers to caste-free Buddhism. Illiterate and impoverished villagers were drawn to their hero, Gandhi, while middle- and upper-middle-class Indians looked to Nehru and his secular and socialist allies (such as the Calicut-born firebrand, Krishna Menon, still remembered at the United Nations for delivering its longest-ever speech: a full eight hours, defending New Delhi's policies in disputed Kashmir). Muslims found their champion in Jinnah, who reiterated his signature phrase, "Islam in danger!" whenever he believed his followers were slighted during the freedom struggle; only in its final phases did he and the Muslim League push for partition. And among the freedom movement's younger recruits was E. M. S. Namboodiripad, who like many of his generation then moved leftward, becoming a founder in 1934 of the Congress Socialist Party, while secretly and simultaneously assisting the then illegal Communist Party of India (CPI).

Our informants were both drawn to Communism by its orderly, humanistic ideology and each took part in strikes and demonstrations in the 1940s, risking arrest or imprisonment (as EMS later wrote, "Jail was my university"). By then, the Communist anthem, the "International," had been translated into Malayalam, along with tracts by Lenin, Trotsky, and Stalin. Newspapers, theater, and popular arts propagated the cause, so that even if the CPI was small in numbers, its influence was pervasive. As summarized by the Australian scholar Robin Jeffrey in a history of the state's leftist movements, "Marxism in Kerala came to fill an ideological void keenly felt by thousands of literate, alienated people. Given glaring class divisions, high rates of literacy and heavy population density, what was crucial in directing Malayalis toward communism was the breakdown of the social system."

"We Namboothiris came a bit late to understand our situation," recalled Subramanian Namboothiri. "But [during the 1940s] we suddenly became aware, and began to study English and other languages. At that time, there was much questioning among youths in the Congress, and some of us went to the extreme and became Communists or

Marxists. I became a Communist." He was affronted by the invidious irrationality of traditional Brahmin taboos: Namboothiri women, known as "the people inside the house," wore veils and ventured outside only to visit close relatives or temples; even so, they were always accompanied by a maid. Inside the house, they were not allowed to wear anything to cover their upper body. The younger Namboothiri sons didn't fare much better than the women. Everything favored the eldest son, as a reform-minded Brahmin, V. T. Bhattathiripad, declared "It is better to be born a dog than a younger son in a Namboothiri family."

In August 1947, India finally rejoiced in its "tryst with destiny" (Nehru's phrase). Universal suffrage became a reality, and four years later the newborn republic anxiously braced for its first general election. Voting was spread over one million square miles and required 224,000 polling booths for some 200 million eligible voters, the great majority illiterate, speaking a score of major languages within a mind-blowing total of 415 defined tongues (as enumerated by Bible translators). In the event, the great gamble succeeded. Violence was negligible, and although the Congress Party secured 364 out of 489 seats in Parliament, more than half the votes went to other parties. (Congress benefited from the British-inherited first-past-the-post formula, since in most constituencies six or more rival candidates appeared on the same ballot.)

Out of this ferment emerged a legal Communist Party of India with strong bases in Kerala and Bengal, geographically distant states with contrary political traditions. Bengal was turbulent, with recurrent communal riots in Calcutta and a germinating insurgency by Maoist-inspired, militant Naxalites in the rural hinterland. The real surprise was the rise of the radical left in Kerala, given its three major religious communities and a Communist Party still defensive about its ideological floundering during World War II.

All this was living history to Vasudevan Namboothiri. He had just left college when he joined the staff of Kerala's Communist newspaper enduring its travails when it was banned for an antiwar stance that persisted until Hitler invaded the Soviet Union.

"Then [the party] named it the antifascist war," he recalled, "and with that the government lifted the ban. When independence came, the party called it only a compromise between Indian officials and the

British imperialists. We won't recognize it. But in two years the Communists changed their minds." He remembered the fierce intramural debates over "left mediation" during a decade of inept and unpopular Congress rule in Kerala. The party's pragmatists prevailed, and Communists increased their vote in successive local elections: from 10 percent in 1948 and 18 percent in 1951, then to 35 percent statewide in 1957, enough to form a coalition regime with EMS as its chief minister.

In office, the leftist ministry freed political prisoners, enacted a far-reaching Land Reform Ordinance, and adopted measures that made primary education compulsory for all Keralites while extending government standards to private schools, many church operated. It was the latter initiative that ignited the most passion. Christian clerics joined with conservative caste organizations in mounting protest marches, sometimes provoking pitched battles with police. Among leaders in New Delhi, none responded more vehemently than Prime Minister Nehru's daughter Indira Gandhi, newly elected as president of the Congress Party. "When Kerala is virtually on fire," she told an audience in New Delhi, "it becomes the Centre's duty to go to the aid of the people; the misrule of the Communist rulers of the state has created a situation which is unparalleled in the history of our country. Such a situation does not brook legal quibbling." (This presaged Mrs. Gandhi's own premiership, when she selectively suspended state governments whose leaders she found wanting, at the cost of undermining India's democratic federalism and her own reputation.)

On July 30, 1959, invoking an article of the Constitution empowering the Centre to dissolve a state government on law-and-order grounds, Nehru seconded his daughter's plea and evicted Kerala's Communist government. In a special election, a record 84 percent of the eligible voters awarded a solid majority to Congress and its Socialist and Muslim League allies. Nehru himself took part in a campaign billed as a choice between "Communism and democracy." Still, it proved a temporary victory for the Centre. Four years later, EMS and his wing of the party broke with their pro-Moscow comrades to form a new Communist Party of India–Marxist (CPM), which chose to remain neutral in the ideological duel between Moscow and Beijing. That same year, 1963, the stubbornly independent voters of Kerala had their own second thoughts. They now awarded 53 out of 133 legislative seats to the newborn CPM, compared with 19 to the CPI, and a mere 30 to the Congress Party, whose record in office was deemed ineffectual and uninspiring. Thus a beaming EMS commenced his final term as chief minister, having forged a coalition with the Muslim League and other independent deputies.

A political cycle commenced: Keralites thereafter switched electoral support to and from Communists and Congress, with Muslims frequently holding the balance of power, an example of give-and-take democracy that has made India as a whole a laudable exception in South Asia.

———

AFTER VISITING PANJAL, we felt we had a firmer grasp on the achievements, the failures, and the paradoxes of democratic change in Kerala. For decades, leftist and centrist governments had promised to reform the state's rigidly stratified social and theocratic system. In this village, they evidently succeeded: not wholly, but substantially. Panjal is no longer a pyramid capped by seigniorial landowners resting on a huge base of landless serfs; it is instead a patchwork of smallholders. Their former Brahmin masters today live peacefully in modest traditional villas; Brahmin sons still learn the Vedas and serve their villages as priests. Those we interviewed approved the redistribution of their ancestral holdings but regretted that the major benefits of land reform had gone to the middle castes instead of the still-impoverished lowest castes (who continued to work in the lands).

To our more parochial benefit, the changes in Panjal have been tracked by a succession of social scientists, led by the American anthropologist Richard W. Franke. Beginning in the 1980s, Franke along with other researchers tried to determine whether the Kerala Land Reform Act (as amended in 1969) had in reality broken up large estates in this typical village. He concluded, in articles and books published in 1992 to 1994, that the reforms had significantly reduced caste inequality. The historic grip of Panjal's Namboothiri Brahmins on land ownership and higher incomes, Franke concluded, had been decisively broken:

The land basis for caste inequality and caste exploitation has been entirely eliminated in land reform. Brahmin incomes have risen far less rapidly than those of other castes. Nair and Mannan caste households have gained the most, while the lowest caste Pulayas have raised their relative position only slightly. Mannans and Pulayas probably have gained more from programs outside the land reform, such as affirmative action.

In Franke's view, the momentum for reform was energized by organized tenants and their allies whose struggles reinforced the leverage of the lowest caste groups. Using tax records, he calculated that the average income of former landlords had shrunk to 1.5 times the overall average in the village, compared with the six-fold ratio prior to land reform.

Equally interesting to us was the way in which Panjal's Brahmins somehow blended Marx with their proud adherence to Hinduism. Midway through our talks, Kunju, Vasudevan's son, offered to take us to his nearby family temple, known in full as Killimangalam Mana Palungil Siva Narayana Temple. We were allowed inside as special guests only because it was owned privately, otherwise temples in Kerala are accessible only to Hindus. The temple, open to all castes since 1951, with its oldest sections dating to the eleventh century, has its costs borne by the Vasudevan family, with the help of the donations of local villagers. It proved to be a large horizontal nest of interlocking chambers leading to the central sanctum where Namboothiri priests perform rituals and offer their prayers and gifts to the gods. As his male visitors donned the obligatory white *mundu*, our host explained that he was the officiating priest, that the temple was sacred to Shiva and Vishnu, that Kathakali dances were still performed occasionally, that its precincts were available for marriages and feasts, that termite damage was an abiding problem, and that his mother had presciently planted the coconut trees in the encircling grounds. He took us to the sanctum sanctorum consecrated to Ganesh, the elephant god, whose devotees arrive daily with offerings "to have their daughters get married or to remove obstacles. Ganesh is very famous for that. It is a sweet thing."

Here, facing the inner sanctum, our host paused. "This has a story. We had another temple, one mile from here, where there is a small river.

During the monsoon season, the *pujari* [priest] could not reach the temple to do the *puja* [a ritual offering to the gods] because the river overflowed. So my great-grandfather said, 'Okay, I'm going to shift that temple here.' But the astrologers said, 'No, no, you can't do that. The deity is not willing.' So my great-grandfather said, 'Okay, if the deity is not willing, he can starve. I don't mind.' After two days, the astrologers came back and said, 'Okay, since we talked, he is willing.'"

And so the Ganesh moved back to its earlier site, a modest victory for pragmatism over the all-controlling stars.

———

ON HEARING THE WORD "astrologer," our ears perked up. We wondered if, as we had been told, the leaders of Kerala's Communist Party (Marxist) still consulted the stars. Shortly after leaving Panjal, we interviewed K. P. Raveendran, the CPM Municipal Chairman of Thalassery (population circa 100,000), a city that boasts it is the birthplace of Indian cricket and the exporter of the world's best pepper. Our meeting with the intense, forty-something municipal chairman took place in his office, where he was flanked by a dozen attentive aides. Obligatory coconuts were passed out and as we sipped the milk from straws, we asked questions about communal harmony in this city, which has a larger than average number of Muslims. Putting our skepticism to rest, Raveendran pointed to his deputy seated next to him. "I am a Hindu, he is a Muslim."

"Suppose a problem happens between Muslims and Hindus," we asked, "do you solve it or do the police?" He responded: "The communal problems are usually created by one or two bad elements perhaps for political or communal reasons." Rumors start and "nothing has happened but just to throw oil on the fire. First the police try and quell the rumors and then they intervene." For example, recently a Hindu procession was going to the temple and somebody threw a *chapal* (a sandal) and there was a rumor that a Muslim did it. Actually it was done by some Hindus in order to cause a problem. The matter was resolved within twenty-four hours. The Hindus were persuaded by the evidence, and nothing happened.

At the end of our interview, we posed a mischievous question: Was it true that CPM office holders consulted horoscopes? A buzz coursed through the room. The municipal chairman paused and exchanged whispers with his colleagues when a senior adviser uttered the authoritative answer: "It's a traditional society, old practices continue."

This mix of scientific socialism with Hinduism's traditional practices has perennially baffled Western visitors, among them Arthur Koestler, the Hungarian-born connoisseur of failed ideologies. While visiting India to research a book on Asia's "culinary and spiritual spices," Koestler turned up in Kerala in January 1959, "the first country under Communist rule that I had visited since I left the Communist Party in 1938." He described Kerala as a "tropical Marxist Ruritania, where Cabinet Ministers were known to consult their horoscopes to deduce the Party-line from the stars." Yet for the author of *Darkness at Noon,* it was not a happy visit. He was unimpressed by his encounters with the state's reigning guru, Sri Atmananda Krishna Menon (not be confused with Nehru's leftist foreign minister) and was evicted after three days from the Mascot Hotel, whose manager insisted that Koestler's travel agent had failed to book a longer stay.

It developed that the misunderstanding was genuine, that it was not a Communist plot, but Koestler's patience's was exhausted. As he wrote to his secretary/mistress/future wife Cynthia Jeffries, Indian democracy was a sham, blighted by mindless obedience to Hinduism, "the root of the spiritual and social crisis, the tragic predicament of India." Democracy therefore had no real future in India. As he elaborated in *The Lotus and the Robot* (1961), "At best it will settle down under a benevolent dictator in the Kemal-Sukarno-Ayub tradition; at worst become a totalitarian state after the Chinese model—see the warning signs in Kerala, West Bengal, or Andhra." (This was not among Koestler's brilliant forecasts.)

Still, we owe to him a timeless, still applicable description of Trivandrum, as Kerala's capital was traditionally known: "The Communist State capital turned out to be the charming tropical suburb to a nonexistent town, its low bungalows hidden among lush coconut-groves. It is true that there were a few huge concrete blocks in the usual Esperanto architecture—administrative buildings, hospitals and clinics—but they stuck out like sore thumbs in plaster casts."

———

KERALA'S CAPITAL REMAINS a work in progress, as elastic as its expanding name. By official decree, its name is now Thiruvananthapuram, the "City of the Sacred Serpent." Its circa 900,000 inhabitants are spread over seven hills linked by a tangled web of tree-lined streets clogged with auto-rickshaws. The capital vibrates with unfocused energy, recalling John Kenneth Galbraith's description of India in the 1960s as "functioning anarchy."

What impressed us about the capital was its immense pharmacopoeia of hospitals, clinics, Ayurvedic pharmacies, and spas. During our exploration, we had been told repeatedly that Keralites were extremely health conscious. In villages and among the elderly, the practice of Ayurvedic medicine, deriving from ancient Hindu practices that try to balance wind, fire, and water within the body, prevails. But increasingly Keralites want Western pills (India manufactures many for the United States market), Western joint replacements, Western open-heart surgery, and Western chemotherapy for cancers. (According to recently compiled data, Kerala has become the coronary capital of India.) As a physician told us, Kerala's health care was once one of the wonders of the developing world. "We did have good primary care. Now it's the best in India, but it's not good enough." We were speaking to Dr. Krishna Kumar, chief pediatric cardiologist at the Amrita Institute of Medical Sciences. "What was achieved in Kerala in the 1970s was by earlier governments which were truly committed to the people. Much of those benefits are being lost, eroded with time because the commitment to primary health care is no longer the same. So Kerala hasn't really made a fundamental advance in its health indices over the last thirty years." Dr. Kumar, who trained at Boston's famed Children's Hospital, laments the current tendency to copy trends in the United States: expensive hospital care and solutions through pills rather than life-style changes.

Our entire health care system is flawed. It's flawed because we are completely devoted to tertiary care that takes care of the upper strata of society. The actual needs, the health needs, of the vast majority of the population is completely unmet. And the answers don't come from high-technology solutions. The answers don't come from knee replacements, or catheterization, or devices, or open-heart surgeries. The answers come from simple preventative services, basic immunization, good health care advice, education, and good primary health care.

Dr. Kumar's criticism was particularly informed since he practices surgery at a state-of-the-art facility near Cochin. Since its inception a decade ago, the Amrita Institute has grown from a small hospital to a health-care center with 50 departments, a staff of 2,500, 500 volunteers, 22 operating tables, and 400 hospital beds. It is a not-for-profit institution "committed to providing outstanding and affordable medical care in a patient-friendly environment" regardless of "race, caste, religion, or economic condition." Its mission was set forth by its still-active founder (as of 2010), the spiritual leader Sri Mata Amritanandamayi, known affectionately to all as Amma. A fisherman's daughter, she is renowned for her charity work in many fields, including health and education. Amma's portrait hangs over the desk from which Dr. Kumar daily supervises the care of scores of ailing youngsters.

Asked why he returned to India instead of pursuing a more lucrative career in the United States, he replied,

Before that I lived in the north of India, and I'd grown up all over India, so it's been really a very interesting journey. I've been particularly interested in situations where I've been able to be with a variety of communities living side by side. And Kerala is probably the best example in India. I think they have assimilated various cultures very well. It turns out that most of our patients are Muslims, for a reason that I can't fathom. And relatively small proportions are Hindus, Syrian Christians, and the Catholics. I don't really understand, for this is a Hindu hospital. It was inspired by Amma, who is a Hindu spiritual leader but again, she really encourages and strongly urges that we should take care of various religious communities as if they are one. In twelve years, I have taken care of over 10,000 patients here. I don't recall a single instance where people have been upset about their religious sentiments being hurt or having made any specific requests on grounds of religion other than small issues. We've had Jehovah's Witnesses who didn't want to have blood transfusions, and we've had a few Muslim patients who have requested the rescheduling of their surgeries during Ramadan, when they wouldn't want to be operated on. Kerala is fairly mature society so you encounter fewer problems here than any other part of the country because the education level is high.

In our discussions with academic, journalistic, and political figures, we began to take account of the underside of Kerala's extraordinary achievements. As the Duke of Wellington ruefully remarked, "Nothing except a battle lost can be half as melancholy as a battle won." In Kerala, every increase in life expectancy has raised the medical costs of an aging population. Fostering a competitive, consumerist society has yielded familiar afflictions: Kerala's suicide rate is the highest in India; alcoholism is now a challenge, along with an ever-rising auto fatality rate (India as a nation leads the world in traffic-related deaths, averaging 100,000 annually). According to physicians we met, obesity is also a focus of concern in Kerala (abetted, in our anecdotal observation, by the general absence of sidewalks, parks, and other safe places to walk, run, bike, or play).

Another perennial worry has been the lack of jobs for India's most literate workers. Kerala's fisheries account for some 22 percent of India's marine exports, and fishing is the source of income for about 330,000 workers in 222 coastal villages, but fishing is declining and otherwise the state has few large-scale, job-generating sectors. Instead, cottage industries proliferate, many of them high-minded and eco-friendly, but few serious exporters. In effect, Kerala is reaping the unanticipated results of its own successes, and is experiencing frustrations that stem from the excessive expectations politicians have raised. Certainly few anticipated that one million or more Keralites, most of them Muslims, would wind up as engineers, construction workers, and service employees in the volatile Gulf Emirates, and that their remittances would exceed their state's fiscal revenues from New Delhi. Still, this has an encouraging offset, since the returning workers buy property and invest in businesses, thus fusing their personal interests with those of Kerala.

Arguably no group remains as ambivalent about the vaunted "Kerala Model" than millions of semiliberated women. This is the only Indian state in which females outnumber males (51 to 49 percent), and where birth rates have declined to the levels of advanced industrial societies. Many analysts attribute this to Kerala's exceptional literacy, which has given women far greater influence on family decisions than their sisters elsewhere. Keralite women have fewer children, live longer, and survive at birth more frequently than men. Still, in the judgment of Australia's Robin Jeffrey, "The willingness of families to educate their daughters and marry them late is the greatest single factor in explaining Kerala's declining birth rate. Yet women still do not play a major role in public politics."

We heard as much from Dr. Praveena Kodoth at the Centre for Development Studies in Trivandrum, a leading authority on gender issues. Before the age of reform, Kerala was still in some respects a matrilineal society, but as Dr. Kodoth remarked, the implicit goal of postindependence education has been to prepare women for a patriarchal society. More than half the students in college are female, yet how many women, she asked, actually held major political office? "There is now one state minister and a handful of women in our state assembly, despite the fact that everybody tells you we have more women than men. In local government, yes, we have a 33 percent reservation [i.e., quota] for women, and it will soon become 50 percent, but that's only at the village level." Don't be taken in by all the talk about female literacy, Dr. Kodoth admonished. "It can also empower patriarchy, and that's what has happened here."

Seconding her view was Dr. G. S. Jayasree, author, editor, and director of the Centre of Women's Studies at the University of Kerala. Did she agree that Kerala was a patriarchal society? "Yes, it's really true," she responded, "because even now we have inherited the colonial system of education, where we are taught to be ideal wives and mothers. But I should also say we have some signs of change in our university classrooms," especially regarding the matter of caste: "Back when we were students, no one ever used to talk about caste, at least in schools and colleges, but my daughter tells me that it is now common. In my own generation, we never mentioned caste as such, and that kind of non-mentioning is not good." As to the negatives, she deplored at length the intolerable pressures on women to excel at school, leading to their borrowing heavily to attend costly private institutes with the aim of migrating abroad, arguably contributing to their higher suicide rate compared to their male schoolmates.

This pressure was crystallized in the ubiquitous highway posters we saw day after day, featuring a smiling young woman next to the words "Work, Study, Migrate."

———

ALL THIS IS GRIST for journalists in Thiruvananthapuram. No other state matches Kerala's passion for newsprint. This is evident in the proliferation of newspapers in Malayalam, the state's vernacular tongue (and surely the world's sole language whose name is a palindrome, meaning it can be spelled correctly either backward or forward). So we sought out Mr. T. Radakrishnan, coordinating editor of *The Mangalam Daily*, a politically independent newcomer known for its investigative reporting. He guides eight local reporters and ten subeditors who turn out four different editions, and he helps determine news and editorial policies, having recently left a bigger established newspaper to join the new daily whose circulation, unlike that of US local papers, is growing.

India's newspapers nevertheless contend with straitened budgets. Hence the concern in 2009 over the revelation that some hard-pressed vernacular dailies are marketing "political advertising," in effect hawking favorable news coverage for a price to politicians and their parties, an ominous precedent. But his own paper is vigilant, and he believes this has not occurred in Kerala, though he continues to press for details.

Finally, we encountered an ornament of Kerala's past in our meeting in the modest but art-filled Pattom Palace with Maharaja Marthanda Varma, the 88-year-old head of Travancore's royal family whose ancestors ruled Travancore until 1971, when a constitutional amendment formally terminated the status of all royal families in India's princely states. Like his predecessors, including his father and long-reigning elder brother, the king is at once a devout Hindu who goes daily to his family's Sri Padmanabhaswamy Temple, and a secular-minded progressive on issues of tolerance and education. We discussed his family's matrilineal tradition, which he defined in a sentence: "I became the maharaja because I was my mother's son, rather than my father's son."

The best measure of the esteem in which he is held is that even as a "pensioner" (his phrase for himself); he is invited to take part in three hundred events each year. Notably, he became the spokesperson in the subsequent current dispute over the newfound temple treasure. In our own encounter with him, we sensed something of the grandeur of a creed with close to one billion adherents, making it the world's third most popular religion. Kerala has been spared the wilder effusions of Hindu nationalists who give the impression of being a besieged minority under virulent attack. Religion in India has become the pretext for riots and hysterical rallies that mock sanity and civility. Parallel with this, as the British author William Dalrymple comments, "There has been a concerted attempt by politicians on the Hindu right to rewrite the history textbooks used in Indian schools and to bring historians and the writing of history under their direct control." Hence the word "saffronization" to describe ongoing attempts to dip accounts of the past in the trademark dye of the BJP.

In a surreal episode in 2004, Hindu militants armed with crowbars smashed into a library in Pune, a suburb of Mumbai, and vandalized 18,000 volumes, including a first-century manuscript of *The Mahabharata*, before police finally arrived. Why? Because a book in the library written by an American academic dared question the legitimacy of a seventeenth-century Hindu warlord named Shivaji Bhonsle who defied the (Muslim) Mughal empire and crowned himself king of an independent Maratha state. Only a Jonathan Swift could do justice to this act of barbarism in the name of India's ten thousand gods. How heartening therefore to meet Sri Marthanda Varma, and to be reminded that his creed is not only the world's oldest, but has nurtured Buddhism, Jainism, and the Sikh religion. And that Kerala stands as testament to the power of reason to tame the furies of misbegotten zealotry.

3

TATARSTAN:
THE CAVE OF THE CLAN BEARS

I am in Asia! I wanted to see this country with my own eyes. In Kazan, there are twenty different peoples who are nothing like each other and I have to sew, for them, one garment to suit everyone.

—CATHERINE THE GREAT TO VOLTAIRE,
WHILE VISITING KAZAN, MAY 29, 1767

MIDWAY IN OUR TRAVELS we reconfirmed an important reality. When judging the relative health of reputedly successful multicultural societies, distances simplify, telescopes mislead, and the movie *Rashomon* provides an essential corrective. In Akira Kurosawa's 1950 masterpiece, filmgoers are offered conflicting versions of a rape and murder in a gloomy forest, each version flavored by the differing perceptions (and self-interest) of the culprits, victims, or witnesses. So we likewise heard firsthand testimonies that smudged the crisp and clear media profiles of our targeted societies, as for example, the Russian Republic of Tatarstan.

Situated to the west of the Urals at the juncture of the Volga and Kama Rivers, roughly five hundred miles east of Moscow, Kazan, the capital, straddles the cultural fault line separating Europe from Asia. Tatarstan's circa 3.8 million inhabitants are nominally divided into two major religions, mostly Sunni Muslims of Tatar origin (53 percent) and

Orthodox Christians of Russian origin (40 percent). Within and around these basic blocs sprout seventy lesser ethnicities and a score of other religions, which helps explain why election ballots are in six languages. Tatarstan forms the historic motherland of seven million Kazan Tatars, who belong to Russia's largest national minority (of whom less than one-third presently live in their titular republic, the rest having spread to Siberia, the Crimea, and the Caucasus, Moscow and the nearby Volga republics: the legacy of wars, migration, and Soviet-era border surgery).

All this is set forth in standard references, along with descriptions of Tatarstan's thriving agricultural sector, its petrochemical enterprises, its shrinking yet still lucrative petroleum fields, and its giant KamAZ truck factory, said to be the world's largest. But what Wikipedia entries, official websites, and gazetteers won't or can't say is that Tatarstan is ruled less by ideology, free markets, or religion than by the oldest of governing systems: blood relations and tribal camarillas. Its polity might be rightly called (with apologies to the novelist Jean Auel) the Cave of the Clan Bears. And yet, wheezes and malfunctions aside, the system so far has worked: Tatarstan has been spared the prolonged agony of another, no longer diverse former Soviet republic, Chechnya.

Unusually among the Russian Federation's thirty-three republics and autonomous districts, Tatarstan wrested from Moscow substantial cultural, political, and economic self-rule, which in good measure (generous fiscal breaks excepted) survived the wary ambivalence of Russia's once and likely future president, Vladimir Putin. But was this a success for bottom-up federalism or rather a case of shadow secessionism? And what does Tatarstan's special status say about the foggiest term in the political lexicon: sovereignty? We flew to Kazan to seek answers.

————

FLASH BACK TO August 2005. Protected by fifteen thousand Interior Ministry troops, thirteen thousand official guests are mingling in Kazan to celebrate the millennium of the Tatar capital's founding. Although Tatarstan remains an integral part of the Russian Federation, President Mintimer Shaimiev hosts a leadership summit of the Commonwealth of Independent States. (Formed after the Soviet collapse in

1991, the fifteen-member CIS includes the five Central Asian "stans" with which Tatarstan is erroneously, and chronically, confused.) The millennium celebration is a five-star fete, replete with fireworks, scholarly conferences, folk dances, horse races at a lavish new hippodrome, concerts, museum exhibits, and the inauguration of a Moscow-endowed, seven-stop subway.

Popping up everywhere is the presidential dynamo, Mintimer Sharipovich Shaimiev, once the republic's Communist boss and now ending his third term as president (twice by election, and then by appointment under Putin's centralizing doctrine of "vertical power"). At age sixty-eight, balding and heavily browed, Shaimiev is expert at exploiting useful anniversaries and the special prestige of Kazan, a city designated by the United Nations Educational, Scientific, and Cultural Organization (UNESCO) as a World Heritage Site and later branded as Russia's "Third Capital" (after Moscow and St. Petersburg). Tatarstan flags flutter along Bauman Street, the major thoroughfare leading to the ancient Kremlin, where a congress of kindred Tatars pays homage to their homeland. By an auspicious (and useful) coincidence, 2005 also marks the fifteenth anniversary of the Tatarstan Parliament's unanimous "Declaration of Sovereignty," which opened the way to a formal treaty with Moscow. Signing for Russia was then-President Boris Yeltsin, who had encouraged Tatarstan's inhabitants to "take all the sovereignty you can swallow." Both his oft-quoted remark and the treaty it helped beget provoked dismissive objections from Yeltsin's successor, Vladimir Putin.

Hence the delight among Tatars, when President Putin begins his principal address at Kazan's State Theater speaking in Tatar, a Turkic tongue. Switching to Russian, Putin recalls the pivotal, if unwilling, role Kazan played in the dramatic expansion of the Tsarist realm after Ivan the Terrible annexed the city in 1552. He also notes that "kazan" derives from the Tatar word for cauldron: an apt image for the capital's rich mixture of faiths and cultures.

The mixture is memorialized by the cathedral and mosque rising side by side within Kazan's thick-walled Kremlin atop a low hill overlooking the River Volga. For the first time in eighty years, an Orthodox service resonates in the newly restored Cathedral of the Annunciation, originally built to commemorate Ivan's conquest. Guests in the sober cortege led by the Orthodox Patriarch Alexius II include not only Shaimiev, but also the Grand Mufti of Russia and assorted imams. The cathedral's onion domes rival in splendor the blue minarets of the adjacent Kol Sharif Mosque (named for the imam who defended the mosque that once rose on the same site before its destruction by the Russians).

For devout Muslims, Kol Sharif's martyrdom remains an unhealed wound. In an open letter to Shaimiev, Tatar nationalists implored the president in 1992 to remember that the various churches in the Kremlin were built "on the graves of Tatars and their mosques." Responding to their demand for a monument to match a Soviet-era memorial to Ivan's Russians who died besieging Kazan, Shaimiev declared that the new mosque completed in 2005 would also serve as a memorial to all Tatar defenders. Built by Turkish contractors with extra funding by Saudi Arabia, Kol Sharif is ranked as one of Europe's two biggest mosques (the other is in Grozny, the capital of Chechnya); it both commemorates and exorcises.

In his dedicatory remarks, President Shaimiev recalls this history and goes on to say that the cathedral and mosque convey "a profound meaning, tied to the aspirations of the multiethnic peoples of the republic, to live in peace and friendship. The edifices stand next to each other as a symbol of mutual understanding between two leading faiths." This is not mere boilerplate. In living memory, there have been no violent eruptions between rival faiths in Tatarstan, an oasis of ecumenical tolerance where remarkably, nearly one in three marriages joins spouses professing different religions and/or ethnicity. Hence our own decision to explore Tatarstan in 2009, where by chance our visit overlapped with a brief stopover by Secretary of State Hillary Clinton.

"Welcome Hillary" and "Hillary Is Coming" proclaimed local headlines in an effusive greeting, marred only by the frosty public statement of a nationalist, self-proclaimed head of a pan-Tatar movement. "Does she know," demanded Ms. Fauzia Bairamova, "that Christianity has become an official religion and is obligatory in schools? [In fact, Tatarstan has no state religion.] Does she know that other nations' religious rights and their rights to an education are being abused? If she knows these things, then what is the United States going to do about it?"

But the ensuing silence suggested that hers was a momentary one-handed clap. For her part, Secretary Clinton inspected the cathedral and the mosque and justly extolled their symbolism. A State Department spokesman, Ian Kelly, rejected suggestions that she was seeking "the dismemberment of Russia." Not at all, Kelly explained to a questioner, since "to understand Russia and its vibrancy and its diversity, you have to get outside Moscow." Yet Mrs. Clinton's instructive visit failed to generate even a blip in the day's Western news cycle; nothing is duller than absence of conflict.

———

FOR OUR PART, from the moment of our arrival we experienced the *Rashomon* effect. What, we asked, about the great fete in 2005? Was Kazan really one thousand years old? Did the celebration proceed smoothly? And what of Shaimiev? Was he a wily negotiator and patriotic peacemaker, or rather (as detractors claimed) a party hack and enabler taking credit for an historic legacy for which he was not responsible? We spoke with friends and foes of the president (whose fourth and final term ended in 2010, when he gave way to a Shaimiev-anointed, Medvedev-appointed successor). We visited the Brezhnev-vintage industrial city of Naberezhnye Chelny, home of the KamAZ truck factory, and nearby Yelabuga, a historic mercantile village evoking the ghosts of Gogol and Chekhov, where the Soviet-era poet Marina Tsvetaeva killed herself in a fit of wartime despair. We spoke with monks, imams, rabbis, backstage wire-pullers, cabinet ministers, journalists, human rights activists, dissident scholars, and student rappers. Little that we heard conformed to the conventional clichés about this intriguing republic.

Once in Kazan, after we checked into our apartment hotel facing Kazan's opera house, we found that official versions of the millennium fete were, so to speak, quasi-official. In fact, as a flustered Tatar cultural bureaucrat confirmed, the thousand-year figure was based on the convenient archeological discovery of ancient coins buried in the Kremlin, believed to date to the late tenth century AD. This buttressed the claims of Tatars who hold that their forebears, known as Volga Bolgars, were founders of Kazan. (Volga Bolgars are also widely believed to be related to Balkan Bolgars, titular ancestors of today's Bulgaria.) Moreover (if the finds spoke truly), Kazan is 150 years older than Moscow, a point the millennium fete was also meant to underline.

In any case, Kazan's early history is a blend of fragments and fable until the thirteenth-century rise of the Mongol empire; the conquest of the Volga peoples by Batu, grandson of Genghis Khan; and their subsequent conversion to Islam as the Golden Horde fractured into autonomous khanates. Indisputably, in the fifteenth century, Kazan emerged as the capital of a Tatar khanate powerful enough to exact ransom from the early-day Muscovite kingdom, whose successive rulers either paid tribute to, or warred with, Kazan's khans until Ivan IV (The Terrible) sacked the city in 1552.

However, as we learned, much of this history is in spirited contention, recalling the old Soviet-era adage that nothing is harder to predict than the past. Thus among scholars there are Bolgarists versus Tatarists, while President Shaimiev deplores reflexive Russian references to "the Tatar-Mongol Yoke" as promoting "a negative attitude towards the Tatars." All sides agree the Tatars were/are not Mongols. As phrased by Shaimiev's biographer, Ravil Bukharaev, Tatars bear the same relation to Genghis Khan "as, say, the modern Danes and Dutch bear to Charlemagne." The Tatar tongue is Turkic, and physically Tatars are hard to distinguish from Russians save for names, dress (at times), and arguably salient cheekbones (as evident in the best-known of modern Tatars, Rudolf Nureyev, bred in Bashkortostan, a kindred republic southeast of Tatarstan).

Moreover, the identity debate is artificially inflated, as we were cautioned by a scholarly Kazan-based ethnologist, Damir Ishakov. "Russian self-consciousness," he told us, "is built on negating the Golden Horde, and this possibly may lead to their understanding that the Tatars are the ethnic group most opposed to the Russians. For their part, Tatars state their own claim, saying the Russians colonized us." In reality, Ishakov contends, Tatars and Russians are "interconnected vessels." How much saner (in his view) if both sides finally recognized that the predatory Golden Horde "was our common parent state." He paused, sighed, and added, "Because the imperial mindset is so strong in Russia at the moment, this interpretation will not be accepted."

———

NOR, IT APPEARED, was the millennium festival as harmonious as official accounts suggested. Little was said, for example, about the exclusion of high-level Vatican dignitaries from the Orthodox cathedral's celebration. As we learned, in a propitiatory gesture, the Holy See in 2005 had returned to Tatarstan a venerated copy of the icon known as the "Our Lady of Kazan." The renowned and long-vanished original was said to have been miraculously unearthed in the garden of a Kazan monastery in 1579. A pious copy, encrusted with jewels, was subsequently exhibited in Moscow and then in St. Petersburg. Believers credited prayers to "Our Lady" with twice helping to shield Moscow from foreign invaders: 1612 (by Poles) and 1812 (by the French). "Our Lady" was among the most popular of Slavic icons, inspiring eponymous Orthodox churches around the world; no fewer than nine replicas were said to be miracle workers. In 1904, thieves snatched the reputed original from its altar in Kazan, and in 1917 either Bolsheviks or devout White Russians (nobody is sure which) made off with the principal copy in Petrograd (as St. Petersburg then was known).

The icon next became known as "Our Lady of the Shadows," resurfacing in New York and finally at Our Lady of Fatima's shrine in Portugal, where in 1993 it was somehow acquired by Pope John Paul II. The pope vainly sought personally to return the icon to the Russian Orthodox Church as a peace offering to mend centuries of schism. Initially, Mikhail Gorbachev and later Vladimir Putin welcomed John Paul's overture, but both deferred to the Patriarch of All the Russians, the Orthodox pontiff, who opposed any papal visit whatever, reportedly accusing His Holiness of covertly seeking converts among the Orthodox.

Trapped awkwardly in the middle was Rafael Khakimov, the learned Muslim director of the Institute of History at the Tatarstan Academy of Sciences, and longtime senior counselor to President Shaimiev. Khakimov was part of a delegation led by Kazan's mayor, Kamil Iskhakov, charged with the fraught negotiations. Speaking for Kazan's spiritual community was Mufti Gusman-hazrat, since the Orthodox hierarchy declined to meet with the Vatican. We were told by Khakimov that the Holy See had pressed for a compromise whereby the Pontiff would make "a very short, several hours stop" at the millennium ceremony. But the Orthodox Patriarch was unyielding, less because he was personally opposed (in Khakimov's view) than "because he was afraid of the synod, the meeting of the archbishops. I know this very well because I was working on the problem, because I went to the Vatican to bring the icon back." A default agreement was struck between Christianity's two most numerous denominations: "Our Lady" was discreetly returned to Russia by a papal legate. Hence representatives of the Vatican were brusquely excluded from the formal repatriation in 2005 of "Our Lady" at the restored Kazan cathedral.

Khakimov's story illustrated the palimpsest nature of multiculturalism in Tatarstan: the smooth outer layer often masks a complex subscript. It took Muslims to mediate the return of "Our Lady" since "the Orthodox could not make direct contact with Roman Catholics because of their terrible relations." As Khakimov dryly elaborated, "I'm a Muslim and icons don't have a special meaning for me, except historical. . . . So this was a Muslim contribution, although nobody ever said thank you." By the same token, when (Christian) Old Believers sought to block the construction of a Roman Catholic chapel adjoining an Orthodox church in Kazan, their demand was rejected as "unacceptable" under a Tatarstan policy of "attentive control, which excludes the more radical extremes." In Khakimov's words, "If you attend an important political or social event here, you will see a mufti and an archbishop nearby, accompanied by Lutheran leaders, Roman Catholic leaders, and a rabbi, side by side. And so this has become part of our culture, not just in Kazan but all around in Tatarstan." And hence as well, a government led by tolerant self-proclaimed Muslims and former Communists somehow transcended the "clash of civilizations" gloomily envisioned by Harvard's Samuel Huntington.

An intense, fluent, and sixty-something intellectual, Dr. Khakimov is both a forceful nationalist and leading theoretician of moderate Euro-Islam (his coinage). His prolific works include a timely volume he edited, *Federalism in Russia,* translated and published in English. Yet the past permeates his book-lined offices. Near his desk is a framed sword forged in the age of the Golden Horde; close by one sees a panoramic map of Eurasia's ancient Islamic khanates; and then a photograph of his father, Sibgat Hakim (1911–1986), a Tatar poet and nationalist who tried to work with the Bolsheviks, only to be thrown into prison; he was later rehabilitated and just before his death was honored as "the People's Poet of Tatarstan."

There were more surprises. At first we could not quite grasp how a seemingly conventional Communist apparatchik, Mintimer Shaimiev (whose first name means "iron" in Tatar, and who supported the attempted coup against Gorbachev in 1991) somehow secured for Tatarstan not only innovative fiscal benefits, significant cultural autonomy, and diplomatic rights, but also is credited with ensuring a softer landing during Russia's free fall to a market economy. And we likewise wondered how a single, vague, and talismanic word helped make all this possible: "sovereignty."

———

"SOVEREIGNTY" MEANS everything and nothing. One is reminded of Karl Marx's attempt to define a commodity, "at first sight, a very trivial thing and easily understood." At second glance, Marx writes in *Das Kapital*, a commodity is "a very queer thing, abounding in metaphysical subtleties and theological niceties." For example, wood is merely an everyday thing until it becomes a commodity; then it "stands on its head, and evolves out of its wooden brain grotesque ideas." Similarly, sovereignty is an idea we intuitively grasp: unmolested self-rule. But when injected into political discourse, "sovereignty" also becomes a queer thing, an abstraction capable of inciting wars or preserving peace; it did both in post-Communist Russia.

The word's power can be sensed in countries whose citizens have endured the agonies of nonsovereignty: Iran, Cuba, Egypt, and China. All were ostensibly sovereign during the high noon of imperialism, a time remembered bitterly in China as "the century of humiliation." Yet as their inhabitants well knew, their presumed sovereignty was a diplomatic facade since on vital matters their emperors, shahs, and presidents were vassals to foreign powers. Over time, popular resentment bred the avenging furies, as personified by Khomeini, Castro, Nasser, and Mao.

A variation of the same word game characterized the Soviet Union's policies toward its predominantly non-Russian republics. Initially, the old empire's principal nationalities were promised "self-determination," a slogan as enthusiastically embraced by V. I. Lenin as by Woodrow Wilson, but which the USSR honored only on its deathbed (in Wilson's case, fair to add, his enthusiasm did not extend to Mexico or the Caribbean). Another elastic phrase was devised in 1918 by Bolshevik Russia's first Commissar of Nationalities, Joseph Stalin, who stipulated that non-Russian "autonomous" republics would be "national in form, but socialist in content." This meant that ethnic traditions and territorial frontiers were to be respected (more or less), but that Moscow Center would approve local party leaders and security chiefs, and determine educational, religious, and language policies. Finally, following the formal birth of the Soviet Union in 1924, all national territories were stitched into a quilt consisting of fifteen union republics (the most favored, nearly all of which seceded from the collapsing USSR), eighteen autonomous republics, twenty-three autonomous provinces, and forty-eight autonomous regions (as the count stood in 1989, before the quilt unraveled).

Soviet propaganda made much of the respect shown for the folkways of a multicultural population spread over one-sixth of the world's lands. Yet until the system verged on collapse, Moscow's party leaders failed to grasp how much discontent festered in their ethnic Potemkin villages. Among the misinformed was Mikhail Gorbachev, who declared in 1985 that "the nationalities problem has been decisively resolved." However, while visiting Washington seven years later, he was asked at an informal breakfast with scholars what proved to be his most difficult problem as Soviet president. Gorbachev replied: "The nationalities issue." When did he become aware of it? "In the fall or winter of 1990."

Two years too late, in the judgment of David Remnick who, as a correspondent for *The Washington Post* and *The New Yorker*, chronicled the old order's demise and the new Russia's birth. As he was told by Galina Starovoitova, a Duma member and an adviser to Yeltsin, disintegration was inevitable: "The Soviet Union brought together one-hundred and twenty-six nations and tried to homogenize them, managing it only superficially. . . . The layer of *Homo sovieticus* was extremely superficial." A valiant campaigner for human rights, Ms. Starovoitova was slain in a gangland-style killing as she was leaving her

Moscow apartment in 1998. Her analysis was confirmed when a flailing Gorbachev wavered between repression and concessions as breakaway popular fronts and nationalist movements spread contagiously in 1988 and 1989. He was beset both by frantic Kremlin hardliners and by more radical reformers led by the post-Communist populist, Boris Yeltsin. In summer 1990, at Yeltsin's initiative, the Russian Soviet Federated Socialist Republic (RSFSR) declared its own sovereignty, and by example encouraged others to follow suit. As they did, the entire structure tottered.

Scrambling to catch up, Gorbachev in early 1991 won referendum approval for developing a new, looser Union Treaty, a heresy that so outraged party hardliners opposed to greater autonomy that in August they conspired to oust him. Their botched coup accelerated a rush to independence by fourteen republics, spanning from the Baltic to the Caucasus and Central Asia. (Even ethnic Russians in eastern Ukraine joined in their republic's 90 percent vote for independence that December, startling Yeltsin himself.) The final ten days that shook the empire were signaled in the *Izvestiya* headlines jotted down by Jack F. Matlock Jr., the US envoy in Moscow: "Struggle for National Self-Determination May Threaten Integrity of Russia" (December 16); "Russian Parliament Takes Over in Kremlin" and "Union Parliament Passes into History" (December 18); "USSR Supreme Soviet Accepts Inevitability of Its Demise" (December 19); and "History of Soviet Union to End in Kazakhstan" (December 20). Four days later, on Christmas Eve, Soviet diplomats vacated their seat at the United Nations, making way for a new entity called the Russian Federation.

It ended not with a bang but with a press bulletin; the Union of Soviet Socialist Republics formally announced its own demise on December 31, 1991. Having named and helped found the hastily improvised Commonwealth of Independent States (CIS), Gorbachev honorably resigned. Yeltsin succeeded to his office in his capacity as president of the Russian Federation, and he was credibly hailed as his country's first democratically chosen ruler. At midnight precisely, the Soviet flag with its hammer and sickle was struck. The tricolor introduced three centuries earlier by Peter the Great once again flew over Moscow.

This astonishing transition posed a new, still unresolved question: What now for the non-Russian supposedly autonomous republics still embedded in Russia's newly sovereign federation? Weren't they likewise entitled to self-determination?

———

A GOOD QUESTION. Even shorn of its Soviet empire, the enormous Russian Federation spans eleven time zones and encompasses 13 percent of the earth's landmass (compared with the Tsarist Empire's 17 percent in 1917). Its total territory is nearly as vast as the United States and Canada put together. Its population, reckoned at 142 million in 2010, is primarily ethnic Russian, but with scores of persisting non-Russian enclaves, notably in the north Caucasus, throughout Siberia, and among the peoples of the Volga basin. With this ethnic diversity in mind, President Yeltsin in 1991 proposed a new Federation Treaty that acknowledged "republican sovereignty" and granted liberal rights to non-Russians. In March 1992, most republics voted to approve this charter, but it was rejected as too little and too late by both Tatarstan and Chechnya. A year later, Yeltsin called for a national referendum to give electoral legitimacy to his presidency; and the same duo barred even conducting a vote in their territories. (Yeltsin prevailed readily elsewhere, encouraging him to put forward a new, ambiguously permissive Russian Constitution.)

Tatarstan *and* Chechnya? Together? Both Kremlin insiders and foreign observers were puzzled. As everybody knew, the Chechens nursed a host of grievances, the most traumatic being Stalin's deportation in 1944 of a half million Chechens on the suspicion they might collaborate with Nazi armies. After Nikita Khrushchev in 1957 permitted Chechen repatriation (having described the deportation as a "mistake"), Muscovites nevertheless tended to vilify Chechens as criminals and killers, or in street vernacular as "black asses." Small wonder ethnic Chechens flocked to the separatist cause championed by former Soviet Air Force General Dzhokar Dudayev. What followed evidenced Boris Yeltsin at his least generous and most bloody minded: he initiated years of warfare in which Russian troops and bombers leveled Grozny, the Chechen capital, forcing Dudayev to flee. In 1996, a Russian guided missile honed in on the satellite signal of Dudayev's phone, killing him and two aides. (Ironically, his satellite call was to a Russian member of parliament proposing a meeting between Dudayev and President Shaimiev, who had opposed the war and volunteered to act as intermediary between Yeltsin and the Chechen leader.)

But Tatarstan? It was commonly assumed that the Volga republic was different. Over the centuries, its predominantly Islamic inhabitants had seemingly learned to coexist peacefully with Orthodox Russians, unlike the fractious tribes in the Caucasus, whose conquest in the nineteenth century provoked the fiercest anticolonial rising in Tsarist times. By contrast, beginning with Catherine the Great, the Russian elite commonly prized its Tatar subjects, often intermarrying with their nobles. (It was even deemed chic in St. Petersburg's salons to possess a touch of Tatar blood.) Strategically, the Volga and its tributaries formed vital passages for trade and conquering armies, and Kazan guarded the gateway: a true jewel in the Tsarist crown. Indeed, soon after its founding in 1804, Kazan University was ranked among the three best in Russia. (Leo Tolstoy, whose grandfather was a governor of Kazan, studied at its Faculty of Oriental Languages before switching to law. In the 1880s, the young Vladimir Ulyanov, soon to rename himself V. I. Lenin, first came upon the works of Marx and Engels in the university library.)

Moreover, Tatar Muslims were not known as firebrands. To the contrary: Kazan's religious scholars in the nineteenth century nurtured Jadidism (from *jadid*, meaning "new" in Arabic), a reformist Islamic movement whose moderating influence spread from Crimea through Central Asia. Jadids challenged the traditional practice of requiring youngsters who knew no Arabic to memorize passages of the Koran. Indeed, as apostles of the printed press, Jadids endowed the written word (even in newspapers) with a sacral aura. As the religious scholar Adeeb Khalid writes in *The Politics of Muslim Cultural Reform* (1998), the Jadid movement evolved into a direct challenge to the authority of the traditionally learned. This helps explain why in Tsarist times Tatars were said be highly literate, with four times as many schools per capita than the Russians. During the Bolshevik Revolution, Kazan's literate populace oscillated from right to left; soldiers and workers leaned to the Petrograd Soviet, while the commercial and ecclesiastical elite tilted to the counterrevolutionary Whites. The rightists predominated in summer 1918, when Kazan was occupied by the anti-Bolshevik Czechoslovak Legion. (The rescue of this wandering legion became the pretext for Woodrow Wilson's decision to intervene militarily in Russia, an episode forgotten by most Americans but indelibly recalled by Soviet historians.)

Czech bayonets literally struck gold in the form of 657 million rubles in bullion and 100 million in banknotes deposited for safekeeping in Kazan by Russia's central bank. Seizing Kazan became an overriding goal for the newborn Red Army and its indefatigable commander, Leon Trotsky. On August 7, he arrived by special train at the Volga front, where he was able to mold undisciplined recruits, with the aid of former Tsarist officers, into what became the Fifth Army, one of the best-disciplined units forged in the civil war. On September 10, 1918, Kazan fell, a day worthy of becoming a national holiday, according to Trotsky's proclamation: "The forces of the Fifth Army have torn Kazan out of the hands of the Whites and the Czecho-Slovaks. This is the turning point. . . . The spirit of the enemy is broken."

It was surely with an eye to the fighting skills of these Volga Tatars that care was taken in the nascent Soviet Union to divide the "Middle Volga Muslim Group" into two distinct republics. Still, the split among Volga Muslims was not wholly of Moscow's making, then or later. Following the overthrow of the Romanov dynasty in February 1917, during the nine months when Russia was ruled by a provisional parliamentary regime, Tatar leaders joined with other Muslims in demanding autonomy for all non-Russian peoples. But Tatars were outvoted at the First All-Russia Muslim Congress, meeting in Moscow in May 1917 by delegates who demanded instead discrete territorial autonomy within a federal state.

In the words of Harvard's Dmitry P. Gorenburg, an authoritative chronicler of a very muddled sequence, "This event marked the beginning of the division among Muslim ethnic groups in Russia, a division that culminated in the Bashkir leaders' refusal to participate in a Tatar-Bashkir republic, and the birth of a separate Bashkir Autonomous Soviet Socialist Republic in 1919." Thus only one-third of the Tatars living in the Volga area became inhabitants of their own titular republic. With Stalin's ascent, constitution making served as a means for rewarding or punishing competing ethnic groups. Every republic's status within the federal hierarchy, and the language rights it obtained, prompted prolonged haggling. Over the decades, Tatarstan gained a bit, being allowed marginally greater autonomy in domestic affairs, plus the right to publish official documents in both Russian and Tatar, while the militant Bashkirs saw their modest privileges pared back. But contrary to Moscow's expectations, the effect of concessions was to whet appetites, so that when the prospect of a real change loomed, non-Russians everywhere demanded greater self-rule.

As Gorenburg recounts, ethnic mobilization in Tatarstan germinated among scholars concerned with preserving an ever-diminishing indigenous culture. On June 28, 1988, activists in Kazan formed a Tatar Social Center to promote discussions and a statewide congress. (Damir Ishakov, the ethnologist with whom we met, was among the center's founders.) Ethnic nationalism surged from an inner cadre of intellectuals to prodemocratic Communist officials, then to ordinary workers, farmers, and civil servants. The long-dormant Tatar-language media sprang to life, rallies proliferated, and the Popular Front Party materialized. Soon demands for some form of sovereignty burst like rockets.

On October 15, 1991, an estimated ten thousand Tatars gathered in Kazan's Freedom Square to protest their parliament's refusal to proclaim Tatarstan's independence. The day marked the 449th anniversary of Ivan the Terrible's conquest, and nationalist passions were cresting. Eleven persons were injured in clashes with police when demonstrators stormed the parliament building facing the square. From the melee emerged an emblematic figure, Fauzia Bairamova, leader of the militant Ittifak (or Alliance) National Party, who challenged demonstrators to prove they were not slaves to the Russians. In the same spirit, Ittifak had previously organized twenty-five protest rallies throughout the republic and led the call for a boycott of Russian elections. In May 1990, along with fifteen comrades, Bairamova undertook a two-week hunger strike. In spirit, she recalled Dolores Ibárruri, celebrated as La Pasionaria during the Spanish Civil War: a gloriously intemperate embodiment of total resistance (notwithstanding Bairamova's populist anti-Semitism, wholly absent in Ibárurri's speeches).

Bairamova excoriated as spineless those moderates who (in her eyes) condoned intermarriage with Russians and accepted an equal legal status for the Russian and Tatar languages. "The great tragedy is that the nation has lost its pride," she lamented in an address that October:

> Would a nation that has any pride really allow such self-mockery in its history; would it really sell the Russians its languages, religion and customs; and would it really accept their much worse traditions? Would a Tatar who had any pride really mix his genealogy with the enemy? Would such a Tatar look on calmly as his sacred lands were parceled out to others? . . . The leaders of Tatarstan pretend to be good fellows, while both the Russians and the Jews laugh at us, mockingly. They eat our bread, but they don't even consider us human beings. Half of Russian territory is Tatar land. . . . The time has come to raise the question of annexing to Tatarstan the lands that belonged to the Tatars of old, lands where they now dwell—the lands of Simbirsk, Saratov, Samara, Astrakhan and Orenburg, the expanses of Ufa plateau, and all of the western slopes of the Urals.

A few months earlier, following the failed August 1991 plot to oust Gorbachev, Tatar nationalists for the first time demanded a complete break with Moscow. And why not? After all, Tatarstan had ample resources (one-eighth of all Russian petroleum flowed from its fields), it controlled vital rail and pipeline links, and it bestrode the Volga. Its skilled workforce manufactured trucks and helicopters, and its farmlands were renowned for their fertility. Besides, nationalists contended, Volga Tatars were in genetic reality a blend of Bolgar Turks, Kipchak Turks, and Mongol Turks, and thus constituted one-third of the triad of great nations that shaped the old Russian Empire. Like Russians and Poles (so it was affirmed) Tatars were also martial by nature and no less skilled at assimilating rival ethnic groups. Not least, total independence would ensure the survival of an imperiled Tatar culture, with its national epics, folk tales, music and dances, plays and poetry, and a language that fewer and fewer young people now spoke, or were allowed to speak, in Russian-administered schools. So why not go for broke? Let a thousand rockets blaze for free Tatarstan!

FROM THIS MINEFIELD of ideas emerged an improbable champion of Tatar exceptionalism, Mintimer Sharipovich Shaimiev. The former chairman of the Council of Ministers of the Tatar Autonomous Socialist Republic (1985–1989) and former first secretary of the Tatarstan Oblast Committee of the Communist Party of the Soviet Union (1989–1990), Shaimiev was from 1991 the elected president of Tatarstan—not the résumé one might expect for the most innovative of post-Soviet constitutional rebels. Nor did Shaimiev sound like a stereotypical insurgent. While visiting Saudi Arabia in 2008 to take part in a forum with other Muslim leaders, Shaimiev (as cochairman) offered this insight into his thinking:

> Russia always occupied a special place in the Islamic world. In Soviet times, global problems were not solved without Russia. Today, the situation has changed, and it is necessary to direct affairs using the intellect rather than weapons, as it used to be. Tatars have a proverb: "The one who is strong will beat one adversary, and the one who is clever will beat a thousand." Our age is an epoch of rivalry of wits, and of modern technologies.

Thus in preparing for his negotiations with Boris Yeltsin, Shaimiev deployed his most effective weapon: his wits. He was well aware of Moscow's strategic advantages. Unlike the Central Asian "stans" or rebellious Chechnya, Tatarstan was locked within the Russian Federation since it shared no frontiers with a foreign state. To be sure, it possessed mineral riches, most especially petroleum, but it was entirely dependent on Russia for access to external markets. Hence in any confrontation with Moscow, a fully sovereign Kazan could expect little meaningful foreign assistance. Ethnic Tatars, moreover, were until recently less than a majority of the republic's population (and even today are barely more than half), blunting the numerical thrust of the self-determination principle. And as every rational Tatar knew, the skills and goodwill of non-Tatars were essential to sustaining a progressive, prosperous, and stable society. Independence would almost surely precipitate an impoverishing civil war.

For his part, however, Shaimiev possessed a potent face card: Moscow's fear of a protracted, violent confrontation with another Muslim people, à la Chechnya. It served Tatarstan's interest to underscore its own separatist/Islamist peril, so much so (as we were told) that the government most probably bussed demonstrators from Ms. Bairamova's base in Chelny to rallies in Freedom Square. Or, as it was put to us in Kazan by Professor Midkhat Farukshin, a political analyst and outspoken dissident, Shaimiev used ethnic separatism "to blackmail the federal center, making his case as follows: if you don't give certain preferences to the regional elites—and please mind you, he was talking about elite privileges only—then we will not be able to curb the further, uncontrollable growth of ethnic self-consciousness that could potentially lead to violence." (Dr. Farukshin's forthright views recently cost him his post at Kazan State University.)

Shaimiev likewise shrewdly manipulated the word "sovereignty," the elastic mantra binding moderates and militants. He named his own proposals "the sovereignty project," and with the aid of a scholarly task force led by his counselor Rafael Khakimov (whom the reader has met), he scoured the world for parallel examples of what political scientists call asymmetrical federalism. High on the list were the Generalitat of Catalonia in Spain, the Province of Quebec in Canada, and the Commonwealth of Puerto Rico in the United States. On August 30, 1990, he won the unanimous support of Tatarstan's Supreme Soviet for a "Declaration of State Sovereignty" that guaranteed equal rights and freedoms to all the republic's citizens, "irrespective of nationality, social origin, belief, political convictions and other differences." Russian and Tatar were each designated state languages, but "the maintenance and the development of other languages are ensured." More broadly, the declaration itself would be "the basis for the creation of that Tatar SSR Constitution, for the development of the Tatar legislation, for the collaboration of the Tatar SSR in the creation and signing of a Union Treaty, [and] for agreements with the Russian Federation and other republics." Missing throughout was the word "independence."

As recounted by Uli Schamiloglu, a scholar of Tatar origin at the University of Wisconsin-Madison, 61 percent of 2.1 million eligible voters on March 21, 1991, approved the following statement: "Do you agree that the Republic of Tatarstan is a sovereign state, a subject of international law, building its relations with the Russian Federation and other states and republics on the basis of equitable agreements?" The vote added populist legitimacy to the Supreme Soviet's declaration of sovereignty.

In essence, Shaimiev's carefully crafted "sovereignty project" envisioned Tatarstan's becoming an "associated sovereign state" within a loose federal framework. Concretely, this meant the republic and its leaders could enjoy symbolic badges of nationhood, for example, flags, anthems, and a limited diplomatic presence—but not a national army or the pleasure of naming relatives and party loyalists as ambassadors, each entitled to the same twenty-one-gun salute as their superpower peers. Shaimiev sought a halfway house with an overriding benefit: peace. In a candid interview in 1995 with the American journalist Trudy Rubin of *The Philadelphia Inquirer*, Shaimiev declared, "I can tell you that in Tatarstan in 1991 and 1992, I went to great nationalist rallies, and they called on me to announce independence. But I knew that complete independence was totally unrealistic, so I braced myself and never once said this word." For his part, Boris Yeltsin escalated the word game; while visiting Tatarstan in August 1990, he brashly invited its leaders "to take all the sovereignty you can swallow."

————

THE "SWALLOWING" consumed two years of negotiations culminating in a bilateral treaty signed in Moscow on February 15, 1994, operative for ten years. Titled "On the Delimitation of Jurisdictional Subjects and the Mutual Delegation of Authority Between the State Bodies of the Russian Federation and the State Bodies of the Republic of Tatarstan," the treaty is a masterwork of adroit evasion. Tatarstan is nowhere described as sovereign, and yet nowhere is its sovereignty denied. In substance, Kazan emerged as the capital of a ministate empowered to pursue foreign contacts on nonmilitary matters. Thus in 1995, a newly established Department of Foreign Affairs, building on earlier initiatives, administered sixteen missions abroad and signed fourteen agreements with external governments dealing with economic, trade, scientific, cultural, and educational issues.

Treading carefully, and raising eyebrows in Moscow, Kazan also entered into cooperation accords with Chechnya and Ingushetia, and with breakaway Abkhazia in Georgia, all regions seeking greater autonomy within a larger state. Call it "paradiplomacy," a noun coined by the American scholar Gulnaz Sharafutdinova for a subnational foreign policy, which amounts to a benign form of status seeking. Who was injured if the republic's citizens were enabled to carry Russian passports embossed with official symbols stating that the bearer was also a citizen of Tatarstan—satisfying pride without precipitating an invasion? (Under the more restrictive treaty later negotiated with Putin, the official symbols were to be imprinted on an inserted sheet, not within the passport itself, but the plural principle survived.)

So how sovereign is Tatarstan? Here is the artful gloss put forward in 2000 by one of the treaty's architects, Rafael Khakimov:

> The essence of Tatarstan's sovereignty lies not in its striving for complete independence (although this option has been discussed in the parliament) but in getting guarantees for the republic's autonomy and establishing new relations with Russia, relations in the interest of the people. Tatarstan does have reason to distrust the central government even if it is headed by democratic forces. . . . There are no guarantees that if someone like [Vladimir] Zhirinovsky [a zealous rightist then making headlines] comes to power in Russia, he will not try to follow Stalin's example, not least since the new Russian Constitution makes the establishment of an authoritarian regime plausible. For this very reason, Tatarstan has become active on the international scene, signing bilateral treaties and opening permanent representations.

Concretely, the treaty awarded Tatarstan full title to the republic's real estate as well as control of the oil, natural gas, and petrochemicals extracted from its soil. Its government was empowered to collect taxes and, crucially, to be the auctioneer of its denationalized enterprises. Critics justly protested that the auctioning was carried out in ways that favored the president's family and his network of former party allies (a matter to be elaborated below). However, in contrast with the convulsive transition to a market economy elsewhere in Russia, the pace of change was slower in Tatarstan, and losers benefited from a more generous social safety net. Deservedly, Shaimiev's accord attracted wider attention. He not only lectured at Harvard on what became known as "the Tatarstan Model," but in 1996, he flew in a presidential jet (along with a representative of Chechnya) to The Hague to preside at a conference jointly sponsored by Harvard and the Carnegie Corporation of New York.

Once in place, and as implemented in successive bilateral agreements, the treaty also triggered a much-debated building boom in Kazan. As detailed by Skidmore College's Katherine Graney, the word "slum" entered the republic's vocabulary via a "Program for Slum Clearance and Modernization" that focused on the inner city at a cost of $685 million. Spinoffs included the beginnings of a mini-subway system, and a "European style" pedestrian mall replete with the obligatory modernist sculptures, fountains, and McDonald's emblematic golden arches (with the Tatarstan seal inscribed on its facade). All these rose rapidly in Kazan, along with a gleaming convention and cultural center known as "The Pyramid," billed as the "only building of its kind in Russia." Plus flashy restaurants, a new concert hall, sports arenas, a racetrack, and many restored landmarks, most notably the Kremlin, with its mosque, cathedral, museums, and government offices. Yet as Professor Graney relates, redevelopment proceeded with scant regard for the rights of the luckless residents living in the path of the bulldozers, who were neither consulted about the demolition schedule nor told where they would be relocated. Needless to add, few ordinary citizens could afford to dance to the electro beat at Club Pyramid or other trendy restaurants meant to confirm (in Graney's words) "the republic's ascension—or at least its pretension—to modern sovereignty."

———

FOR AMERICAN VISITORS, Kazan's facelift can be oddly unsettling. Embedded downtown in the city's ongoing urban redevelopment are the spectral ruins of an old prerevolutionary grand hotel, its brown bones retaining a dignity noticeably absent in its Stalin-era successors. Strange wrinkles of the Soviet past anomalously survive post-Communist surgery—that is, a major downtown avenue still named for Felix

Dzerzhinsky, the Polish-born "Knight of the Revolution" and first chairman of Cheka (the precursor of the KGB), remembered for his zeal and his ruthlessness. (We wondered whether his name survived because he was famously non-Russian. As the old Polish joke goes, "Q: Who was the greatest Pole of them all? A: Felix Dzerzhinsky, because no Pole killed more Russians.")

Such wrinkles are not only evident in the physical landscape; they mottle the body politic as well. This became clear in our meeting with Igor Sholokhov, chairman since 2006 of the Kazan Human Rights Center. (He had earlier served for fifteen years as an officer in the Tatarstan penitentiary system.) His unmarked offices are located in a nondescript residential suburb for good reason: the center's previous, more visible quarters had been raided in 2004 by unidentified masked intruders who smashed computers and trashed files. "It was clearly an act of intimidation," Sholokhov elaborated, adding with a tight smile, "We found an unexploded grenade near the door, as a kind of warning."

The Kazan Human Rights Center's primary concerns, its chairman told us, have been the harassment of demonstrators, the abuse of conscripts in the Russian army, and the failure of the republic's officials to enforce adverse court rulings. Yet when we asked for the center's estimate of the number of political prisoners, Sholokhov replied, "We don't have them in Tatarstan." In Soviet times, Natan Sharansky had been among the better-known dissidents jailed in a local "psychiatric" hospital, but in post-Soviet Tatarstan (in the center's judgment) no such fraudulent pseudo-institutes exist. In parting, we were given copies of the center's pocket-size, hundred-page booklet detailing what the police lawfully can or cannot do in sovereign Tatarstan, for use by dissenters of every persuasion.

And what of the media? How high does Tatarstan rate in terms of press freedom? Our grade, based on our interviews, is C plus. The government owns or controls all local television channels and most of the print media, but at the margins contrary views are boldly voiced. No pall of fear induces self-censorship in talking with foreigners, or so we found. At no point did our critical informants freeze, speak in whispers, or ask not to be quoted. Police surveillance is widespread, but very typical was the attitude of Rhasbulat Shamsutdinov, then-chief editor of

The Evening Kazan, when we asked if we could record our conversation: "Everything is being recorded anyway," he shrugged, "so the old KGB system is still as it was—you can ask them for a backup. You know, here you can just turn your face to the ceiling in your hotel room and say, 'Please, I want this.'" His robustly independent daily is neither controlled nor subsidized by the state; it is sustained by 32,000 subscriptions to its print edition, constituting one-third of its revenues, with advertising accounting for the balance. In his summary, "Other newspapers are government newspapers—or they are very careful."

Fifty-something and open-collared, Shamsutdinov proved agreeably argumentative. When asked why Tatarstan was so unlike Chechnya, he voiced "deep surprise" at our repeating so commonplace a question:

It's absolutely incorrect to compare Tatarstan with Chechnya, because Tatarstan was always a European place. Kazan was always a European city. It was never a place where Islam would predominate. Chechnya is such a long way from here; it's something very different. It's impossible to compare. So when people come and say, 'Wow, you're so tolerant. How could you manage this high level of tolerance?' The obvious answer is that it has always been like that.

Still, the chief editor did express concern about "the tendency, the spreading trend" toward giving employment preference to Tatars in professional posts in schools and hospitals, a cause of considerable unrest among ethnic Russians. "You should understand me correctly—I consider myself cosmopolitan—you must understand that people here are pressured not in the ideological sense, but in the economic sense. They are afraid to start a public protest because they are afraid they would lose their job, or their children would suffer somehow, or they would be thrown out of their business." Yet he himself in no way seemed intimidated; before we left, like other visitors, we were each given a T-shirt and a white "gimme cap," bearing his paper's proud name, *Vechernyaya Kazan.*

Another example of what can rightly be called repressive tolerance was described by a veteran broadcaster, Rimzil Valeev of Azatliq Radiosi, the director of Radio Free Europe/Radio Liberty's Tatar language service. We asked whether and/or how local officials expressed displeasure about his reporting. "I am sure the authorities do not like what we say," he told us, "and our writers often face the following: silence, cold silence. There is no feedback, and it is very bad when you don't get invited to briefings, so when there is a big visit from a high-profile guest and the pool of journalists is being formed, they just forget about you. And later on, you call, and they say, 'Sorry, sorry, we just forgot about you.' So it's very tangible punishment [when] stations and channels are always competing for the best coverage of information, and you really feel this."

Pressing further, we asked how many journalists had been murdered in Tatarstan, an egregious commonplace elsewhere in Russia where (as of this writing) not a single killer has yet been tried and convicted. "We had one case ten years ago," Valeev recalled, "where a journalist starved or froze to death in the streets during winter, while he was drunk. Although some people would say he was killed because of his profession, everyone knew that he often returned home late and drunk."

We asked Valeev about his personal relations with state officials. "I'm actually quite loyal, but because I work for Radio Liberty [the US-financed broadcasting service based in Prague], lots of officials would say I'm subversive, that I'm an American spy. . . . When we have a personal meeting, and drink together, they would never have the courage to fling this accusation to my face. But officials are very conservative, and you cannot change this except over generations, and there are some who always want to restart the Cold War."

On the debit side of press freedom, there is the case of Irek Murtazin, formerly Shaimiev's press secretary, who in November 2009 was convicted by a district court in Kazan of defamation and incitement to hatred. After resigning in 2002, Murtazin broke with the president, joined the opposition, and wrote a book titled *Mintimer Shaimiev: The Last President of Tatarstan*, which was excerpted in a fifteen-part series published by *The Evening Kazan* in 2006. He eventually became an opposition blogger and in September 2008 he rashly posted a news flash claiming that Shaimiev had died suddenly while on vacation in Turkey. "Frankly speaking, I can't believe it," ran his comment. "To be precise, I don't want to believe it. Because, if it's true, then there will be such a mess, such a serious struggle to get into the vacant seat that the peasants' forelocks will be cracking here and there. And it's because of these prospects that Shaimiev's closest circle will try to conceal this information—to win time, to regroup (or even to leave the country). That is why the official information, I think, will appear not earlier than a week."

In truth, later the same day the president's rumored death proved an exaggeration, but not before shares of an oil company allegedly owned by the "Shaimiev clan" plunged. Three months later, Murtazin was charged with defamation and a year later the forty-five-year-old blogger was found guilty in a Kazan court and sentenced to twenty-one months in a penal colony (not a prison, but a less onerous community of prisoners). He filed an appeal to the European Court of Human Rights, still pending as of this writing. Anent this dispute, a Westerner may fairly remark that if every false, exaggerated, or premature report on the blogosphere carried a similar penalty, not a penal colony anywhere would have space for the resulting grand army of scribblers.

––––––

ALL OF THIS POSES a still-unaddressed question. Just who is Mintimer Shaimiev? Opportunist or genuine reformer? And what is likely to happen now that he has stepped down after completing his fourth five-year term? Concerning his family history, we have a detailed account in a 1999 biography by Ravil Bukharaev of the BBC Russian Service, who tracked down Shaimiev's rural origins and interviewed his family and friends. Mintimer Sharipovich Shaimiev was born on January 20, 1937, in Anyakovo, a nondescript Tatar village, the ninth child of Sharifulla Shaimiev, who for twenty-six years served as chairman of the local collective farm. As a Red Army recruit, his father was wounded in the 1941 battle of Moscow and returned to a hungry village during a wartime food crisis. His commissars would accept no excuses for a bad harvest, and the succeeding postwar years were almost as fraught. In 1949, Shaimiev's father was arrested for the supposed crime of distributing seeds to hungry villagers and was charged with squandering public wealth. He was acquitted, Bukharaev asserts, because the succeeding harvest was so abundant that his case was dismissed. Equally formative was the fate of Shaimiev's grandfather, who was among the untold tens of thousands killed, jailed, or dispossessed as class enemies during Stalin's collectivization drive. In the 1930s, he lost land, livestock, home, and dignity.

Thus Mintimer Shaimiev grew up knowing (1) that Soviet justice was brutally capricious, (2) that the first priority for any government is to feed its people, and (3) that the loyal support of an agricultural base could be a vital asset for an upward-striving Tatar. In the decade ending in 1967, Shaimiev worked on his village farm, attended agricultural school, studied economics by correspondence, became an engineer in a regional technical service center, and he married. His wife and lifetime partner, Sakina, recalls him saying, "Sakina, I would not promise you mountains of gold. You know, I graduated from the Agricultural Institute, and my whole life is dedicated to the village. The only thing I can promise is that I will always love you." Soon his talents were noticed, and in 1967 he was in Kazan serving as Minister for Land Improvement and Water Resources. The pasture irrigation schemes he pioneered and the vegetable farms he propagated as minister all flourished, and he was duly rewarded in 1983 with a pivotal new post as secretary of the regional Communist Party. Within two years he was Tatarstan's Prime Minister and so presided over the 1990 parliament that proclaimed the republic's sovereignty. (His rural antecedents were not exceptional for Soviet leaders; Mikhail Gorbachev, also a villager, graduated from Stavropol Agricultural Institute in 1983, and a memorable highlight of Nikita Khrushchev's 1959 American tour was his visit with the Iowa farmer Roswell Garst, with whom he shared a passion for hybrid corn.)

Yet there is another dimension in Shaimiev's upbringing. He is steeped in his ancestral heritage and is fluent in the Tatar tongue and its literary classics. His family observed the basic tenets of Islam, and like most village children he was taught traditional Muslim prayers. Inscriptions in an Arabic script are carved on the marble tombstones of his parents in their village graveyard. Asked about correct relations between mosque and state by *The Muslim* magazine, Shaimiev's response was a model of calibrated prudence: "Religion, albeit separated from our *state*,

is not separated from our *society*. . . . Therefore, our destiny is construc-
tive cooperation. We should safeguard what we already have and create
the necessary material conditions for spiritual revival."

Taking his cue from Rafael Khakimov and other secular-minded
Tatars, Shaimiev approved the establishment in 1998 of the Kazan
Islamic University, reputedly the first of its kind in the new Russian
Federation. We talked with its present rector, Rafik Mukhametshin,
who explained that his university did not propagate Euro-Islam or
Jadidism, or any other Muslim doctrine. In his guarded words, "To give
wide currency to Jadidism, you must have a society ready for discussing
complex religious issues. You need a lot of educated people who would
understand all the intricate differences among these theories. So
Jadidism is an intellectual search among the Muslim intelligentsia, but
our society does not consist only of intelligentsia." In other words, some
subjects cannot be frankly discussed by Tatarstan university rectors.

But should any importance be given to Shaimiev's biography? In
formerly orthodox Marxist-Leninist historiography, class origins were
the controlling matrix, while postmodernist scholars insist that history
is mostly an agreed-upon fiction, and psychohistorians seek a master
clue in oedipal conflicts. How interesting, therefore, that the academic
journal *Ab Imperio,* published in Kazan, revisited the musty "Biographic
Turn" and argued in a 2009 editorial that "there is a growing interest in
the inner world of people of the past that is paralleled by a common
mistrust of both traditional psycho-history and structuralist
approaches." In sum, biography might again throw a revealing beam on
recent history, as it arguably does in Tatarstan.

Still, as a tough-minded leftist radical might observe, these relative
liberties at the periphery are fine, but who really controls Tatarstan's
economic and political life? It is to this question we now turn.

———

BY ANY FAIR RECKONING, Mintimer Shaimiev's negotiating
strategy opened a safe path through a threatening wilderness. His leadership held at bay rule-or-ruin extremists. Like a prudent farmer, he
kept the silos full during a turbulent transition from a failed socialist

system to an unsteady market economy, and he did so without resort to police-state thuggery. Yet it would be a stretch to characterize Tatarstan's chief as either a political or social democrat. More accurate to say he supplanted Communist hegemony with an ethnic ruling class rooted in his own rural origins, with bonus benefits to his (very) extended family.

Nobody has tracked the emergence of a clan-based regime more sedulously than Dr. Midkhat Farukshin, who contributed a detailed account to a Texas-published symposium, *The New Elite in Post-Communist Eastern Europe* (1998). He begins by noting that when the Soviet Union collapsed, 80 percent of the industrial enterprises in Tatarstan were subordinate to all-union bodies, and only 2 percent were controlled by the republic. "As a result of decentralization and the incessant drive for autonomy," he writes, "Tatarstan gained administrative control over sixty-five percent of the state property located within its borders." Given this leverage, Shaimiev and his associates could influence day-to-day prices and the auctioning of state-owned enterprises. As a result, in Farukshin's view, they became the republic's new ruling class:

> Two-thirds of the Tatarstan elite are originally from rural areas. If we add those originally from small towns, the figure climbs to eighty-six percent. Naturally, these people brought with them a "village culture" that permeates all relationships within the elite. This culture features traditional customs of servility; disdain for dissent and opposition; favoritism for people from the same milieu, especially nepotism; distrust for "strangers," particularly the urbanites and the more educated stratum of society; self-righteousness; and narcissism. This culture is antidemocratic at its very core. Practically all members of the ruling elite have higher education. However, their background is heavily skewed toward the agricultural or veterinary schools, and only thirteen percent are university graduates. . . . First in line to replace the present leaders of Tatarstan are the very same people from the villages who once assumed top-level positions. They will propagate others in their image from the younger generation of villager dwellers.

Such was the solid phalanx sustaining Mintimer Shaimiev in his initial encounters with an incoming, glacial-eyed President Vladimir Putin in 2000. At the outset, Putin made plain his determination to bridle Russia's regional overlords, together with their allies, Moscow's super-rich oligarchs. As Russia's biggest and most affluent ethnic republic, Tatarstan was a prime target, especially since its "sovereignty project" provided the precedent others followed, notably the adjacent and irritatingly pugnacious Bashkir republic. A key element of Putin's centralizing strategy was his support of the recently formed United Russia party, which checked efforts by regional leaders to launch their own all-union movement. Slice by slice, the Kremlin's new overlords shaved back the fiscal, legal, and symbolic privileges of the ethnic republics, including most especially the popular election of regional leaders; henceforth Moscow would appoint these presidents, subject to the approval of mostly docile local parliaments.

As before, President Shaimiev moved with the changing tide. Power sharing became the new mantra. He signed up with United Russia, loyally delivering Tatarstan's votes to Putin's party in lopsided elections; he prudently dropped plans for issuing separate passports; and he secured Moscow's collaboration for costly urban redevelopment schemes and for the full-throated, two-billion-dollar celebration of Kazan's putative millennium. As his republic's decade-long pact with Boris Yeltsin neared its end in 2004, Shaimiev came to the table with a team of battle-hardened negotiators, and came away with a new treaty that reversed the earlier 73–27 percent division of local taxes, with Kazan roughly retaining the lower proportion.

But the new treaty, as signed in 2007, did not dislodge Tatarstan's village-based elite; rather its hold was tightened. The principal instrument for clan dominion proved to be a shadowy holding company known as TAIF, short for Tatar-American Investment and Finance Company. Founded in 1995, TAIF currently controls an estimated 96 percent of the chemical, petrochemical, and gas industries of Tatarstan; it employs 40,000 persons and its consolidated revenues in 2010, according to its own data, totaled 340 billion rubles, more than the republic's state budget.

TAIF is generously staffed by Shaimiev's relations; one board member is his younger son, Radik, who reportedly also owns 5 percent of the shares in Tafnet, the chief producer of crude oil in Tatarstan. As reported in 2000 by *Novaya Gazeta,* Russia's preeminent investigative journal, "Clan Shaimiev directly or indirectly controls more than seventy percent of the economic potential of the republic." (As of 2011 Russia's *Forbes* magazine estimated Radik Shaimiev's wealth at $550 million.) "You should know," Dr. Farukshin told us in 2009, "that besides TAIF, Shaimiev's relatives control key positions in the regional and municipal administrations. For example, [Ilsur] Metshin, the mayor of Kazan, is married to the niece of Shaimiev's wife; the current minister of land and property is Shaimiev's nephew; and the mayor of Chelny is another nephew. I can't name all of his nephews and what they are doing."

Hence it was not surprising that the presidential baton passed to a tested protégé following Shaimiev's resignation in January 2010, as he neared completion of his fourth term. His successor is Rustam Minnikhanov, a village-born Tatar, formerly the republic's minister of finance and since 1998 the chairman of its government. A graduate of Kazan's Agricultural Institute, a doctor of economic sciences, Minnikhanov holds numerous state awards, including the Order of Merit of the Fatherland. As Professor Farukshin foresaw in 1998, members of the governing elite have propagated a successor in their own image; and as Ravil Bukharaev discovered, a time-honored Tatar tradition known as the pie ceremony conveys something of the underlying character of village-based politics. In Bukharaev's words,

> The pie in its iron bed sits at the centre of the table, as the veritable king of the meal. First you have to cut the roof in the [pie's] centre, revealing its juicy contents and, as the aromatic steam curls out of it, cut the rest of the pie into segments, so that everyone at the table receives a piece of the pie cover. Then the luscious inside is divided, and if there is a guest from afar, he or she receives the first portion. . . . There was nothing especially solemn about the pie ceremony, which dates back hundreds of years. But the mere sight of the pie crowning the table of local produce, be it organic tomatoes, cucumbers or fresh sturgeon and other fish of the Belaya River, had an air of solemnity and homage, if only for my gullible poetic soul.

One is touched by this bucolic scene, as if sliced from a Brueghel painting of a peasant carnival. Still, a nagging and prosy second thought intrudes: just who sits at that round table? And aside from the honored guest, to whom and to what is homage rendered? In the Cave of the Clan Bears, the ticket of admission appears to be fluency in the language of the host, the cook, and their village.

———

IT IS HARD TO overstate the importance of language rights as a political third rail within post-Soviet territories. In the Russian Federation, an estimated 70 percent of its numerous languages are said to be "moribund"; that is, in the final generation of native-born speakers, inspiring urgent demands for multilingual schools. The controversy is reversed in the Baltic, the Caucasus, and Central Asia, where arguments center on the linguistic plight of surviving Russian-speaking minorities. To complicate matters, modalities remain in dispute. For example, in this ongoing debate, what constitutes "pure" Tatar, as compared with the spoken vernacular corrupted (or enriched) by Russian or other non-Tatar words?

Interspersed is a long-standing preoccupation with identifying categories within a diverse population. In Tsarist times, for example (as Dmitry Gorenburg relates), census takers distinguished between serfs, non-Russian natives (*inordotsy*), servants of the state (*sluzhilye*), and members of the local elite with a status equal to Russians—and moreover, serfs were divided into "crown serfs" and those belonging to a specific person. No surprise, therefore, that in the post–Soviet 2002 census, Tatars were divided into forty-five subgroups within three major categories: Tatars, Kreshens, and Mishars. Of particular interest in Tatarstan is the precise definition of Kreshens, the one hundred thousand or so Tatars whose forebears converted to Orthodox Christianity centuries ago. Are they true Tatars, or what? In 2002, some Kreshens complained that against their wishes, they were registered as Tatars, which could tip the latter group just over the 50 percent census total (which in fact occurred). Adding to the richness of this ethnic pie are other minorities also counted by census takers: Chuvash, Ukrainians, Mordvins, Udmurts, Maris, Bashkirs,

Belorussians, Azeris, Germans, Uzbeks, Kazakhs, Armenians, Georgians, and Moldavians.

Few Americans have more closely explored this linguistic maze than Suzanne Wertheim, who learned Tatar and reported her findings in a dissertation for the University of California, Berkeley. Through what she calls "the logic of oppositional identity," Tatar purists reject most Russian loanwords while pointedly salting their prose with archaic Arabic and Persian terms, causing a philologist to protest, "[I]t has become more difficult to read Tatar newspapers and journals from one end to another in one sitting. After picking up a newspaper and starting to read, you must stop and busy yourself with foreign words that are meaningless in Tatar." Ms. Wertheim found that her own lack of a Russian accent led Tatars to assume she was a "young Tatar girl" who had led a "clean village life." As she elaborates in her *Ab Imperio* essay, "This idealization of village life, and of the village as a protected enclave of Tatarness, is quite a common one, particular noticeable in Tatar-language comedies and musicals produced in Kazan theaters." (We attended such a comedy, centering on a farmer seeking a suitable husband for his comely daughter. We were given earphones offering successive translations in Russian and English. Thus three waves of laughter followed each comic turn: first a loud guffaw among Tatars, then a resonant ripple among Russian speakers, followed by scattered titters among Anglophones.)

Yet the most stubborn linguistic dispute concerns orthography. In Soviet times, party ideologues could not decide which alphabet, Cyrillic or Latin, was politically correct in various ethnic republics, so Tatarstan endured three changes of script in less than a century. As part of their post–Soviet sovereignty project, Kazan's rulers in 1999 restored the Latin script and allowed Latin letters to appear on street signs and in schoolbooks. Going further, acting on appeals from scholars and young Internet users, Kazan approved a complete orthographic conversion to the Latin alphabet (some Tatars contended that Latin letters formed a better phonetic match for their Turkic tongue).

Moscow's response was swift and categorical: the shift was condemned as divisive, separatist, and an unacceptable sop to the West. At Putin's urgings, the Duma in 2002 ordained that all Russia's state languages were to be rendered in Cyrillic. Resistance ensued in Tatarstan, led by a movement called the Latin Front, whose leaders encouraged Tatars to study the disputed alphabet. Moscow struck back: the Education Ministry removed all non-Russian languages and cultures from the national education "standard." The struggle persisted. In 2009, the Russian Supreme Court ruled that all official Tatarstan documents and announcements were to be printed in both languages, even those pertaining to Tatar cultural events. A year later, Moscow's Education Ministry barred five Tatarstan secondary schools from taking part in an annual contest for designing Russia's best websites, because the student entries contained no Russian—the latest skirmish in an unresolved duel along Russia's unsettled linguistic frontier.

Given this obsessive concern with ethnic and language rights, we could not help but wonder about the power of minorities. We frequently asked whether the Obama phenomenon might occur in Tatarstan; that is, whether a candidate of the ethnic Russian minority could arguably become president. The negative consensus was emphatically expressed by Rhasbulat Shamsutdinov, the editor of *The Evening Kazan*: "It's impossible, even if such a candidate could speak fluent Tatar—and I'd like specifically to emphasize that there are quite a number of Russians who can speak fluent Tatar. Still, it's impossible." His was an informed rejoinder to Tatar nationalists who contend that Shaimiev somehow gave away the linguistic store by agreeing to Moscow's demand that a presidential aspirant's fluency in Tatar should not be subject to demonstration, but was to rest on the candidate's assertion. Yet this was not the only criticism leveled at the outgoing president's treaty negotiations.

————

"THE SECOND TREATY IS pure fiction," our insider informant asserts. "It's a fig leaf for covering the fact that Shaimiev needed to capitulate. So the existence of the treaty is Shaimiev's business card, it's his political face—he could not have refused it. But if you actually look at the text, there is no 'treaty/agreement' at all—it's as if you and I sat down together and 'agreed' that you will have a cappuccino and that I will have an espresso." As it happens, we are all seated in one of many

crowded coffee shops in the heart of Kazan. The speaker is Lev Ovrutsky, a freelance writer and winner in 2004 of Russia's Union of Journalists' Golden Pen Award, and the author of *When Republics Were Big*, a
critical survey of Russian federalism. He describes himself as a lapsed
Communist and a secular freethinker; a onetime fan of Mikhail Gorbachev; a former contributor to *Ogonyok*, once the trademark pere-
stroika journal; and a Jew. His contention is that Shaimiev's second
treaty achieved nothing: "If you study carefully any document that is
signed by federal ministries and the regional ministries, you will see
there is no reference to the new treaty, which is a sure sign it is not
needed."

And yet, with the same knowing voice and a complicit wink, he
acknowledges that Shaimiev did in 1994 astutely exploit his "situation
to the utmost, when Russia actually capitulated." With a shrug, he con-
cedes that in fact all Tatar history is a tangle of contradictions, and that
politicians habitually dissimulate (he supplies details). Of Shaimiev,
Ovrutsky goes on to say, "He's extremely cautious. And you must
understand that he's been more so since the trauma he experienced
when he supported the coup [against Gorbachev] in 1991. Actually, I
quite appreciate his cautiousness. As a father and a grandfather, I would
like to see political decisions made cautiously and slowly, rather than
fast and spontaneous."

Half sighing, Ovrutsky elaborates that for all Shaimiev's faults,

> He likes to listen to different opinions. I consider him something of a
> spontaneous democrat. He doesn't have a lordly view of others. He
> may not fully value democratic institutions, but he's got a kind of
> peasant democratic attitude. Once, when I was doing a piece on
> Shaimiev, I ironically suggested that I wasn't surprised to learn that
> his favorite pastime was digging potatoes from the ground. [And]
> when I was interviewing him in 1992, he confessed that he had one
> dream that had not yet come true—which was to learn to play the
> accordion.

This grudging ambivalence marked many of our interviews. Nearly
everybody with whom we talked (save officials) had complaints, but

their criticism was uttered without rage or sulfur. Almost everybody older than thirty graphically recalled the turbulence in the Caucasus in 1991, after former Soviet Air Force General Dzhokar Dudayev famously announced he had no intention of being a "wedding general" (a general invited as decoration to the proceedings) and seized power in Chechnya. In his first decree as president, Dudayev proclaimed Chechnya's independence. His cheering supporters hoisted a new flag (white and red, emblazoned with a wolf and full moon). In Moscow, President Yeltsin responded by declaring a state of emergency. The massive flight of ethnic Russians from Chechnya began. In December, Dudayev's forces stormed KGB headquarters, triggering a twenty-month siege in which Grozny became (in the words of the subsequently murdered Russian journalist Anna Politkovskaya) "a small corner of hell."

The death toll is reckoned at 160,000. Chechens and Russians vie in conjuring horrific statistics: Grozny was said to be the most bombed-out city in Europe (85 percent of the Chechen capital was leveled), more Russian tanks were lost in the siege than during the final battle for Berlin in 1945, and more Russian soldiers fell in Chechnya than in the decade-long Soviet war in Afghanistan. In 1992, both Tatarstan and Chechnya were the sole republics refusing to sign the all-Russian treaty with Moscow. Both were led by presidents who attained office in 1991. Both initially had strong separatist movements, but who can dispute that when the road forked, Kazan took the more civilized course?

As we were told by Shaimiev's longtime adviser, Rafael Khakimov, during the first year of the Chechen war, Grozny's Minister of Culture undertook a three-day visit to Kazan. "At the end of the third day," Khakimov recalled, "he came to me and said, 'Dudayev wouldn't even want more than what you already have.'" Tatarstan thereafter enjoyed an honorable, and mostly uncelebrated resolution, of which its inhabitants are justifiably proud.

This affirmative outcome became clearer to us in our meeting at a noisy pizza restaurant with two college-age rappers, Tamir and Rassik, the former an ethnic Russian of Orthodox descent, the latter a Muslim of mixed parentage. (He chose to be a Muslim, as law and custom now permit, and married a Christian despite fervent appeals by mullahs urging Tatars not to marry outside their faith.) As Rassik phrased it, "In

Soviet times, we were not very proud to say that we were from Tatarstan. Now everybody here is proud to say, 'We are from Tatarstan, and we come from Kazan.'" Yes, acknowledged Tamir, rappers have to watch their tongues in protest songs: "Of course, you have to remember that if you are doing some real, straightforward protest, you may find it hard to be invited to a big event, because they will sideline you. . . . So we do lots of stories, relational things about friendship. We do some things about the Georgian war, and we do some things about [World War II] veterans, because they are forgotten now." And what of Russia's Afghan war conscripts? His words deserve quotation:

> That's about grandfather-era veterans. We don't have the memories: this is being erased, this is being lost, and people suffer from a deficit attention to each other. We hear stuff about the [current crisis] every day on television, and on the other hand we have this consumerist propaganda—you buy this, you buy that. There is an absence of personal relationships. That is what we are writing about. We're not protesting, so much as we're emphasizing those things that should not be forgotten.

To which we add, Bravo Rassik and bravo Tatarstan! It would appear that Our Lady of Kazan's protective powers ecumenically endure.

4

MARSEILLE:
BLACK, BLANC, *BEUR*

*It was good to be in Hassan's bar. . . . Whoever came
there to drink a pastis sure as hell didn't vote for the
National Front. And they never had, not once, not like
some others I knew. Here, in this bar, every single one
of us knew why we were from Marseille. . . . Friendship
mixed with the smell of anise and filled the place. We
only had to exchange glances to know we were all the
children of exiles.*

—JEAN-CLAUDE IZZO, *SOLEA,* THE THIRD BOOK
IN HIS MARSEILLE TRILOGY (1998)

IT WOULD BE AGREEABLE to report that Paris, city of light
and seat of reason, nowadays resembles Hassan's bar. But the scent of
sulfur rather than anise fills the room whenever the political class
debates such issues as headscarves (*l'affaire du foulard islamique*), secularism (*laïcité*), or the rights of the Roma to settle in the Fifth Republic. For Americans to look down their righteous noses at perceived
French intolerance is unwarranted. Similar issues ignite wrangling in
our own country, where opinion polls suggest that roughly one fourth
of the adult populace suspects that President Barack Obama is a for-
eigner or a Muslim, or both. Moreover, French insistence on assimilation, a one-size-fits-all approach to citizenship in the "public space," is
in partial atonement for the country's wartime complicity in the

Holocaust. Ethnic labeling in occupied France and its collaborationist Vichy partner made possible the fatal deportation of sixty-five thousand Jews. This contributed to France's decision to ban census questions related to religion and ethnicity in favor of universalism: all French citizens are statistically and theoretically the same. In early 2004, consistent with this principle, a National Assembly lacking a single Muslim deputy, voted 494 to 36 (with 31 abstentions) to forbid the wearing of ostentatious religious insignia (i.e., headscarves, skullcaps, or large crosses) in public schools: a law plainly directed at the largest Islamic minority in any European state.

Let it be stressed that French citizens of goodwill found themselves on all sides of this vexed controversy. Were Muslim students voluntarily wearing headdresses, or were they yielding to peer and parental pressure? Or was the new law a liberal outgrowth of France's historic struggle to entrench secularism in a predominantly Roman Catholic country? Or instead, was the *loi sur le voile* (as everybody called the law) a crumb opportunely tossed by centrists to appease and defuse the right-wing, anti-immigrant populism of Jean-Marie Le Pen's flourishing National Front? What hampered the debate, given the prohibition on census questions, was the absence of certifiable data on the size, location, origin, and economic status of France's growing Islamic population. To get around this void, social scientists and municipal officials rely on names, postal codes, and word-of-mouth to identify Muslims: a curious example of a country that cherishes reason choosing willfully to blind itself.

––––––

STILL, FOR A WONDROUS moment in 1998, France seemed very like Hassan's bar. On July 12, auspiciously close to Bastille Day, everybody rejoiced in France's spectacular World Cup victory. In a parade unmatched since the liberation of Paris in 1944, an estimated one million fans marched down the Champs-Élysées, rejoicing in the defeat of Brazil (a soccer superpower) at the Stade de France in Seine-Saint-Denis, a suburb synonymous with immigrants. Seventeen players on the winning team had origins in Algeria, Tunisia, Martinique, Guyana, Senegal, New Caledonia, or Guadeloupe. Headlines proclaimed that Les Bleus (the French national team) had become "*l'Équipe Black, Blanc, Beur*" (the Team of Blacks, Whites, and North African Arabs). France's superstar, Zinédine Zidane, the twenty-six-year-old son of an Algerian Berber (Muslim, but not Arab) grew up in La Castellane, a working-class neighborhood in Marseille (the standard French spelling, which we will use). "Zizou" scored two of the three goals in France's 3–0 victory. His image, proudly singing "La Marseillaise," appeared nightly on television. As his teammate Emmanuel Petit later reminisced, "He was perfect for the role because his parents were immigrants. He became the star of the political message saying, 'Look at Zidane, he has Algerian origins, be like him, be proud to be French, and you will be integrated into French culture.'" It was a moment of "national communion" marveled the Bleus's coach Aimé Jacquet, a sacramental sentiment reinforced by billboards (for sneakers) proclaiming, "There is not one god, but eleven" (the number of players on a soccer team).

Flash forward to 2010, twelve years and three World Cups later. Multiculturalism is in full disarray. The Bleus are now derided as "*Les Imposteurs*" in *L'Équipe*, the leading French sports daily, alluding to the team's shaming early losses in the World Cup with hardly a goal. For their part, the players refused to practice after their coach Raymond Domenech exiled a teammate for swearing at him. Critics faulted Domenech for repeatedly fielding a team lacking talented *beurs* in key matches; cameras panned to captain Patrice Evra, the son of a Senegalese diplomat, his lips sealed during the singing of "La Marseillaise." (Sympathetic bloggers noted a possible racist innuendo in the anthem's refrain, "Let impure blood water our furrows.") Responding to "*la débâcle des Bleus*," President Nicolas Sarkozy summoned a cabinet meeting, at which his (then) junior sports minister Rama Yade (born in Senegal) proposed that all of France's players should thereafter be obliged to sing the national anthem. Taking a different tack, (then) Secretary of State for Urban Affairs Fadela Amara, herself a Muslim, cautioned, "We are building a highway to the National Front." To learn what immigrants themselves were saying, the center-left daily *Le Monde* sent a reporter to Corbeil-Essone Taterêts, a diverse neighborhood southeast of Paris. "They want to find scapegoats," journalist Anne Reheu was told.

"Fortunately, there were no *rebeus* [slang for *beurs*] on the team, so they cannot Islamize the failure of the Bleus." As another resident complained, "When the team wins, the players are French; when it loses, they are 'Africans of French nationality.'"

Two intervening events played a pivotal role in undoing the national communion of 1998. In 2006, France lost the World Cup to Italy after the team's sainted captain Zidane damaged his halo by head butting an opposing player who may have insulted his mother and/or sister (accounts differ). The final game went into penalty overtime without "Zizou," arguably permitting Italy to win 5–3. So blame fell on the "African of French nationality." Worse, the debacle followed a year marked by riots and car burnings in Paris and hundreds of other cities and towns, an eruption that polarized the immigration debate. Our own inquiry into its causes and aftershocks took us from Paris to Marseille. There we learned how the least typical of major French cities twice in the past century set an example of courage, patriotism, and tolerance under outstanding mayors (with organized crime playing a paradoxical backstage role). And our interviews underlined the salient importance of history and geography in abetting traditions of civility. We also found that pervasive local enthusiasm for soccer and rap music helped explain what didn't happen in Marseille.

———

IN THE SPIRIT of Jean-Claude Izzo, Marseille's master of detective fiction, we were mindful in recalling France's violent autumn of 2005 of the oft-invoked if overworked dog that didn't bark in the Sherlock Holmes adventure (*The Silver Blaze*). What didn't happen in multiethnic Marseille was the curious incident that mattered most as other French cities were gripped by riots, rage, and car burnings. Marseille seemed especially vulnerable. Its 839,000 inhabitants (as of 2006) included as many as 240,000 Muslims, by far the most in any European city, plus an estimated 80,000 Jews (mainly of North African ancestry) and some 80,000 Orthodox Christians (of Armenian or Greek origin). Add to the mix Corsican, Italian, Spanish, Portuguese, Maltese, and (most recently) Comorian communities. As important are the thousands of families of *pieds-noirs,* the European settlers who fled newly independent Algeria decades ago. These former colons and their offspring are, if often unjustly, assumed to be partisans of Jean-Marie Le Pen's xenophobic National Front.

Was Marseille a Mediterranean bonfire awaiting a match? So it seemed. Yet France's major port remained quiet, save for a night early in November when fourteen cars were reportedly torched in Marseille's northern suburbs. When Kader Tighilt, one of the city's social workers and a Muslim, heard the news on his radio, he cried, "The bastards! They've done it!" In fact, the report was misleading; the burnings occurred not just in Marseille proper but throughout its wider department, the home of nearly two million persons. It proved a spark quickly contained. Why the predominant calm? Many who addressed the paradox cited as a metaphor Marseille's signature dish, the bouillabaisse, a stew of fish, crustaceans, and vegetables flavored with garlic, orange peel, basil, bay leaf, and saffron.

Dwelling on this culinary cliché led us to a deeper insight. Back in 1962, *The New Yorker's* resident Francophile A. J. Liebling became curious about a scorpion fish known in Marseille as the *rascasse,* said to be essential to the bouillabaisse. He checked with culinary high priests and was informed by Waverley Root, author of *The Food of France,* that the *rascasse* "is a coarse fish, armed with spines, which lives in holes in the rocks, and would be allowed to stay there if it were not for the *bouillabaisse.* Alone, it is not particularly good eating, but it is the soul of the *bouillabaisse . . .* it has the gift of intensifying other flavors." It is an apt metaphor for Marseille's multiple personality. The port's denizens, some armed with spines, are content to reside in their own niches, but collectively they intensify each other's distinctive flavors.

With the help of friends and colleagues, we began our quest for more information in Paris, where we interviewed deputies, a Muslim cabinet minister, a key mayor, and human rights activists before proceeding to Marseille, where we met with office holders, social scientists, community organizers, writers, transit executives, publishers, rap artists, and devotees of soccer. Doing so, we came to appreciate the cohesive role played by Marseille's beaches, sports, civic activism, schools, hip-hop, and (silently, in the shadows) its criminal caste. But consider first the origins and outcome of the convulsive events that gripped France in 2005.

The prologue occurred on October 25 in Argenteuil, northwest of Paris, home to many poor and frequently jobless youngsters of Arab and African origin. On that day Nicolas Sarkozy, who then was interior minister, visited Argenteuil to appraise new measures against urban violence. On his arrival, he was pelted with stones and bottles, provoking his retort that crime-ridden neighborhoods should be cleansed with the high-pressure hose known as a Kärcher aimed at youthful rebels he derided as *racaille* (an abusive word, variously translated as "scum," "riffraff," "thugs," "hoodlums," or "rabble").

Two days later, three teenagers were roaming the streets of Clichy-sous-Bois, another *banlieue*, one of many outlying suburbs encircling Paris. It was early evening, during the final week of the Muslim holy month of Ramadan, and none of the boys had eaten. Bouna Traoré, a black from Mauritius, and Benna Zyed, an Arab from Tunisia, were practicing soccer with a third friend, Muhittin Altun, a Kurd from Turkey, when sirens began screaming through the canyon-like corridors of Clichy's high-rise projects. None of the boys carried mandatory identity cards. They feared arrest and possible deportation if picked up and questioned. Soon barking dogs and flashing lights merged with the wail of police sirens. Muhittin fled down a street. Bouna and Benna desperately sought refuge in a high-voltage power substation. They stumbled into a steel maze, and both were electrocuted. (Muhittin suffered electric shock but survived. He tried to explain the boys' frantic behavior to the police and was sternly lectured, "When one has nothing to reproach, you do not run.") The deaths of the two youngsters stirred instant rioting among other jobless immigrants living in housing estates that perforate the suburban Parisian horizon, like a forest of ziggurats.

Riots and car burnings blew across nearby Seine-Saint-Denis as hundreds of marchers mourned Benna and Bouna, many wearing T-shirts reading (in French) "Dead for Nothing!" On October 30, Sarkozy vowed "zero tolerance" for the rioters, who retaliated with hundreds of car burnings. The disorders leapt to other French cities. On November 8, President Jacques Chirac proclaimed a state of emergency. A record deployment of 18,000 police imposed curfews as turbulence spread to three hundred cities and towns, among them Toulouse, Lille, Rouen, Orléans, Strasbourg, Saint-Étienne, and Lyon. By the time the violence ebbed in mid-November, 2,900 rioters had been arrested ("by all means necessary"), two were killed, 126 police were injured, and as many as ten thousand vehicles torched (the official toll of 8,973 is deemed conservative). Scores of public buildings were firebombed, and schools and hospitals were shuttered, spreading the security fears that helped ensure Interior Minister Sarkozy's defeat of his Socialist opponent Ségolène Royal in the 2007 presidential election. (In justice to Sarkozy, whose father was a Hungarian immigrant, he has guardedly tried to address the alienation of jobless newcomers; once in Élysée Palace, he initially brought three Muslim women into his cabinet and reiterated his support for minority scholarships, a tentative variant of US affirmative action programs.)

———

BY CONSENSUAL JUDGMENT, the riots were the worst since the leftist eruptions of May 1968 that brought down the government. Yet as Molly Moore of *The Washington Post* reported on November 8, "While many French leaders depict the rioters as simple criminals, many French citizens see the fires that are burning across the country as reflecting a growing identity crisis in a nation where social policies have not kept up with rapidly changing profiles in religion, race and ethnicity." She quoted a forty-three-year-old music teacher in a northern suburb of Paris as expressing a widespread minority view: "It's similar to the U.S. civil rights movement in the 60's. The integration policies of this country do not work."

The parallel has a rough justice. In his monumental *An American Dilemma,* the Swedish scholar Gunnar Myrdal in 1944 contrasted the founding values of the United States with the racism he observed everywhere. He quoted "a Negro political scientist" (Myrdal's then little-known assistant Ralph Bunche) as remarking, "Every man in the street, white, black, red or yellow, knows that this is 'the land of the free,' the 'land of opportunity,' the 'cradle of liberty,' the 'home of democracy,' that the American flag symbolizes 'the equality of all men.'" Yet Myrdal comments, "American Negroes know they are a subordinated group experiencing more than anybody else, the consequence of the fact that the Creed is not lived up to in America." Such was the American dilemma, only partly acknowledged and tardily addressed by Johnson–era civil rights legislation.

Hence an American's inescapable sense of déjà vu in visiting France. The tricolor is synonymous with the republic's founding commitment to liberty, equality, and fraternity, just as France's former empire claimed a redeeming *mission civilisatrice*. As the Swiss author Herbert Luethy marveled decades ago, every anticolonial rising had its roots in the French Revolution: "Hence the phenomenon, astonishing at first sight, that the most radical advocates of independence in the French Empire continually emphasize their love of France—not the France represented overseas by French Residents and Governors-General, but the France of the 'ideas of 1789.'"

The contradiction persists. Beginning in the 1960s, the former colonial subjects began migrating to demographically challenged France in quest of jobs and a better future for their children. Once there, they everywhere encountered the claim that France was color blind, and that every newcomer's overriding duty was to integrate. In Sarkozy words, "Freedom is the rule in the private sphere, republican conformity the rule in the public sphere." Yet as decades passed, few non-European immigrants or their offspring were to be seen as members of the governing political class, graduating from elite *grandes écoles*, or assuming seats on corporate boards. The meritocracy's glass ceiling was reflected in the pale complexion of the journalists reporting the 2005 riots (reminiscent of America's overwhelmingly white press corps in the 1960s).

Reflecting on this, we were led to a wider observation. During the 2005 riots, Marseille seemed a throwback to a past when Mediterranean cities were celebrated for their thriving diversity, examples being Alexandria, Beirut, Salonica, Smyrna, Sarajevo, Trieste, and Córdoba. In different centuries and ways, each succumbed to ethnic cleansing, fratricide, and "population exchanges" (a code phrase for forcible expulsion). So how and why did Marseille escape? Put briefly, our research suggested that pragmatism trumped tribalism. Marseille adopted a Gallic version of America's ethnic bartering to accommodate successive waves of newcomers. What French scholars now term Marseille's "political clientism" secured jobs and housing, honored an immigrant's dignity, and eventually offered the ambitious a winning slot on all-important party voting lists.

———

AGE, MYTH, SIZE, AND GEOGRAPHY all combined to set Marseille apart. By consensual tradition, Marseille is France's oldest metropolis, founded in or around 600 BC by seafaring Greeks from Asia Minor. Legend asserts that the Hellenic colony of Massalia had its origins in the marriage of the Phocaean sea captain Protis to the Ligurian princess Gyptis. Their coupling is said to have presaged the advent in Gaul of writing, currency, and the cultivation of wine and olives, thereby initiating a new age of fruitful Mediterranean interbreeding.

The historic port's physical markers were evident to us from the moment of our arrival from Paris via a sleek TGV bullet train (now a three-hour trip). Warily descending the stairway from Gare Saint-Charles, we looked northward at the craggy mountains that shelter the city. Not only did these peaks discourage landward invasions over the centuries, they also curbed urban expansion. Marseille does have a growing north-south social divide; its poorer inhabitants have moved northward as middle-class householders gentrify southern districts. Yet overall, Marseille remains a metropolis without Parisian-style *banlieues*. Instead, after the medieval port burst its confining walls, a patchwork of densely populated villages emerged. These evolved, over time, into Marseille's 111 administrative districts, each retaining its original name, traditional fêtes, and distinct flavor. All became building blocks for a municipal structure rooted in clans, ethnic solidarity, and religion. And over time, the northern districts would emerge as underclass enclaves.

Basic to this evolution was the city's welcome to foreigners. Shielded from the mainland by mountains, Marseille has been immemorially accessible from the normally equable Mediterranean. Beginning with Greek galleys, ships have continuously crowded its Old Port, where smaller vessels to this day form a forest of masts. Nearby is the New Port, the adjoining quays where freighters and container ships are off-loaded daily. Aggregately, the harbor presents a cinematic montage of cafés, hostelries, and the impressive Hôtel de Ville (dating to the sixteenth century, a prize example of Provençal Baroque). At the Old Port's entrance lies Fort Saint-Jean (the traditional point of departure for Foreign Legionnaires) and further out rises the fortress, Château d'If (abode of the fictional Count of Monte Cristo). On nearby quays, double-decker buses and impatient guides await an unceasing procession of tourists from cruise liners. Most day-trippers will visit the Basilica of Notre-Dame-de-la-Garde, built in the nineteenth century in then-fashionable Romano-Byzantine revival style, reachable by buses crawling up and around the spidery John F. Kennedy Corniche. Crowning a high promontory, the basilica has become Marseille's signature image, its steeple topped by a welcoming statue of Our Lady.

Yet her welcome is not a pious fiction. Walking along Marseille's crowded downtown districts (le Panier, le Canebière, and la Plaine) we were impressed by the pedestrians, their animated diversity and the absence of tension. Males of every sort, from bankers in double-vented Armani suits, to unshaven youths in Adidas warm-ups, mingled with young females in flip-flops, along with cheerfully bloused mothers whose children tugged at their skirts and a sprinkling of older Muslim women wearing black or brown headscarves. (There was not a single spotting of the controversial head-to-toe burqa.)

The street theater could hardly be livelier: sidewalk artists, fast-food vendors, teenagers aboard Vespas and skateboards, activists handing out fliers and, in the early evening, fans of every origin gathering at outdoor sports bars in the Canabière district to cheer the football *étoiles* of Olympique de Marseille (OM). With typical Marseille impudence, someone has planted a Socialist poster reading *"La Gauche ne se relévera pas sans toi!"* ("The Left Cannot Rise Again Without You!") on a stonewall enclosing a distinctly bourgeois church graveyard.

Above all, we were struck by the relaxed confederacy among residents of a mercantile city where differences of creed, color, and political persuasion have long been a matter of course. This helps explain why so many immigrants chose to remain permanently in their port of arrival. "Marseille belongs to exile," Jean-Claude Izzo writes in *Chourmo*, the second volume in his Mediterranean noir trilogy. "The city will never be anything else, the last stop of the world. The future belongs to those who arrive. Not to those who leave." Thus Marseille absorbed refugees from Mussolini's Italy, Franco's Spain, and Hitler's Reich. (During the wartime Vichy era, the port also served as a primary escape route for imperiled artists and intellectuals, their path cleared by two young Americans, Varian Fry, an unofficial volunteer, and Hiram Bingham IV, a career diplomat, who cheerfully ignored State Department guidelines in providing visas).

Over the years, Marseille's tolerance hardened into the attitude that has become the port's trademark. Social scientists have confirmed the importance of civic identity among Marseille's teenagers. In 2005, a team of French researchers asked a diverse sample of students whether they identified themselves as "French," "Marseillais," "Algerian," "Comorian," or "Muslim." As the psychologist Alain Moreau of the University of the Mediterranean reported, "Young people from Marseille, particularly those of North African origin, often stressed that in matters of social identity, they declare themselves first and foremost as 'Marseillais.'" By contrast, the consensus among those questioned in Paris was that few youngsters of non-European origin living in outlying projects would identify themselves as Parisians. (We also learned that a generic term increasingly used by newcomers is "Maghrebin," since it also includes Berbers, who are Muslim but not Arabic.)

These findings were elaborated in 2011 by a cadre of researchers recruited by the Open Society Foundations for its voluminous study, *Muslims in Marseille,* compiled by Françoise Lorderie and Vincent Geisser (hereafter cited as "the MIM report"). On the vexing identity question, MIM quotes this telling summary of a prevalent French attitude, as defined by Tariq Modood, a British sociologist of Pakistani origin:

In France, you can be of any descent, but if you are a French citizen you cannot be an Arab. Composite identities like Arab French are ideologically impossible. The giving up of pre-French identities and assimilation into French culture is thought to go hand-in-hand with the acceptance of French citizenship. If for some reason assimilation is not fully embraced—perhaps because some people want to retain pride in their Algerian ancestry, or want to maintain ethnic solidarity in the face of current stigmatization and discrimination—then their claim to be French and equal citizens is jeopardized.

Still, Marseille's more inclusive attitude was not preordained by the city's geography or its mercantile pragmatism, as the fate of its Mediterranean counterparts suggests. Civility also requires human agency. In the port's case, the three principal agents have been the long-serving Socialist Mayor Gaston Defferre; the bridge-building Mayor Robert Vigouroux; and the incumbent centrist Mayor Jean-Claude Gaudin. Less formally acknowledged is the offstage role of the Union Corse, the name given by French authorities to the secretive criminal syndicate known to insiders as le Milieu. Over the decades, Corsican *pacteri* (or peacemakers) within le Milieu worked with Mafia godfathers, made and traded heroin, engaged in human trafficking and sophisticated smuggling, fought gang wars, played a major role in the wartime resistance, cooperated with the US intelligence agencies in combating Communist-led trade unions, helped divide political spoils, and tacitly partnered with police in curbing urban riots. To ignore the Milieu would be like performing *Cyrano* without its nasally troubled Gascon (or filming *The French Connection* without Gene Hackman).

———

A MOUNTAINOUS OFFSHORE island populated by Italian speakers, Corsica was simply sold to France by Genoa in 1768, an attachment consecrated the following year by the birth in Ajacio, the capital, of Napoleone Buonaparte. Even as Corsica dwindled into one of many French departments, its inhabitants were renowned for their fierce clan loyalties. As noted in the classic 1910 edition of the *Encyclopedia Britannica,* the Corsican is "implacable towards his own countrymen when his enmity is once aroused, and the practice of blood feud or vendetta has not died out." Every islander belongs to a specific family or clan, as noted in the article, and those who break ranks risk serious retribution.

From the early nineteenth century, Corsicans streamed to nearby Marseille, where by current estimates their community still composes a tenth of the city's inhabitants. But the islanders' influence always exceeded their numbers, in good part because Marseille was the gateway to France's overseas empire. "It's all family oriented," the Provence-based social scientist Jean Viard told us. "As Corsicans like to say, 'We even share the same cemeteries.' They've been politically organized since colonial times. Colonial civil servants, gendarmes, and custom officers were mostly Corsicans, so they were already inside the state system before they entered the political system."

All this mattered, Viard continued, "Because you have to know that in Marseille most jobs are in the public sector. There are thirty thousand municipal employees alone, and [in local elections] the difference between left and right can be four hundred votes. So, for example, the municipal employees' trade union can decide who is elected—if you get them to work for you, you win."

We spoke with Viard in the offices of his publishing firm, Éditions de l'Aube, located in the bucolic provincial village of La Tours-d'Aigues. A prolific scholar, he is also a Socialist participant in Marseille's complex polity. "Complex" seems an understatement. Itself a prefecture within the French department of Bouches-du-Rhône, metropolitan Marseille comprises 111 districts bundled into 25 cantons, 21 communes, and 16 arrondissements. The latter are sorted into eight "sectors," each with its own mayor, town hall, and council, while every canton is administered by a councilor. Adding to the mix, each department elects sixteen members to the National Assembly. Some double as sector mayors, while Jean-Claude Gaudin, Marseille's overall mayor, has been simultaneously a vice president of the French Senate.

What distinguishes Marseille (as the Open Society's MIM study stresses) is that succeeding migrant communities settled in the city's central area, so that newcomers have long been clearly visible near administrative and political headquarters. Given Marseille's twenty-seven (at a minimum) defined ethnic groups, its phalanx of labor unions, and its fractious political parties, scrambling for office is continuous. "What's terrible is that nobody wants to do anything," Viard remarked with resignation. "Most of our time is spent preparing for the next election, and we almost never discuss our current projects. That's a bit annoying, even very annoying." Within this electoral maze,

Corsicans not only benefited from their clannish discipline, but also from the prudent respect accorded to the Milieu's captains. Jean-Claude Izzo's Marseille Trilogy is salted with the nicknames of Corsican godfathers known locally to all: Francis le Belge; Jacky le Mat; Gaëtan Zampa; Tweety Colonna; and Mémé Guérin, the latter belonging to the city's premier crime family, known also by their Italian names as the Guerinis. Its longtime dons, Antoine Guérin (1902–1967) and his brother Bartholomew (alias Méme le Doux, 1908–1982), were among Europe's most powerful syndicate bosses (or *les vrai Monsieurs*) from the 1940s onward. Bonded by common interests, these and other underworld chiefs entered into an informal liaison with Marseille's long-dominant Socialists and later, with the CIA—even as the port's laboratories processed some 90 percent of the heroin consumed in the United States.

(Before piously throwing their hands up, Americans should recall that their outlaws have long been folk heroes, from the days of Jesse James and Billy the Kid, continuing through the eras of John Dillinger and Willy Sutton, and culminating in popular fascination with John Gotti, the Teflon don of the Gambino crime family; Crazy Joe Gallo, of the Colombo syndicate; and Tony Soprano, fictional boss of the New Jersey mob.)

———

THE MILIEU'S DISCREET enabler was Gaston Defferre (1910–1986), "the Lion of Marseille." Seven times mayor, five times a national cabinet minister, Defferre was the arch-pragmatist once touted as the moderate Socialist superman who, some hoped, might unite all French centrists "between Mount de Gaulle and the Communist peak." So writes de Gaulle's biographer, Jean Lacouture, who characterized Defferre as a poor speaker; an able administrator; and "a sporty, open, forthright *bon vivant.*" The favored son of a wealthy Protestant family, Defferre was a young lawyer, demobilized (for health reasons) in 1940 when he joined de Gaulle's nascent Free French movement, at a moment when the tall soldier cast a very slender shadow.

Unexpectedly and unwittingly, Hitler in 1940 spurred recruitment to Marseille's underground by offering Mussolini the bait of retaking

Corsica, Nice, and Tunisia should Italy enter the war—which the Duce did on June 10, only days before the fall of Paris. The prospect of again becoming Italian subjects dismayed Corsicans who had reaped exceptional benefits from their French citizenship. Still, all was confusion. Hitler and Stalin were ostensibly at peace; Britain's defeat seemed imminent; distant America was nervously neutral. Although formally part of Vichy France, Marseille was ruled by Berlin's surrogates until 1942, when Germany assumed direct control of the vital port. Typical among the city's opportunists at this time was Simon Sabiani, a crowd-pleasing Corsican demagogue who in the 1930s switched from Communism to a Gallicized brand of populist Fascism. (A onetime mayor, in 1931 Sabiani ended as the arch-collaborator; at war's end, he fled abroad and died in Spain, having been sentenced to death in absentia).

Marseille's Communists were quiescent until the Nazis invaded the Soviet Union in June 1941, overnight energizing the Marxist FTP (Francs-tireurs et partisans français). Socialists had already joined the CAS (Comité d'action socialiste), while the London-based Free French worked with the British SOE (Special Operations Executive) even as de Gaulle struggled to speak for a discordant resistance. In Marseille, Corsicans flocked to the *maquis* (their own word for the island's scrubby hinterland, soon to become the generic term for all *résistants*). By 1943, Libération-Sud was viewed as France's most effective resistance front, thanks to its alliance of Socialists, Communists, and the Milieu, plus principled patriots and diverse refugees. The port's fighters then took the lead in forming the Brutus Network, a national resistance group tasked with sharing intelligence—whose leader, at war's end, was Gaston Defferre, the pragmatic leftist who emerged in 1944 as provisional mayor of a free Marseille.

All Marseille's complexities resurfaced when General de Gaulle arrived as liberator on September 15, 1944. Free France's leader found the atmosphere "ominous." The Old Port's center lay in ruins, its populace divided and destitute. Moreover, as de Gaulle later wrote, Communists had taken advantage of "old local dissensions and the persecution inflicted by Vichy agents" to establish "an anonymous dictatorship" that made arrests and even "performed executions without the public authority's decisive opposition." Still, de Gaulle took heart from his warm popular reception and from his meeting with the thirty-four-year-old Mayor Gaston Defferre, who "seemed quite pleased with my firmness [regarding the Communists] which made every problem seem simpler."

Defferre's combative zeal proved his most vital asset during a time of paralysis and confusion. Among his distinctions, the deceptively cherub-faced Socialist twice fought duels in the name of honor. On the second occasion, in 1967, his sword wounded a fellow deputy in the National Assembly who was outraged at being called a "slob" during a heated debate. ("He's still a slob," Defferre taunted after the duel, said to be the last of its kind in France.)

Buoyed by his wartime record, and alert to shifting political winds, Defferre now distanced himself from his former Communist comrades. He assembled a Socialist machine that tapped into Marseille's diverse ethnic communities, ranging from Corsicans to newly arrived refugees. His strategy is described as "political clientism" by Cesare Mattina, a social scientist at the Université de Provence-Aix-Marseille. "Clientism" is short for distributing public goods, providing "social housing" (i.e., tenancy on favorable terms), and awarding offices among defined ethnic communities. In Mattina's phraseology, "Political clients have been for the Defferran leadership a means of operating a social reclassification of the city, thereby ensuring the rise of certain segments of the popular classes, ameliorating the social situation of the lower and middle classes, and consolidating the privileges acquired by certain liberal professions. It thus reinforces a heterogeneous social bloc."

A dexterous juggler of offices as well as ideologies, Gaston Defferre lost out as mayor to the Communists in the post-liberation election of 1945, but he won a seat in the National Assembly, held secondary ministerial posts, and became proprietor of *La Provençal*, the region's most influential daily. A mayoralty victory in 1953 rewarded his legerdemain; he was reelected five times, serving until his death in 1986.

From the outset, Defferre's Socialists cultivated ties with ethnic minorities. As a gesture to the Armenian community, for example, the mayor renamed a street "April 24th 1915," the date memorializing the genocidal slaughter of Armenians by Ottoman Turks during World War I. "Gaston Defferre personally felt close to the Jewish cause," Mattina elaborates. "He did not fail to support Jewish associations, both secular and religious." In a revealing afterthought, Mattina adds, "The idea of seeking the support of communal voters is not generally part of the political life of France. It rather exists as a tradition around the political machines and the electorates of American cities." Indeed.

———

A STRANGE DETOUR followed as the Cold War dawned, Moscow and Washington began covertly funding their respective French allies in the Communist-led CGT (Confédération général du travail) or the non-Communist FO (Force Ouvrière). Marseille became a major battlefield. In 1948, CIA operations chief Frank Wisner flew to Paris to confer with Jay Lovestone, the veteran ex-leftist who headed the Free Trade Union Committee, and his AFL-CIO partner, Irving Brown. Together they funneled funds to both FO and the Milieu. As recounted by *The New York Times's* Tim Weiner in his history of the CIA, "Payoffs in the gritty ports of Marseilles and Naples guaranteed that American arms and military materiel would be off-loaded by friendly longshoremen. The CIA's money and power flowed into the well-greased palms of Corsican gangsters who knew how to break a strike with bare knuckles." In effect, the Milieu's dons agreed to harass the CGT in France's principal port in exchange for a tolerant wink concerning narcotics (it being understood that their heroin was solely for export). Few scholars have probed more deeply into the CIA's Corsican connection than the University of Wisconsin-Madison historian Alfred W. McCoy, who recounts what happened in Marseille during a 1947 general strike:

> Through their contacts with the Socialist Party, the CIA had sent agents and a psychological warfare team to Marseille, where they dealt directly with Corsican syndicate leaders through the Guerini brothers. The CIA's operatives supplied arms and money to Corsican gangs for assaults on Communist picket lines and harassment of important union officials. . . . At one point, the American government threatened to ship 65,000 sacks of flour meant for the hungry back to the U.S. unless the dockers unloaded them immediately. The pressure of

violence and hunger was too great, and on December 9, Marseille's workers abandoned the strike. . . . The Guerinis gained enough power and status from their role in smashing the 1947 strike to emerge as new leaders of the Corsican underworld.

———

BY THE MID-1950S fears of a Communist-led insurrection in France had ebbed, and the ongoing colonial wars in Indochina and Algeria had become major concerns. This paralleled a shift of allegiances among leftist intellectuals, many of whom were smitten by the Third World (a French coinage, as in *tiers monde*), in which seemingly purer Maoism rivaled Stalinism as a new lodestar. For their part, centrists in the National Assembly briefly rallied under Premier Pierre Mendès-France, who skillfully negotiated France's withdrawal from Vietnam, Cambodia, and Laos. His premiership then foundered in "*immobilisme*," exemplified by his own aging Radical Socialist Party, whose policies proved as opaque to foreigners (a wit remarked) as the tragedies of Racine.

By 1960 a search was under way for a middle-roader presidential nominee who might revitalize the torpid French political system—as John F. Kennedy had done in the States. Leading the quest was Jean-Jacques Servan-Schreiber, the photogenic editor of the newsweekly *l'Express,* who announced in 1965 that he had discovered "Monsieur X," a Third Force paragon capable of uniting Socialists, Christian Democrats, and Radicals. His name: Gaston Defferre, the mayor of Marseille.

It was not to be. Like the city he governed, Defferre remained an outlier: too gritty, forthright, and provincial for the political elite in Paris. In 1965, he lost out as Socialist presidential nominee to François Mitterrand (later to preside for nearly fourteen years in the Élysée Palace). When Defferre finally did win his party's presidential nomination in 1969, it came in the wake of rioting students and leftist general strikes. A majority of French voters turned to the reassuring de Gaulle–anointed banker, Georges Pompidou. Defferre garnered only 5 percent of the vote, a record low for a Socialist candidate. And yet, from today's vantage, it would appear that this mostly forgotten figure possessed a surer vision of his country's diverse future than his many Parisian adversaries, left or right. The policies he pioneered still define his city as a place apart.

———

MORE THAN ANY other French city, Marseille felt the furious initial backlash of France's 1962 defeat in Algeria. Beginning in the sixties and continuing through the seventies, Marseille's interethnic peace was tested as bitter returning European settlers, the *pied-noirs*, and uprooted Algerians swarmed into the Old Port. Colons and civil servants, teachers and soldiers, winegrowers and workers, all arrived by tens of thousands, many of them joining the Marseille police force; alongside arrived Muslim families whose members had cooperated with the French during the revolution led by the FLN (Front de Libération Nationale). For contrary reasons, each group felt betrayed, less obviously in the case of the Muslims, now scorned by their Algerian compatriots as *harkis* (a derogatory name for Algerians who had fought for France) who were herded into French detention camps by their wary former employers. Then, in August 1973, a mentally distraught Algerian immigrant knifed to death a Marseille bus driver, an episode that ordinarily might have been a "*fait divers,*" a news item—but not at this tense moment.

The French historian Yves Gastaut relates what followed (as cited in the MIM report): "A dark climate of an 'Arab hunt' gradually spread all over the place. . . . The local press played a major role, most notably *Le Méridional,* the right-wing daily." Its editor, Gabriel Domenech, had close ties with the *pieds-noirs.* "Folly is no excuse," he stormed on the day after the incident: "We have had enough. Enough of Algerian thieves, enough of Algerian thugs and vandals, enough of those bragging Algerians, enough of those Algerian troublemakers, enough of syphilitic Algerians, enough of Algerian rapists, enough of Algerian madmen, enough of Algerian killers. We have had enough of this savage, uncontrolled immigration that brings to our country all the riff-raff from the other side of the Mediterranean."

(A predictable corollary, documented in MIM, is that the *pieds-noirs* flocked into the Marseille police force, and harassment of Muslim immigrants became routine.)

In the estimate of the Open Society research team, continuous media fusillades abetted a surge of support for Le Pen's National Front and its local copycats. During a fraught decade, anti-immigrant candidates reiterated that Muslim immigrants could only be "fifty percent Marseillais." A major target in these attacks was a proposal to build a Grand Mosque. Yet in one of the unpredictable swerves that make French political history so fascinating, a left-of-center republican named Robert-Paul Vigouroux, a former physician—and a published poet, novelist, and essayist—was elected mayor in 1989 and served until 1995. During his tenure, as crime rates dropped, the economy grew and Mayor Vigouroux promoted Marseille Espérance (Marseille Hope), a forum in which leaders of all ethnic communities could candidly communicate. With less success, he favored building the Grand Mosque. Nevertheless, Vigouroux set in place the reconciling foundations for Marseille's renaissance under his successor, Mayor Jean-Claude Gaudin.

———

OUR FIRST MEETING IN MARSEILLE, as it happened, was with Mayor Gaudin. A former professor of history at the local Saint-Joseph College, and a founder of the center-right UMP (Union pour une Mouvement Populaire), Gaudin was now midway through his third term. We met in his spacious office adjoining the city hall's vast vestibule, its marble staircases lined with mythic statues adorned in Grecian robes. "Welcome," said Mayor Gaudin, bidding us to sit as he took from his desk a fossil oyster, explaining that its gnarled shell (like Marseille) was twenty-six centuries old.

As we talked, he was twice interrupted by urgent calls from the Vatican, regarding arrangements for a forthcoming official visit. His voice, a colleague remarked, fills the room, as does his beaming demeanor. Did we know that a decade ago only a hundred thousand passengers on cruise liners stopped in Marseille, while in the current year the total exceeded a million?

Preliminaries over, we initially asked how the mayor explained the relative calm in Marseille during the nationwide riots of 2005. "You can find many explanations which would not suit me," he responded. "True, we have [easy access to] the beaches, of which you no doubt have heard." More important in his view were economic realities and urban geography. "In Paris, you have the richest areas almost in Europe, but it is ten minutes as the crow flies to the poorest neighborhoods. This proximity of extreme wealth and extreme poverty creates extreme tensions. In Lyon, it's exactly the same. You have a very bourgeois downtown, and very poor neighborhoods all around."

By contrast, he went on, Marseille is not only economically mixed but is surrounded by mountains. "The big 'projects' [as everybody calls high-rise apartments] are within the city, whereas other French cities have at their center a town hall, a cathedral, pedestrian streets, flower markets, brasseries, cinemas, theaters—and ten kilometers away, you have those big projects." How different was Marseille. Here civility was also fostered by difficult-to-define urban associations, financed by city, region, and state "such as Marseille Espérance, which is funded by the city and brings together representatives of all its religions."

Thus on the day after 9/11, Gaudin summoned Espérance's leaders to agree upon a timely response to possible attacks on the city's Muslim population: "They all got together in the room next door and talked to the press. The aim was to maintain friendship among the communities." Besides, he continued, "You also have Olympique de Marseille, which is about much more than soccer. At OM games, sixty thousand people meet. Everybody is together, which makes the players a factor in integration, very particularly in Marseille." (The 2011–2012 team consisted of thirteen French-born players; eleven of African origin; two Brazilians; and one each Spanish, Dutch, Belgian, and Argentine.) Plus, he added, "We have strong links with all neighboring countries in the Mediterranean. Marseille is twinned with Marrakech and with Tunis—and also with Glasgow. We have lots of cultural and administrative exchanges. This is probably what led to our being named [the European Union's] Cultural Capital in 2013." (It should be added that Gaudin finally secured approval for construction of the Grand Mosque, a signature goal of Marseille's observant Muslims.)

Granted, riots that happened elsewhere could also erupt in Marseille. "Police arresting somebody in a bad neighborhood can get stoned here, as in any other city, but this happens less in Marseille. Our hardest night is July Fourteenth, our national holiday. Why? Because it's hot, and in poorer areas there will be fireworks, and youngsters setting fire to trash. That's the night I ask the police to be more visible, and limit the damage."

"Those are real reasons," he said. He hesitated, then added, "Another one exists. As you know, we have a little bit of underground drug trafficking, and the people involved don't want to see the police coming into their neighborhoods, so they do their own enforcing. We don't like to say it, but it exists anyway." (His candid acknowledgment of an awkward reality surprised other leaders with whom we spoke, a frequent comment being "Did the mayor really say *that*?") Otherwise, Gaudin articulated the official explanations for Marseille's equipoise during a national trauma. As we learned, there were other, more self-critical views.

———

OUR IMPRESSION, after many interviews in Marseille, was of a vibrant political class struggling to reconcile France's official ideology ("we do not discriminate") with the palpable obstacles facing migrants in Marseille. "The fact in France is that we are very hypocritical on these subjects," we were told by Karim Zéribi, a former professional footballer, a Muslim and since 2008, the chairman of the Marseille Transportation Authority (RTM). "Because, were there no discrimination in this country, you would find diversity at all levels—not only among bus drivers in the north [of Marseille] but here, too. When I became president of the RTM, I was the only person of Maghrebin origin in the entire building. And I'm the president, not a bus driver. There were two hundred people here, but nobody from the Maghreb."

So how did Zéribi encourage change? The impressively fit RTM chairperson leaned forward and explained: "Since by law we are not allowed affirmative action, we have to lure people from [diverse] communities and tell them to come to us. And they do come and send their résumés. So we have three criteria [for 'positive discrimination'] without admitting it: the home address, the name, and the skin color (even if it's not something you're supposed to say)." As a union member for twenty years, he regretted acknowledging that "the unions in this country are very conservative." But in mitigation, he elaborated, "It reveals something that is not American or French, it is human. Anything that is different from you is scary, and you try to keep it away. And maybe once the Maghrebins are settled enough in this society, they will probably do the same thing to newer immigrants."

He might have cited the plight of the most recent migrant wave, the eighty thousand or so newcomers from the Comoros Islands in the Indian Ocean, a day's sail from Africa's east coast. Most arrivals come from Mayotte, the only island of the four whose inhabitants voted in 1974 to reject independence and remain within the French community. Dark-skinned and predominantly Sunni Muslim, Comorians are now assertive newcomers in France's ethnic politics. We spoke with a rising leader, Nassurdine Haidari, deputy mayor of Marseille's first and seventh districts, an imam, a Socialist, and a member of its youth and sports commissions. Yes, he told us, the city does have Marseille Espérance, but when you also have drug trafficking, "Do you think putting a rabbi, an imam, and a pastor together solves a neighborhood's cocaine problem? I don't think so. It's another kind of drug."

Fluent and self-assured, the thirty-something Haidari sketched this critical picture: "Marseille wants to sanitize its social landscape. You have Marseille Espérance on one side and OM [the soccer team] on the other, but it's like putting our problems in drawers. It's going to blow up. The current generation won't accept it. It's the difference between me and my dad. My dad would say, 'We're just waiting, I don't expect anything.' I'm not going to wait, and a new generation is coming along that keeps being asked to wait for reforms. They want to live, and so at a certain point things could explode."

Nor was Haidari sanguine about the healing powers of hip-hop or rap music, a theme about which we were to hear more:

It's just another means of sanitizing society. You have in France the voice of the rapper, and it has become a way to channel rage. They [the rappers] should become part of our society instead of only using their anger to sing. They sing about our situation, but once they get their money, they leave their neighborhood, and it's over.

We heard a different view from Kader Tighilt, a social worker. We met at the School for a Second Chance, a place for students who have failed academically. It is located in the northern district known as Saint-Louis where the remains of a defunct slaughterhouse are being cleared for construction of the Grand Mosque of Marseille, which at a cost of $30 million and at 92,500 square feet is expected upon completion in 2012 to be the largest mosque in France. A secular-minded Muslim, Tighilt is credited with a major role in countering extremist rhetoric among the neighborhood's youngsters. Yet he was dismayed by the effects of Marseille's ethnic segregation. As he complained to us,

> The problem today is in our southern neighborhoods, the [newly fashionable] downtown parts, where people try to empty the areas. So they send [immigrants] to the northern neighborhoods, and so you have neighborhoods for Arabs, Gypsies, Comorians, Turks, and so forth. So how can you claim to be a republic if people don't mix? And then people are astonished when there is a rise in fundamentalism. . . . It's hard to call yourself a republic when you ghettoize—and I don't want to call it "ghettoize," "concentration" is a better word—and here it's called "gentrification."

In France, gentrification has "a very pejorative meaning." People nowadays remark, that in northern Marseille more Muslim women appear to wear the veil, yet in fact, he continued, "Women wearing veils in former times used to live everywhere in the city. What happened is that downtown became more expensive to park, and local taxes doubled—that's called 'gentrification'—and people become economically segregated." Still, he agreed that what distinguished Marseille from Paris was the sea: "It's an extraordinary defuser. Here a kid can take a bus and go to the beach for one euro, where he can meet with someone else—and that's a defuser [of tension]." As to soccer, our fluent interviewee had his own take: "A lot of people are wrong when they say that OM is a factor. It's not OM that made Marseille, but Marseille that made OM. The crowds at the stadium represent Marseille, not the reverse."

We traveled next to the bustling offices of Samia Ghali, the mayor of Marseille's 15th and 16th arrondissements in the proletarian northern sector. She is one of three Muslim senators currently in the Paris parliament, becoming Marseille's first representative of Maghreb origins to be elected to France's second chamber. (Yet as of 2010, there were no Muslim deputies in the more potent first chamber.) Born in 1968, Ghali is a rising star, an articulate daughter of Algerian immigrants and a non-college-educated self-starter who earned a leading slot on the Socialist electoral list (with an assist from Jean Viard). When we sought her views on Marseille's comparative lack of violence in 2005, she replied,

It's not true that Marseille isn't exploding. It *is* exploding, but in a different way. In Marseille, everyone closes their eyes to the underground trade, the drug dealing and the parallel economy. You also have to reckon with the nonprofit voluntary [local] associations in Marseille that are advanced and very much family based. So in any neighborhood you won't burn your neighbor's car because, even if you don't know the owner, you know somebody who knows him. A study was done a few years ago by a journalist showing that if you are from Marseille, and you meet someone else from Marseille, you always find you have at least one person in common within your own circle of friends—and this was a scientific study.

Concerning the peacekeeping role of organized crime, Ghali found Mayor Gaudin's remarks "scandalous." In her words,

It's unacceptable because it's like making time bombs. You close your eyes for years, thinking it's not your problem (like Algeria) and then it blows up, and you are surprised you let it happen. You have to know that in this neighborhood we have kids with weapons, military weapons. There is definitely a problem when kids shoot at each other, but in Marseille we have a tradition of being able to suffocate things [we don't approve of].

Regarding criminal clans, in her view, "The Corsicans used to be the big Mafia, but then they were taken over by the Maghrebins, and so the Mafia still remains a really big power."

In her interviews with MIM researchers, it should be added, Ghali officially rejected ethnic references and stressed that she did not wish to be defined by her origins. She said her position is unwaveringly universalist and republican: "I have never wanted to play the community card, nor play the same game as other *beur* politicians, who wanted to join forces for the construction of a mosque." And she spoke with an anthropologist's detachment about the electoral manipulation of immigrant communities:

> The Italian immigrants certainly have no monopoly over the setting up of networks and clans. The French community of Corsican origin and the Armenian community also created networks of mutual aid and solidarity. . . . In Marseille, these issues are still taboo as an object of study, as if the clannish organization was by its very nature soiled, dirty, or as if the secret of the clans (a sort of *omerta*) still had to be maintained. There is no doubt that through its underground, occult dimension, the clan system could provide cover for more or less suspicious activities.
>
> But this type of social structure reaches way beyond the realm of crime-related news. We speak, in fact, of a mode of social regulation that infiltrates all the official organizations. The political life, the trade unions, the clubs, and societies were all dominated by such practices, the marks of which are still deeply imprinted in the realities of today.

All of which became clearer in our successive encounters.

———

"YES, MARSEILLE HAS peace and diversity, but it takes a lot of work, and not being naive, to keep this diversity peaceful." We were interviewing Dr. Clement Yana during a break between patients in his offices where he practices oral surgery. The son of Tunisian Jews who settled in Marseille in 1963, Yana is president of CRIF (Conseil représentatif des institutions juives de France), representing the Jewish community and his views paralleled those of other community leaders. He recalled an incident a few years earlier when a Jewish school was firebombed in what appeared to be part of a surge of anti-Semitism. But on investigation, it developed that three youngsters were responsible "and it wasn't because they were Muslims but because they were twelve years old." He therefore remains cautious about sounding alarms regarding anti-Semitism whenever such incidents recur.

To be sure, pursued Dr. Yana, graver hate crimes have shaken Marseille, notably in March 2002 when a synagogue in the city's northern district was torched. But whenever such acts happen, "People from the Muslim community have joined with the Jewish community in protests." (Dr. Yana at the time conferred with Kader Tighilt, and to defuse tension they jointly initiated what then became an annual sports event between Muslim and Jewish youths.) We asked a litmus question: When you have a wedding, or a bar mitzvah, do you invite Muslims? Do Muslims invite Jews to the feast of Eid? "Yes, if they are friends. They are not Jews or Muslims, but friends first of all. And at the end of Ramadan, Muslims invite some members of the Jewish community [to the feast of Eid]. . . . In all this, there is mutual knowledge of each other's customs, going back to our shared origins in Tunis, Algeria, or Morocco."

Indeed, as we later learned, Marseille's Union of Muslim Families has for five years supported "Eid in the City," to share the festival marking the end of the month of fasting. In 2008, 106 associations partnered and 25,000 persons joined (as MIM researchers found) in "a big festival geared to families, in an atmosphere of sharing, concerts, shows, movies, debates, an exhibition and a workshop in Arabic calligraphy, and a tea dance for the seniors."

We next proceeded to Marseille's bohemian quarter, St. Julien, to meet with Varoujan Arzoumanian, director of Les Éditions Parenthèses, publishers specializing in art and architectural books. Worldly and witty, Arzoumanian deplored the stereotypical portrait of Marseille promulgated by "the big media in Paris." In his words, "They interview the same person over and over, it's always the same woman selling fish at the Vieux Port—you'd think that sums up Marseille. Thick accents, selling fish, that kind of thing." Nevertheless, he allowed with a grin, there were benefits in the heavy Marseillais argot: "It's a big factor in cohabitation and identity. You feel a strong bond with somebody from here because you speak the same language that nobody else can understand."

And, so he pursued, there is the shadowy stabilizing role of the "underground network" that has long existed, and which still makes the Vieux Port a city within a city: "It's not controlled by the mayor. Each neighborhood has its own small narcotics commerce. The mayor no longer has the same links he used to have with local groups. Now each area does its own thing—and local trouble is never good for this kind of commerce."

Forget Marseille's opaque complexities, Arzoumanian went on: "When you see the way people live here, it's extraordinary how well it works." Speaking of his own ethnic community, he emphasized that during a turbulent century the port always offered a refuge to Armenians. Still, with a grunt and a parting shrug, he did complain that city authorities were shoveling too much money into promoting the year 2013 (when Marseille is to become Europe's Cultural Capital) at the expense of supporting the city's financially stressed museums and galleries. "It's not funny. . . . I hope we will still be alive in 2013," he said, waving stoically at nearby tables piled high with his firm's latest titles.

We next sought the perspectives of a mainstream centrist politician. Relaxed and affable, Jean Roatta, is the seventy-year-old mayor of Marseille's upscale 1st and 2nd arrondissements and an influential deputy in the National Assembly. His grandfather emigrated from Italy in 1923; his mother was also Italian. "The Italians integrated really fast, because they accepted right away the new country they entered," he told us as he outlined the city's immigration history. A second wave of immigrants followed from Spain, during and after its civil war. Post-1945, the port absorbed its third wave: French colons from Algeria, Tunisia, and Morocco, along with other Europeans departing from former Portuguese Africa. "That caused few problems since the French, Italians, Spaniards, and Portuguese all had the same religion—and there was a common bond since everybody vacationed in each others' countries. We were all [European] Mediterraneans."

The real test came with the fourth wave, the predominantly Muslim newcomers who "sustained a certain pain from the Algerian war, if less so from Tunisia and Morocco [where France's exit was peaceful]." What lessened the pain, Mayor Roatta continued, was the Mediterranean, "a sea that unites more than it divides. The Maghrebin community [soon] felt more Marseillais than where they were from." During the 1960s, France became the new home of a roughly a million and a half immigrants of Algerian ancestry, a million of Moroccan origin, some three hundred and fifty-thousand Tunisians, around one hundred thousand from elsewhere in the Arab Middle East, and an estimated quarter of a million from sub-Sahara Africa. As a result, France today has more Muslim inhabitants than any other European country.

More important, the mayor said (echoing a near-universal consensus), "You're Marseillais before you are French. When you ask a youth from a migrant community where he is from, he says, 'I am from Marseille,' and not France. The nuance is important. There is a strong distinction between being Marseillais and being French, which is why we don't have the problems they had outside Paris. . . . And another factor is the way Marseille is built between the hills and the sea—no *quartier* is far from the sea."

Still, we asked, what did the mayor think about the proposed and controversial Grand Mosque, with its projected eighty-plus-foot minaret, which on its scheduled completion in 2012 would rival Notre Dame-de-la-Garde as Marseille's visual trademark? We reminded the mayor that elsewhere in the non-Islamic world—from Ground Zero in New York to otherwise hard-to-agitate Switzerland (whose citizens voted in 2009 to ban future minarets)—the very word "mosque" is percussive (literally, in fact; shots were fired in April 2010 at a mosque in the southern French city of Istres, fortunately without casualties). In Marseille, the right-wing politician Ronald Perdormo called the projected Grand Mosque a "symbol of non-assimilation." Reporter Edward Cody of *The Washington Post* quoted a retiree as lamenting, "Marseille is finished. There is nothing left but blacks and Arabs."

Adjusting his chair while frowning, Mayor Roatta begged to differ: "The Grand Mosque is being built at our wish. Respecting all religions is important to us. Although we have twenty places for Muslims to pray downtown, they often have to use garages or other inappropriate sites. So Mayor Gaudin wanted this mosque. The city provided the land without cost [on the site of the former slaughterhouse] and the Muslim community itself will provide the [construction] funds. We have a comptroller who will make sure that the money does not come from shady people." Indeed, he stressed, similar arrangements have long existed in building mosques in Paris, Lyon, and Strasbourg.

Moreover, he went on, despite all the talk about secularism, the city of Marseille, as everywhere in France, underwrites the preservation of its Catholic and Protestant churches as well as synagogues built before 1905. Here a relevant digression is essential. *Laïcité* is not synonymous with secularism as understood in the United States. True, the French state is officially neutral regarding religion, as decreed in the republic's 1905 law on separation of church and state. But existing religious edifices then became the property of city councils, with their maintenance subsidied by the state. Sectarian services are not supported. Ever since, discord has been continuous on how or where to draw the line between "negative" and "positive" *laïcité*. What about official holidays, school menus, state broadcasts, armed forces chaplains, prayers, or meetings with avowedly clerical organizations? And with the growth of a Muslim immigrant community, a new minefield of contention has emerged involving public security, dress codes, census data, and the perceived menace of Islamic law.

Mayor Roatta broached the subject of public security: "At the Grand Mosque, worshippers will have to inscribe their names as they enter—those who aren't fundamentalists won't mind, and those who just come to pray don't want to be associated with those who have a different agenda." But, we rejoined, worshippers who enter churches or synagogues don't have to sign in. "No, that's right. It's evolutionary. I hope that once the Grand Mosque is built, we won't need the names of those who enter. It was the decision of the community, not of the city or state." He went on to discuss other rules regarding background checks and noted that in existing smaller mosques there are too few controls.

Our sense was that this problematic issue is still in the first trimester of political pregnancy. We found, by contrast, that on another matter, few informants differed: urban rappers in Marseille constitute a sort of modern equivalent to a Greek chorus. While an older generation speaks in standard grammar via print, television, and the radio, ascendant youngsters commonly blog, twitter, and upload via YouTube or Facebook; and their universal vernacular is rap.

BLUE JEANS arguably aside, few American exports are more perva-
sive than rap, spawned in the urban slums of New York's South Bronx.
There in the early 1980s, the pulsing cadences of black America, the
Caribbean, and Latin America fused. Usually sung to a 4/4 beat, often
accompanied by a disc jockey's sampling from a recorded source, rap
emerged from noisy neighborhood parties. Afrika Bambaataa, an
African-American disc jockey who came of age in the crime-ridden
South Bronx, is commonly credited with introducing hip-hop to
Europe. A onetime warlord in the Black Spades, said to be New York's
premier street gang, Bambaataa won an essay contest whose first prize
was a trip to Africa. On his return, he became a political activist and
renamed himself in honor of the Zulu warrior who led a sustained
revolt against British control of what became South Africa. In 1984,
Bambaataa and his troupe toured Europe and founded a French branch
of "the Zulu Nation" in a Paris suburb. His principal disciple was a
Senegal-born rapper, MC Solaar, soon to become the voice of the North
African underclass in France, his style honed by the tapes he and his
cohorts brought back from pilgrimages to the South Bronx.

In Marseille, homegrown rap spread among Maghrebins, many of
whose parents were born in Algeria. Most popular was IAM, a group
whose lyrics permeate the Marseille trilogy by Jean-Claude-Izzo (1945–
2000). The self-taught son of a Spanish seamstress and a Naples barman,
Izzo was attuned to his city's corruption, its violence and its anti-Arab
prejudices, yet his trilogy remains a loving paean to Marseille. Izzo's fictional hero is Fabio Montale—*un flic de banlieue*—a cop whose beat is
the tough northern district, who swills *pastis* at Hassan's bar. Rap is as
central to the trilogy as his friend Honorine's delectable *soup au pistou*.

IAM's name, one theory holds, derives from an early album (*De la
Planete Mars*) with tracks that include "I am from Marseille," or Mars
for short. Another scholar claims IAM is an acronym for Imperial Asi-
atic Men, or possibly Independents Autonomous Marseille, or that it
simply echoes Descartes's "*Cogito ergo sum.*" IAM's concerts in the
Dôme de Marseille proved so popular that the Ministry of Culture
awarded the group a major prize, partly in tribute to the poetic skills of

lead rapper Philippe Fragione. Although IAM's performers are by origin Italian, Algerian, and Malgache, each rapper assumed an ancient Egyptian name: Akhenaton (Fragione), Shurik'n (Geoffroy Mussard), Khéops (Erik Mazel), Imhotep (Pascal Perez), and Kephren (François Mendy). According to André J. M. Prévos (a scholarly authority on French rap), the group's "pharaohism" is meant to emphasize its Arabic origins while avoiding the negative stereotypes associated with Islamic extremism— and moreover, serves as a nose-thumb at Paris.

"The two scourges of Marseille," Izzo quotes IAM as collectively remarking, "are heroin and the National Front." In the author's words, Marseille is "a place where people liked to talk a lot. . . . The rappers talked the way people talked in bars: about Paris or the centralized state, the decaying suburbs, the night buses. Their lives, their problems. The world seen from Marseille." As an IAM riff puts it:

> *You hear the rhythm, that's the rhythm of rap,*
> *We hit it hard 'cause we don't take no crap.*
> *All they think about in Paris is power and money,*
> *But us kids down here don't think that's funny.*
> *I'm 22 years old and I'm better than those mothers,*
> *'Cause never in my life would I betray my brothers.*
> *I have to go now, but make no mistake*
> *I ain't working like a slave for no fuckin' State.*

Belying Marseille's sun and sand imagery, "melancholic" is the word usually used to characterize its rap. Unlike Parisian rap, Marseille's beat is generally slower and its words bluer, suggesting the influence of Raï, a form of folk music native to Algeria that combines "regional, secular, and religious drum patterns, melodies, and instruments [which] were blended with Western electric instruments." Among the port's other eminent rappers is M'Roumbaba Saïd, otherwise known as Soprano. (His name and lyrics reflect his fascination with the HBO television series, *The Sopranos*.) One of his hit tracks is "Melancholic Anonymous." "I can't help it, expressing my feelings, my melancholy, in my lyrics," he explains. "I can laugh at my sadness. It helps.")

Other rappers branched out to a reggae-ragamuffin style derived from the Caribbean, notably from Jamaica, typified by the group called Massilia Sound System, or MSS (The title of Izzo's second book, *Chourmo*, is taken from an MSS album). Massilia's success, along with that of the soccer team OM, is credited with changing the image of Marseille in the 1990s from being a city of criminals and losers to a metropolis proud of its mixed identities. A former tobacco factory called La Friche, near the Saint-Charles rail terminal, served as the venue for MSS concerts, in which half the songs were in the Provençal dialect—a fitting prelude to Marseille's assimilation of a musical tradition that has leapt across oceans into the hearts and throats of a restless new generation.

———

TO LEARN MORE, we sought out Marseille's premier female rapper, Keny Arkana, age twenty-nine. With her olive skin and signature headscarf, she looks more Arab than Latin. However, her origins are Argentine; her parents emigrated from the town of Salta, near the Bolivian frontier. She is nonetheless quintessentially Marseillais: "I could talk for hours about Marseille. Did you know that Mary Magdalene lived her last thirty years in the mountains around here?" We met in a busy outdoor café in one of Marseille's trendiest quarters, Cours Saint-Julien. Squeezing between crowded tables resounding with chatter, we were repeatedly interrupted by fans and friends requesting photo-ops and/or autographs. She was gracious to all, even as she chain-smoked and spewed French like bullets. Everyone called her Keny.

It was while living in a Marseille "foyer" (a juvenile home) that Keny first learned to rap. She was fifteen when she became a student in a hip-hop writing workshop taught by a rapper especially for teenagers: "There were two workshops a week. It gave me a certain sense of discipline, because then I was living in the street and wasn't doing anything." She had found her calling.

Keny's passion centered on the wrongs inflicted by callous Westerners on a hungry Third World. Her first single, "La Rage," released in 2006, echoed the anger vented in France's riots: "Rage is the essence of

revolution." Yet her songs were less aggressively militant than the underclass rap heard in and around Paris. Asked whether she preferred standard French to Marseille slang, she said, "I write the way I speak, but I
try to make it accessible to a wider audience. Of course, there will be
bits of slang, but by now, there are a lot of Marseille expressions known
everywhere in France—also there is Marseille argot known only in a single neighborhood, so I'm not going to use them—African words, Gypsy
words, we might use them, but not too many. . . . In Paris, the big thing
is *verlan*, in which you reverse syllables. That's how the word *beur* [itself
derived from slang for Arab] becomes *rebeu*. To say someone is *louche* in
Paris, they say that person is *chelou*. Here we also use Gypsy words like
gajo [a contemptuous term for non-Gypsies]—which can be a man or a
woman."

Between cups of coffee, we repeated the harsh words of other interviewees about organized crime and residential segregation. She understood what they meant: "Marseille is [figuratively] a Mafia city. When
the Opus Dei comes to France, they don't go to Paris, they come to
Marseille—it's also a big city for Masons. There's a lot of underground
networks." She paused, and pursued:

> So you may also notice that the richer areas are in the southern part.
> Marseille has always been divided because of the bourgeois Mafia—
> the poor part is really poor, and the rich part, which is small, is really
> rich. The city also has rich people who are not Mafia related, there's
> even a side that's almost monarchical. And it's always been true that
> the poor live among themselves in the northern quarter, and rich
> among their own selves, more than in Paris. In Marseille, there's
> almost no way you can rise above your social class.

Hearing this indictment, we asked why in 2005 the young, angry,
and oppressed in Marseille did not join in the national epidemic of car
burnings. Her reply captured the ambivalence we encountered on every
side in this fascinating but conflicted metropolis:

> The first thing is that here everybody knows one another, so you
> won't go down and burn your brother's car. Even if I were French for

ten generations, I'm still Marseillais first. In a sense, we don't have the same problems as Paris, since we have a really strong identity as Marseillais—and nobody came and told us "You are French, or not French." You are Marseillaise. . . . We are less confused than the people in Paris, who don't know if they are Algerian French, or French, or not French. We are Mediterranean, we are at home—and *they* are not at home. . . . And it's not chauvinistic but true to say that Marseille does not have a history in common with any other French city. It's always a welcoming place. There's lots of sun. . . . We have a good climate, the sky, and so we're not so tense.

———

HER WORDS, it seemed to us, mirrored a wider ambivalence afflicting France's political class in striving to reconcile long-cherished doctrines with the demographic realities of an aging populace and a shrinking birthrate. Providing services, jobs, and homes for younger immigrants is not just an option; if France is to grow and prosper, it is the *only* option. Still, where should newcomers live? Once again, Marseille led the way, if inadvertently and perversely. Its planners pioneered an efficient if soulless method for sheltering migrants at discount rates in high-rise projects—the HLM's (habitation á loyer modéré) that spawn gangs, drug addiction, and political rage.

This was surely not the intention of Charles-Édouard Jeanneret, the Swiss-born master builder better known as Le Corbusier (1887–1965). Few projects meant more to him than l'Unité d'Habitation, a twelve-story apartment complex on Marseille's southern fringe at whose opening he presided in 1952. To its creator, this lofty concrete edifice, mounted on platforms supported by ingeniously slanted columns, was a "Virgilian dream." He believed it satisfied every basic human need ("sociability, mutual assistance, protection, security and economy") despite its windowless kitchens and bathrooms. ("Why do you want sunshine in the bathroom, when you are only there morning and night?" he protested. "What's wrong with the smell of food if the cooking is good?") Le Corbusier envisioned similar "vertical communes" rising everywhere in Radiant Cities (*les Villes Radieuses*). However, his vision was hijacked by imitators who seized on his elegant model to manufacture innumerable prefab apartment complexes, whose style deservedly earned the epithet "brutalist."

Ironically, l'Unité d'Habitation was meant as Le Corbusier's homage to the city that captivated him from his first sighting, at age twenty-seven in 1912. As he wrote to a Swiss friend, Marseille was not merely "the gateway to the East" that "swarmed with life," it was also "a port, but what a port! Negroes, ships, waves, fish with fantastic scales, shellfish, masked crowds, Chinamen, Gurkas and Kamerat!" Yet when we visited Le Corbusier's homage to a port swarming with life, it was like coming upon a swath of vanilla in an urban rainbow. The project's vertiginous lines are elegant but chilly, reflecting its creator's devotion to mathematical logic at the expense of what Immanuel Kant called the crooked timbers of humanity.

No great modernist was more enamored of mathematics. Le Corbusier's 1954 manifesto, *The Modular*, is subtitled "A Harmonious Measure to the Human Scale Universally Applicable to Architecture and Mechanics." This mirrored the universal doctrines so hopefully promulgated during the French Revolution, which nurtured a universal calendar, the metric system, decimal coinage, and a theoretically purely rational religion. Successor French regimes propagated a uniform legal code, a nationwide school curriculum, and endorsed the linguistic rules set forth by the forty members of the Académie Française, known (half-jocularly) as the Immortals. Even so, by 1900 barely half the Third Republic's inhabitants were fluent in French; the rest grew up speaking Celtic, Germanic, or other Romance languages. Simply defining citizenship perplexed politicians from the Revolution onward, a debate intensified when France in the 1890s became Europe's first "country of immigration." Should the test of citizenship be parentage, place of birth, length of residence, or assimilation? In a carefully researched study, the French political scientist Patrick Weil concluded in 2008 that France "has changed its laws more often and more significantly than any other any other democratic nation has, and policies governing French nationality have been the object of continual political and legal confrontations."

In all this, urban planning played a crucial supporting role, especially after 1853, when soon-to-be enthroned Napoleon III named Georges-Eugène Haussmann (1809–1891) as prefect of the Seine. With the future emperor's support, Haussmann razed much of medieval Paris, thrusting boulevards through clogged neighborhoods to reinvent the city as a capital rivaling imperial Rome (and also to ensure swift military access in the event of a future urban rising). Whole districts were gutted, and Parisians saw a new world emerging before their eyes, but (in the view of Andrew Hussey, a longtime British resident and astute Francophile), "The city built by Haussmann was both superb and chilling, representing a triumph of organization and technology over the past."

We had a firsthand sighting of the results of modern urban planning in Parisian *banlieues* while visiting Éric Raoult, the mayor since 1995 of Le Raincy, one of six municipalities in the department of Seine-Saint-Denis, just north of Paris. (Since 2002, Raoult has represented Seine-Saint-Denis as a center-right deputy in the National Assembly, where he holds the office of vice president.) "My constituency is a melting pot," he told us in Le Raincy's town hall, a solidly traditional edifice dedicated in 1909. Raoult explained that roughly one-third of Le Raincy's residents were legally French owing to their origins in former colonies. Few issues were of greater concern to his own voters, he said, than the HLMs. The key issues were how high, and with what quota for subsidized tenants, especially the public housing near wealthier neighborhoods. He then escorted us to his car and driver, and together we drove from Le Raincy's bourgeois downtown to next door Clichy-sous-Bois's high-rise slums, where some of the worst car burnings occurred in 2005. "Here we are on the frontier," the mayor warned. Everywhere we saw graffiti, much of it crudely obscene, for example, "Fuk the Polis," surely not an epitaph Le Corbusier would have welcomed.

In touring the *banlieues*, we sensed the echoes of interrelated arguments over what might be shorthanded as immigration, Islam, and identity. What should a European state reasonably ask of its non-European immigrants? How ought a secular republic deal equitably with Muslims, given fears among conservatives that Islam itself poses an existential threat? Was it possible, finally, for a loyal citizen to have multiple identities? Questions like this (writes Patrick Weil in *How to Be French*) remain "fraught with contradictory representations, beliefs, and stereotypes." And all such questions are interwoven with France's unresolved entanglement with Algeria, a history that even now is generally little known.

———

FOUR TIMES THE size of Metropolitan France, Algeria before 1830 was nominally a province of the Ottoman Empire, though its true governor was the Dey of Algiers, a prince whose power derived from managing pirates and slavers. In 1827, the incumbent Dey Hussein lost his temper while arguing about grain prices with the French consul, whom he swatted with a fly whisk, deriding him as a "wicked, faithless, idol-worshipping rascal." So doing, he affronted national honor as well as France's last-reigning Bourbon, King Charles X, who seized on the incident to wage a popular war. In 1830, a punitive armada carrying thirty-seven thousand French troops and ninety-one field cannons invaded Algiers and ousted the insolent dey. This resulted in the first European annexation of a Muslim state in the Mediterranean, by any measure an epochal event. But the conquest did not benefit Charles X; it coincided with a long-gestating internal revolt against that monarch, who fled as his non-Bourbon rival Louis-Philippe was crowned as "Citizen King."

What now should be done with France's mostly uncultivated and overwhelmingly Muslim realm? "France upbraids us with the misgovernment and oppression of India," jibed *The Times* of London on July 14, 1830. "We should be curious to know how she will govern Algeria." The new Citizen King wasn't sure either. Absent a consensus, France equivocated and relied on force to suppress what became a fifteen-year rebellion in western and central Algeria. No quarter was given, and the French military's scorched-earth policies stirred a censorious outcry. These perplexities were compounded in the revolutionary year 1848 when Louis-Philippe was in his turn deposed and France's Second Republic proclaimed. Its leaders now rashly decided to incorporate Algeria as an integral part of France, dividing it into three departments. "It was a historic, indeed unique step," writes the evenhanded military historian Alistair Horne, "and one which thereby set up for successive

French republics a deadly trap from which they would find it well nigh impossible to escape."

The trap's deadliness arose from the Second Republic's (1848–1852) decrees asserting that Algerian Muslims were henceforth French subjects, but *not* French citizens. Ted Morgan distills this tangled matter in *My Battle of Algiers* (2005), writing, "A Muslim could not be a citizen unless he repudiated the law of Islam, and accepted the French civil code, which the vast majority refused to do." The trap deepened some years later when France's newborn Third Republic (1870–1940) earmarked fifty million francs to encourage European colonization of Algiers, especially by refugees from Alsace and Lorraine, provinces annexed by Germany after its 1871 rout of Napoleon III. The newcomers provoked a rebellion in Kabylia, the fertile homeland of Algeria's principal Berber tribe. Other settlers began arriving en masse from Spain, Italy, Malta, and Germany. By 1917, it was estimated that only one in five Europeans in Algeria was of true French origin. Colons became collectively known (half-pejoratively) as *pieds-noirs,* literally meaning "black feet."

Algeria's two-tier system of citizenship nevertheless survived two world wars, Woodrow Wilson and his idealistic Fourteen Points, and FDR and his anticolonial Atlantic Charter. From 1914 to 1918, Algerian Muslims provided the Allies with 173,000 soldiers and 119,000 factory and field-workers (to replace Frenchmen serving in the armed forces) yet they received negligible postwar rewards. Granted, as colonialism's defenders tirelessly reiterated, Algeria did benefit from schools, hospitals, roads, railways, and an expanding agricultural economy as a result of French colonization. Yet all this was counterbalanced by the absence of any freely elected Muslims in the French parliament, even though Algeria was an integral department of France.

As the settler population increased, so did its leverage within the National Assembly where the so-called colonial lobby of 120 deputies in 1897 more than doubled by 1935 to 250 out of 608 deputies. Its members were united in their vehement opposition to liberalizing Algeria's suffrage. In 1936, a progressive-minded former governor-general of Algeria, Maurice Viollette, proposed offering full citizenship to twenty-five thousand Muslims out of a population of six million, a reform approved by French premier Léon Blum's Popular Front government (in which Viollette was a minister). The *pieds-noirs* response was volcanic. Angry marches and inflammatory editorials denounced "Parisian ignorance" of purported realities in Algeria, a specimen statement being, "We will never tolerate, in even the smallest commune, that an Arab might be the mayor." Blum, France's Socialist (and Jewish) premier, pulled back as did his own party's support for the reform. For his part, Viollette penned a prophetic warning:

> When the Muslims protest, you are indignant; when they approve, you are suspicious; when they keep quiet, you are fearful. *Messieurs*, these men have no political nation. They do not even demand their religious nation. All they ask is to be admitted into yours. If you refuse this, beware lest they do not soon create one for themselves.

In 1945, after yet another global war fought (in the West) in the name of democracy, the epilogue proved familiar. During the war, when France was either occupied or under Vichy rule, North African Muslims and their Senegalese partners accounted for as much as 90 percent of Free French forces in the Mediterranean. On May 8, 1945, as all Europe rejoiced in Nazi Germany's surrender, Algerians massed to demand the political rights they assumed they had been promised. Most demonstrations ended without incident, but not in the market city of Sétif. There, on Clemenceau Avenue, colonial police tore down banners proclaiming, "Long live a free Algeria!" and "We want to be your equal!" Days of rioting followed in which (at least) 103 settlers were killed and martial law was proclaimed; Foreign Legionnaires rushed in, resulting in an Algerian toll of 1,300 fatalities (the official French figure) or 45,000 dead (the Algerian nationalist figure). Everything about the incident has remained in dispute, with hardliners on each side believing the worst of the other.

This pattern of irreconcilable perceptions hardened during Algeria's 1954–1962 war of independence, during which one million or more persons perished according to the Algerian estimate, or in the minimalist French reckoning, 300,000 persons died, including 12,000 rebels killed in internal purges and 66,000 Muslims slain by the FLN. Undisputed is the war's other legacy: a massive wave of colons and their Muslim allies totaling more than one million (of whom one-tenth or so were *harkis*) crossed the seas to resettle in France. They and their descendents survive as memorials to Algeria's two-tier citizenship system and of France's lost war, a conflict waged on both sides with a disregard for the legal rights of civilians and treatment of war prisoners.

———

IS THIS ALL ancient history? In postcolonial times, does anyone really believe "the Algerian question" still simmers? Our own sense is that despite much soul-searching, France has yet to address fairly her historic demons. This is scarcely unusual among nation-states. Coming to terms with abuses past is always difficult, vide Japan's reluctance to acknowledge war crimes in China and Korea; Turkey's resistance to addressing a former regime's genocidal slaughter of Armenians; and (not least) American tardiness in confronting the infamies of slavery, the prolonged tolerance of Jim Crow, the dispossession of indigenous inhabitants, the "manifest destiny" annexation of California and Texas, and the internment of US citizens of Japanese ancestry during World War II.

Moreover, heated arguments over both Islam and the rights of immigrants nowadays reverberate in traditionally tolerant Denmark, Norway, Sweden, and the Netherlands. In normally stolid Germany, Chancellor Angela Merkel, exasperated by disputes over Muslim migrants, declared in 2010 that multiculturalism had "utterly failed." Still, no Western democracy seems more conflicted than France by its growing Muslim minority and its own colonialist past.

At the 2010 Cannes Film Festival, to cite one example, riot police were summoned to restrain a thousand-strong right-wing demonstrators enraged by a film entitled *Hors-la-Loi* ("Outside the Law"). Made by a Frenchman of Algerian descent, Rachid Bouchareb, the film accepts the FLN version of the 1945 riots in Sétif (described above), focusing on three brothers who were radicalized by police killings and then settled in France to pursue vendettas against former colons, the gendarmerie, and other Algerians. The film was chosen as the Algerian entry for the 2011 foreign-language Academy Award. Coincidentally, France submitted as *its* entry an equally anguishing if quite different film, *Des Hommes et des Dieux* ("Of Gods and Men"), dramatizing the ordeal of seven Trappist monks who had remained after Algerian independence only to be abducted in 1996 by presumed jihadists, and subsequently beheaded.

Reflecting on the two films, *The New York Times's* Steven Erlanger described France's entanglement with Algeria as "a wound that never quite seems to close." He cited the concurring judgment of Benjamin Stora, a leading French historian of the colonial era: "It is a wound. Algeria is France, it is part of the history of French nationalism. Algeria continues to obsess people and still torments French society." The dominant center-right view remains that no apologies are necessary. As phrased in July 2007 by President Sarkozy before embarking on his one-day (and only) visit to Algeria, "Certainly there were a lot of sufferings and injustices during the 132 years France spent in Algeria. But that isn't all there was. I'm for recognition of the facts, but not for repentance, which is a religious notion that has no place in relations between states." Besides, Sarkozy explained in his interview with Algerian journalists (as reported by Reuters), young people in both countries look to the future and not the past "and what they want are concrete things. They're not waiting for their leaders simply to drop everything and start mortifying themselves, or to beat their breasts over the mistakes of the past because, in that case, there would be lots to do on both sides."

Sifting through many such remarks over the past half century, we were struck by a persistent failure to acknowledge the original sin of dispossessing millions of non-European Algerians. To ghettoized immigrants and their offspring, such statements are understandably deciphered as an appeasing bow to the anti-immigrant National Front, whose votes continue to decide close elections. Indeed, these coded ambiguities surfaced in the unresolved and otherwise (to Americans) baffling disputes attending the birth of la Cité Nationale de l'Histoire de l'Immigration, France's new immigration museum.

———

IT SEEMED A SPLENDID idea in 1989 when an immigration museum was initially proposed by Zaïr Kedadouche, a retired footballer, a second-generation Algerian, a political centrist, and a municipal councilman in Paris. The United States was about to dedicate in 1990 a similar museum on Ellis Island, the gateway for twelve million immigrants from 1892 to 1954, a project so popular that New York and New Jersey vied for legal title to the island (a Supreme Court decision led to joint custody). Moreover, a ferry stop away rises the Statue of Liberty, her benign gaze and welcoming torch, conceived, wrought, and financed in France.

Kedadouche's proposal was nonetheless shelved as too risky by President François Mitterrand, who, by most accounts, feared a National Front backlash. But in 1998, buoyed by the euphoria over France's World Cup soccer victory, Prime Minister Lionel Jospin, also a Socialist, bravely revived the museum proposal. He obtained the vital blessing of Gaullist President Jacques Chirac, the Fifth Republic's first chief of state to officially visit independent Algeria. Nicknamed "Le Bulldozer" and roguishly unpredictable, Chirac helped find a home for the new museum at the edge of the Vincennes forest in eastern Paris. However, the home proved a curious choice: an Art Déco pavilion built for the 1931 International Colonial Exposition.

When the 1931 exposition opened, the French Union and its Foreign Legion mystique were at their apogee. Thanks in part to German colonies mandated to France by the Versailles Treaty, France's empire, if not territorially bigger than Britain's, was the world's most extensive. It comprised forty-seven states whose official language was French, all of whose leaders in varying degrees were obligated to France. France's "civilizing mission" was glowingly described by the exposition's commissioner-general, Marshal Hubert Lyautey, the celebrated former proconsul in Morocco. "To colonize does not mean merely to construct wharves, factories and railroads," he proudly stated. "It also means to instill a humane gentleness in the wild hearts of the savannah or the desert." This beneficent task was portrayed in sculptured friezes that still today adorn the pavilion, showing industrious natives— brown, black, and yellow—being raised from ignorance and poverty by kindly colonial officials.

This paternalistic mystique continues to haunt France. In early 2005, the ruling conservatives passed a "Law on Colonialism," requiring secondary school teachers and their textbooks "to acknowledge and recognize, in particular, the positive role of the French presence abroad, especially in North Africa." An outcry over the law arose in former colonies and among French human rights activists, mainstream pundits, prominent historians, and educators. More than one thousand professors and their students signed a petition declaring "NO to Teaching Official History." President Chirac finally broke with his own party and ordered the repeal of the offending language. In April 2006, a grumbling National Assembly majority complied.

As France headed into the 2007 presidential elections, the aging Chirac bowed out and Nicolas Sarkozy became the right-center nominee. Socialists put forward the personable Ségolène Royal, but the wild card once again was the National Front's Jean-Marie Le Pen. Five years earlier, to widespread dismay, Le Pen, the idol of the Islamophobes, who had fought as a paratrooper in the Algerian War, bypassed Socialist Lionel Jospin in the first round, qualifying him for a runoff in which left-center voters, teeth gritted, voted decisively for Chirac. But in 2007, Le Pen fell back to his customary 10.44 percent in the initial poll, and in the second round Sarkozy prevailed by pandering simultaneously to the left and right.

In office, however, the new president's basic impulse was confirmed by the appointment of his close friend Brice Hortefeux, a law and order hardliner, to head a newly named "Ministry of Immigration, Integration, National Identity, and Cooperative Development." This emphasis on "national identity" so troubled the panel of academic advisers to a still-unborn immigration museum that eight of its ten members resigned, including Patrick Weil, its preeminent authority on citizenship. Their forebodings were confirmed when Hortefeux ordered a police roundup of undocumented aliens to meet a new mandatory annual goal of twenty-five thousand deportations. Prominent among these were Romas (Gypsies), despised by many in France. Hortefeux proposed DNA tests to check the family unification claims of North African immigrants, tests not proposed for immigrants from other regions. Detention centers swelled with immigrants, raids were ordered on suspected illegal Roma settlements, and the rules of political asylum narrowed. All this outweighed "Sarko's" modest proposals to widen non-European access to elite schools and his naming of three Muslim women as ministers, all since departed from office.

Thus as its opening approached, the immigration museum had become an embarrassment. President Sarkozy managed to be elsewhere on its debut in October 10, 2007, as did Immigration Minister Hortefeux. Their absence dominated press accounts. Perplexed critics noted the museum's makeshift air and the continued presence of an otherwise unrelated aquarium in its basement. The main gallery showcased both the positive achievements of (mostly European) immigrants, as well as France's recurrent outbursts of xenophobia. Striving to stress the positive, *Le Monde* praised the museum for "bearing witness that 'French identity' exists, but that it has always been mixed." Foreign perplexity was expressed by *New York Times* critic Michael Kimmelman, who was informed by the museum's president, Jacques Toubon, that its mission was to "tell the story of immigration" and not the history of slavery or colonization. To an American, wrote Kimmelman, "that sounded like devising a museum for African-Americans or American Indian cultures but skipping gingerly over slavery, segregation and Manifest Destiny."

Of the controversies most visibly minimized at the museum (as we found on our visit) was the dispute over dress codes for Muslim females in state schools. Of numerous illustrations in the museum's official handbook, only one depicts the image of a young woman wearing a headscarf, and she is not a real person. She is instead a life-size mannequin in a post-modern artwork titled "A Machine of Dreams," by Kader Attia, a young French artist of Algerian origin born in Seine-Saint-Denis. His tableau depicts an adolescent Muslim girl gazing wistfully at a vending machine crammed with forbidden but tempting snacks. As in the tableau, what has been routinely neglected in the headscarf debate, has been the plight of adolescent Muslim women trapped in the middle.

———

L'AFFAIRE DU FOULARD ISLAMIQUE burst into headlines in September 1989 when three girls appeared in headscarves on the opening day of their secondary school in Creil, a town near Paris. The principal asked the students to remove them. When they refused, they were expelled on grounds that the scarves compromised "the *laïcité* (i.e., secularist) neutrality of the public schools."

This incident came at a moment when aggressive Muslim fundamentalism was much in the news. Only months before, Ayatollah Khomeini had issued his fatwa calling on believers to slay Salman Rushdie for purported blasphemies in his novel, *The Satanic Verses,* prompting riots, book burnings, and death threats to publishers. This unrest happened as North African guest workers who had migrated to France seeking jobs had become permanent residents, feeding fears of a new enemy within. Not only did the traditional right sound the alarm; the barometric left-wing weekly *Nouvel Observateur* headlined its October 5 cover story on the Creil incident "Fanaticism: The Religious Menace." As headscarf disputes multiplied, its permutations scrambled the usual political divisions. Leading feminists argued that banning headscarves infringed a woman's basic freedom of choice and would limit access of observant Muslims to higher education. Others retorted that absent a mandatory ban, all Muslim females would be pressured by their peers, husbands, and parents to don headscarves. So intermingled were the pros and cons of the issue that major political figures who initially opposed the headscarf ban (e.g., Sarkozy) later swiveled around to become its ardent advocates.

As the debate post-9/11 intensified, concerned ordinary citizens appealed to legislators to "do something" (which in France means form a commission, then enact its proposal). An American anthropologist, John R. Bowen, author of *Why the French Don't Like Headscarves* (2007), attended rallies, monitored hearings, and measured the inches of press coverage. In April 2003, a speech by then–Interior Minister Sarkozy France's "chief cop" singled out "the unwillingness of Muslims to follow the law as the major obstacle to their becoming full citizens of France." The law in question concerned removing head coverings for identity photos, but Sarkozy's reasoning effectively linked the offending scarves to the perceived refusal of Muslims to embrace the Fifth Republic.

In July, President Chirac appointed a high-level commission to examine the various issues associated with *laïcité*, with special attention to headscarves. Known as the Stasi Commision after its chairman Bernard Stasi, a respected ombudsman and onetime civil servant in French Algeria, it consisted of nineteen members. They included the veteran ideologue and reformed Marxist Régis Debray; the immigration policy expert Patrick Weil; the scholarly authority on Islam Gilles Kepel; and the panel's only Muslim, Mohammed Arkoun, known for his academic writings on Islamic philosophy. The Stasi Commission heard testimony from educators and school principals, from Interior Minister Sarkozy and Urban Affairs Minister Jean-Louis Borloo, and from its sole Muslim witness, Saïda Kada, leader of the Lyon Muslim Sisters, who urged the commissioners to widen their attention beyond headscarves to the plight of Islamic immigrants in ghettoized neighborhoods. At no point (according to Bowen) did the Stasi Commission directly question any of the Muslim teens who chose to wear the *voile*. Most teachers testifying stressed the disruptive effect of headscarves, but in Bowen's view, their experiences were hardly representative: "Indeed, 91 percent of all teachers in France had never even *encountered* a student in a headscarf at their current school. Nevertheless, the teachers who testified tended to generalize their sense of crisis to other teachers and other schools."

This sense of crisis animated the commission's final report in December 2003. With one dissenting vote, its members offered twenty-five recommendations, many of which creditably addressed the testimony of Saïda Kada. These urged the government to promote social inclusion and break down ghetto walls, to respect all interfaith festivals and the burial customs of Muslims, and to deal honestly with the negative legacy of colonialism. Only the final recommendation focused on headscarves:

In schools, middle schools and high schools, appearances and signs displaying religious or political affiliations should be forbidden, conditional on respecting the freedom of conscience and the specific nature of private schools under contract with the state. All sanctions to be proportional and taken only after a pupil has been asked to meet his/her obligations.

An explanatory addenda states that *"signes ostensibles"* included crosses and *kippas* [yarmulkes] as well as headscarves. Smaller medallions, crucifixes, stars of David, hands of Fatima, and tiny Korans were deemed acceptable as displays of religious affiliation.

However, only the twenty-fifth and final recommendation, endorsed by President Chirac, was presented for legislative action. Polls indicated that the ban was approved by 69 percent of French voters who were questioned. Speaking bravely for dissenters, *Le Monde* contended that any such measure would "stigmatize, marginalize and exclude a part of the population when the country has more than ever a need for integration." As the National Assembly prepared to vote, only the victory margin was in doubt; the count was 494 in favor, 36 against, and 31 abstentions. (Let it be added that some seasoned social scientists such as Patrick Weil, endorsed the commission's findings, suggesting how difficult and complex are the issues regarding dress codes for female students.)

The action was followed by a related second decision in July 2010, when the National Assembly voted overwhelmingly to prohibit any clothing worn in public places that conceals one's face, that is, the burqa (335 in favor, 1 against, with the rest of the members boycotting the poll). In April 2011, it became unlawful in France to wear face coverings, except in places of worship or as a passenger in a car; any person forcing a woman to disobey the law faces a year's imprisonment or a fine of 30,000 Euros—both penalties to be doubled if the woman involved is under eighteen. The "burqa ban" is believed to affect fewer than two-thousand women in France, and Open Society researchers managed to find and question thirty-two of them, in a report titled *Unveiling the Truth*. All but three were born in France, eight were converts to Islam, and most were of North African origin. Although the ostensible reason for the ban was to protect women who had been forced by males to shroud themselves, the report found that "the majority of women interviewed freely chose to wear the full face-coverings. They made the decision despite strong family opposition, with only one woman encouraged to wear it."

In reading the Open Society interviews, one is struck by the literate thoughtfulness of the women and by the absence of boilerplate clichés.

Here speaks Latifah, age twenty-seven, one of several respondents living in Marseille:

> The values of the Republic are shaped according to the people who live in the Republic. So 50 years ago, all the nuns were covered, and being topless [on the beach] was shocking, while today it's normal. The women who are displayed on billboards with their naked breasts don't represent the values of the Republic of 50 or 60 years ago. The evolving Republican values do not take into account the diversity of people who live in France. This is reductive, because [in France] there aren't only people who look like them. But in fact, they don't want Islam, that's it! Even in England, when the debate [on the burqa] started, [the English] said, "no, we can't [adopt a law]; there is diversity, and we accept it." In France, they want a country where everyone looks like Pierre, Paul, Jacques, and where [everyone] is dressed the same.

Fundamentally it is the affront to dignity that appears most hurtful. Even in Marseille, as several Muslims remarked, it is routine to address them as "tu," a condescending pronoun otherwise used either for intimate friends or children.

———

VEILS ARE MENTAL as well as material. Excluded from much of the debate over headdresses are complicating realities. As a leading British authority on contemporary Islam, Malise Ruthven, has long contended, North African Muslims are no less susceptible to European cultural influences than other immigrant groups, such as Slavs, Sikhs, Hindus, or non-Muslim Africans. He cites voluminous supporting studies by such scholars as Aziz al-Azmeh, Tariq Madood, Philip Lewis, and Jytte Klausen which refute the cliché of a homogenous immigrant community (in al-Azmeh's words) "innocent of modernity, cantankerously or morosely obsessed with prayer, fasting, veiling, medieval social and penal arrangements." Closer to home is the data compiled by Farhad Khosrokhavar, director of France's École des Hautes Études en Science Sociales, who estimates that roughly one-fifth of France's

Muslims do not practice Islam at all, and that only 70 percent claim they fast during Ramadan, among the creed's most basic duties. Yet the image of a monolithic, impermeable, hostile Muslim cancer remains a press cliché.

How curious (Americans are permitted to ask) that the French so gravely underestimate the appeal of their own culture? Would the Fifth Republic totter if adolescent students were allowed to wear headscarves? And why does the political class in Paris seem so indifferent to the lessons of Marseille? Periodically, ordinary citizens are drawn to Marseille's remarkable past and present. Most recently, a nightly soap opera titled *Plus Belle la Vie* has mesmerized one-fifth of the France's television viewers. The series is filmed in a multicultural bar whose habitués have origins in Algeria and Spain, or are Holocaust survivors. It is indeed a microcosm of Marseille.

Ours is hardly a new observation. In the 1920s, one of Europe's shrewdest journalists, Joseph Roth, was mesmerized by Marseille. The city, he wrote, "is New York and Singapore, Hamburg and Calcutta, Alexandria and Port Arthur, San Francisco and Odessa." As he marveled to his German-speaking readers,

> Sugar, soap, chemicals, vinegar, brandy, porcelain, cement, and dyes are all manufactured in Marseille. A tailor will run you up a suit in eight hours. In twenty-four hours a street may utterly change its appearance. . . . One shop sells food, the next love. The poor boatman's craft bobs alongside the great oceangoing steamship. Shellfish lie next to the jewelers' displays. The cobbler sells Corsican knives. . . . Every tenth wave washes a man ashore, like a fish. The Algerian Jew talks with a Chinaman in the café. . . . The continuous mixing of races and peoples is palpable, visible, physical and immediate. . . . This isn't France anymore. It's Europe, Asia, Africa, America. It's white, black, red, yellow. Everyone carries his homeland underfoot, and the soles of his feet carry him to Marseille.

It hasn't changed.

5

QUEENS:
EMBRACING DIVERSITY

*What is the glory of Rome and Jerusalem, where all
nations and races came to worship and look back,
compared with the glory of America, where all races
and nations come to labor and look forward?*

—ISRAEL ZANGWILL, *THE MELTING POT* (1911)

QUEENS A GLOBAL MODEL? One can hear an incredulous
gasp from the average native of Manhattan. A borough synonymous
with clogged airports, depressing cemeteries, a losing baseball team, and
television's stereotypical bigot (Archie Bunker)? Can Queens truly serve
as the harbinger of multiethnic peace in an otherwise feral world?

We dare answer "yes" answer to all the above. As New York City is
to America, Queens is to its parent metropolis: a crucible of creative
diversity. That Queens is so generally underrated (locally and nationally) remains a puzzle, given its aggregate of superlatives. Consider a
short list. With its population (2.3 million as of the 2010 census) and
territory (120 square miles), a separatist Queens would rank as America's fourth largest city, trailing only Los Angeles, Chicago. and its sister borough, Brooklyn, (population 2.5 million as of 2010). More
languages are spoken (138 by last count) in Queens than anywhere in
America, and globally its only credible rival is London. Half the borough's residents speak a tongue other than English at home, yet an
Esperanto of civility prevails on its sidewalks. Churches, mosques,

synagogues, and temples proliferate, continuing a tradition of religious tolerance that has roots in the borough's Dutch colonial origins. In 1657, the freeholders of the village Flushing, partly because they needed more farmers, appealed to Governor Peter Stuyvesant to allow heterodox Quakers to settle and worship without hindrance in New Amsterdam, the Dutch settlement that grew into New York. "Old Silver Leg," as the governor was dubbed, was an unyielding Calvinist, and he rejected out of hand the petition later known as the Flushing Remonstrance. Unfazed by abuse and imprisonment, the remonstrators boldly appealed to the directors of the Dutch West India Company to reverse the governor's ruling, which in time the company did. The victorious Remonstrance, today framed and preserved in the New York State Library in Albany, is consensually viewed as the precursor of America's commitment to religious freedom.

This was not the last time that Queens anticipated the shape of things to come. Early in the twentieth century, Astoria preceded and then rivaled Hollywood as the first movie capital of the United States. Its rise coincided with the debut of the equally innovative Garden Cities, among them Kew Gardens, Forest Hills, Jackson Heights, and Sunnyside Gardens. During World War II, long-standing residential color bars eroded when Louis Armstrong and other jazz pioneers settled in lily white Corona, Elmhurst, and St. Albans. Two World's Fairs (1939–1940 and 1964–1965) bloomed in a reclaimed refuse dump known as Flushing Meadows; their exhibits heralded the advent of television, computers, robots, and superhighways. Vacant pavilions from the first World's Fair became the temporary home of the newborn United Nations (1946–1950), and in these improvised quarters the world organization's founding delegates crafted the Universal Declaration of Human Rights, still the yardstick by which autocracies are still measured and censured.

––––––

LITTLE OF THIS is known or remembered in the privileged precincts of Manhattan, where the Masters of the Universe are more likely to remark that one should visit Queens only if accompanied by luggage or a corpse. This condescension owes much to the borough's unprepossessing physical appearance. Queens has no centralized downtown, no signature skyscrapers or boutique-lined thoroughfares. Instead, at first glance from an elevated subway car, the borough seems a blurred amalgam of expressways threaded among regimental rows of single-family homes and standard-issue, medium-rise brick apartment houses, many crowned with satellite dishes and peppered with oversize billboards and gnomic graffiti. Pedestrians stroll past innumerable health clinics, lawyers' offices, mom and pop druggists, and diners, their wares advertised in at least eight scripts (Latin, Cyrillic, Arabic, Hebrew, Greek, Hindi, Korean, and Chinese).

With the arguable exception of Flushing Meadows—the locus of two museums, the remnants of the two World's Fairs, and a clutch of sports stadiums—Queens is bereft of "there." So we were cautioned by Professor Andrew Hacker, a sage political scientist at Queens College, who informed us, "Nobody lives in Queens." The borough is essentially a patchwork of fifty-plus neighborhoods, five of which are designated as "towns" by the US Postal Service: Long Island City, Jamaica, Flushing, Far Rockaway, and Floral Park. Alone among New York's five boroughs, these towns and villages serve as distinct postal addresses; letters addressed to "Queens, New York" are likely to be returned marked "Address Unknown."

This was amplified by Andrew Jackson (also known as Sekou Molefi Baako), director of the Langston Hughes Community Library and Cultural Center in Corona: "Queens has its own branding process. You're proud of being from Queens, but the real borough is based on the individual communities. We've always been branded by our own community, so Queens has always been very unique in this respect." Or, in the words of Columbia University's Kenneth T. Jackson (no kin), the scholarly doyen of Gotham historians:

> Queens is not really a place in the usual American sense. It is not politically independent, and it does not have a distinct personality, it does not have a single post office address, and its sports teams are known by another moniker—the New York Mets rather than the Queens Mets, for example. Revealingly, Queens has two of the most important airports in the world—John F. Kennedy and La Guardia— but neither uses Queens in its name.

Yet this nameless entity "is in fact one of the most exciting, most diverse, most American, and most promising places on earth."

It's true. For upwards of a century, Queens has absorbed massive waves of newcomers from every corner of the globe, culminating in a post–World War II tsunami that peaked following passage of the 1965 US Immigration Act. The new legislation widened the door to Asians, Africans, Latinos, and West Indians, liberalizing America's long-standing, quasi-racist quota system. Non-Europeans began surging in unprecedented numbers through JFK International Airport, the heir to Ellis Island as principal gateway to the land of the free. In a few decades, the migrants doubled the borough's million-plus population as many newcomers resettled within convenient range of the airports. When the arrivals increased, so did concern about rising crime, ethnic strife, and degraded citizenship, concerns grimly foreshadowed in the widely publicized fatal stabbing of Catherine (Kitty) Genovese.

On the predawn morning of March 13, 1964, a twenty-eight-year-old barmaid known to friends as Kitty Genovese walked from her parked car to her home in middle-class Kew Gardens. She was tracked, assaulted, and raped near the entry of her two-story, pseudo-Tudor apartment house by Winston Moseley, a demented sociopath. Thirty-eight witnesses, so *The New York Times* related, did nothing for thirty minutes as she was knifed seventeen times. When a neighbor finally lifted a phone, it was too late; she was dead on arrival at the hospital. Arrested two days later, Moseley confessed and talked volubly of his previous sexual attacks. His initial death sentence was commuted to life after an appeals court ruled that the trial judge failed to allow sufficient testimony regarding the defendant's mental condition. (A Queens historian and Kew Gardens resident, Joseph DeMay Jr., has challenged much of the foregoing account, which nevertheless persists as a parable of urban callousness, prompting books, academic studies, a dozen stage and television dramas, and a new phrase, "the Bystander Syndrome.")

The Kitty Genovese story was among the defining markers of New York City's social, political, and economic turmoil from the 1960s through the 1980s, an era locally synonymous with street crime, power blackouts, municipal insolvency, ethnic polarization, feminist sit-ins, transit strikes, campus turbulence, and anti–Vietnam War demonstrations (even on Wall Street). A headline in *The Daily News* in October 1975 caught the edgy and defensive local mood, "Ford to City: Drop Dead," provoked by President Gerald Ford's opposition to federal aid for the bankrupt city. (Ford protested that he said no such thing, but the headline helped explain Jimmy Carter's 1976 victory in New York's presidential vote.) In Queens, the same years were fraught by bitter lawsuits over alleged racism in selecting tenants for the huge apartment complex called LeFrak City, by the prosecution of the borough's supposedly dominant Italian-American crime families, by waves of arrests for narcotics trafficking, and by white-black violence at Howard Beach (the latter contributing to the rise to national prominence of a fiery African-American preacher named Al Sharpton).

Nevertheless, shoots of hopeful change were evident in Queens. Contrary to expectations, the borough turned to its advantage what many viewed as the source of its discontents: the arrival of so many migrants speaking a babble of tongues. Not only did the populace and politicians learn to cope with exotic strangers, they came to delight in their stew of cultures. When Queens Borough President Helen Marshall greets visitors, she routinely bestows a button reading "Visit Queens— See the World." By embracing diversity, Queens County (its alternate official title) has pioneered resourceful public libraries, an innovative school system, and a welcoming civic culture. As Kenneth Jackson found, Queens suffered fewer homicides during the past decade than Atlanta, Memphis, New Orleans, Washington, and Baltimore, although none of these cities was even "a third as large as the unappreciated jewel of New York."

So what explains this turnaround? To find out, we made repeated forays to America's unappreciated jewel. We sought representatives of various ethnic groups, consulted with scholars and shopkeepers, and sampled a score of cuisines. We found that in Queens, heroes truly possess a thousand faces, that hyphens are not daggers, that schools can both integrate and celebrate diversity, that libraries do serve (in Andrew Carnegie's phrase) as lighthouses of the poor, and that the borough's political system now accommodates gays along with other minorities. We also found that the engines of change in Queens have been community boards and civic associations, and as elsewhere, that the bards of rap soothe the pains of a polyglot populace.

Yet these highlights should not blind one to the persistence of the borough's downside. Queens may boast a Utopia Parkway (home at Number 37–08 to the magician of mysterious boxes, the artist Joseph Cornell, from 1929 until his death) but there is a far side of this semi-paradise: grubby backwaters where illegally converted housing, packed with immigrant tenants, sinks into antiquated sewage and power lines. As in greater New York during the current global downturn, foreclo-sures in Queens peaked and jobless rolls swelled. What remains unchanged are the odds favoring those of every origin who are eager to rise. Their mobility is still assisted by the triad of forces that have long shaped this fascinating borough: the market dynamics of real estate; the reach of rails, roads, subways, and bridges; and the visionary passions of a hybrid populace.

———

TO AN EXTENT often unrecognized, American cities and their poli-tics have been defined by the covetous and sometimes inspired machi-nations of property developers, whose immemorial holy trinity is "location, location, location." This is true of the sprawling hinterlands of Queens. Prior to the 1890s, the district was essentially a conglomer-ate of pastoral villages with a sprinkling of budding industries. Its circa 87,000 inhabitants were largely of Irish and German origin. Among them was Heinrich Engelhard Steinweg (Americanized to Henry Stein-way) who in 1853 founded a piano factory in Manhattan whose instru-ments earned so many medals and patents that in 1877 he moved to grander quarters in today's Astoria. There he created a model village covering four hundred acres that featured workers' housing, a post office, library, church, kindergarten, and a public trolley. His plant adjoined the waterfront on which his company floated the logs used to manufacture pianos, and his village became an American variation of similar worker towns in Germany, notably in Jena (Zeiss) and Essen (Krupp).

Steinway's success proved an auspicious augury as the borough flour-ished. In 1894, the male householders of Queens voted in a closely fought nonbinding referendum to approve amalgamation with New York City. After protracted haggling, the merger was consummated on January 1, 1898, when Queens joined Manhattan, Brooklyn, the Bronx, and Staten Island as the fifth borough of a growing metropolis of around 3.5 million souls. Within a dozen years, Queens was physically joined to Manhattan by a tunnel under the East River, and then by the Queensboro Bridge, while a newly electrified Long Island Railroad reached out to the borough's far corners. In succeeding decades, the railroad was followed by (at points) the twelve-lane Queens Boulevard and a network of subways and elevated lines that brought much of the borough within rapid reach of Manhattan (fare: five cents). And the boom was just beginning.

Arguably, no individual left a deeper imprint on Queens than Robert Moses (1888–1981), for forty years New York's iron-willed master builder. It was Moses who transformed the Flushing dump (likened in F. Scott Fitzgerald's *Great Gatsby* to a "valley of ashes") into the sturdy underpinning of two World's Fairs. With the 1936 completion of the Triborough Bridge (now renamed for Robert F. Kennedy), Moses not only soldered Queens to Manhattan and the Bronx, but intentionally gave a substantial edge to motor vehicles; no provision was made for rail transit on his expressways. Two more bridges, Bronx-Whitestone and Throgs Neck, along with two major parkways, indissolubly welded Queens to its siblings. "If a person is driving in New York on a road that has the word 'expressway' in its title," writes Robert Caro, the builder's critical biographer, "he is driving on a road built by Robert Moses." In the crucial years from 1955 to 1965, a decade when spending spigots were wide open, 474 miles of new highways were built in New York, but nothing was spent on mass transit.

For good and ill, present-day Queens rides on its network of roads and rails. On the plus side are the model cities that sprang up in the early twentieth century, all of them real estate ventures. In 1901, New York's Yiddish-language newspaper, *The Forward,* carried full-page ads for the Utopian Land Company, whose investors acquired fifty acres in Flushing to establish an ideal Jewish community. The project failed, and its sole memorial is Utopia Parkway, which snakes through northeastern Queens. More successful was the Garden City movement conjured by an Englishman, Sir Ebenezer Howard (1850–1926), who observed first-hand the rebuilding of Chicago after the Great Fire of 1871. He was favorably impressed by the newborn city's array of parks, and on return-ing to England proposed the creation of "garden cities," limited in size and population, that could be linked to greenbelts circling overcrowded industrial centers. Essential to his vision was a rapid transit system con-necting the towns to an urban center.

Howard's proposal was taken up by New York developers, and in 1908 Jackson Heights became the site for America's first Garden City complex. Its English origins were signaled by its named buildings (Cambridge Court, the Towers, Manchester, and Plymouth Court) and its desired tenants cued by its amenities: tennis courts, a golf course, and a clubhouse. Jackson Heights still retains the aura of the Anglophile village that the aging Howard inspected in 1924 while attending a con-ference in New York of the International Garden Cities Association. Small shops crowd its downtown, and its apartment houses with their period motifs proclaim their cultural roots in Albion. So does a popular site for visitors: the Community United Methodist Church, where in 1931 Alfred Butts, a local resident, first tried out the English-language game he called Scrabble—an event memorialized by a plaque and by the stylized Scrabble lettering on the nearby street sign.

By a splendid and ironic twist, this formerly hyper-WASP neighbor-hood, whose realtors once imposed restrictive clauses to prevent the sale of local property to blacks, Jews, and Catholics, is presently renowned for its peaceful mingling of creeds and colors. Jackson Heights had become a "utopia of diversity" according to a 2005 report in the real estate pages of *The New York Times,* a community where fewer than 20 percent of the residents speak only English at home. Its religions include Judaism, Islam, Sikhism, Hinduism, and most Christian denominations (Scrabble's Methodist cradle now doubles as a commu-nity center and offers church services in English, Korean, Spanish, and Chinese). The community's forty thousand–plus residents are approxi-mately 57 percent Hispanic, 17 percent Asian, 21 percent white, and 5 percent black.

Jackson Heights is within easy reach from Times Square via the New York Transit Authority's Number 7 Line, now known locally as "the

Orient Express" owing to its final stop in Flushing, the home of many East Asian immigrants. A few downward steps from the elevated station at Seventy-Fourth Street and Broadway (in Queens) and you are in the heart of South Asia. Here, along two impossibly crowded blocks known as Little India, you can choose among fifty subtly different varieties of rice at the Patel Brothers food market, buy DVDs of the latest Bollywood films, sample an Indian buffet at the celebrated Jackson Diner, or try on golden bangles in a multitude of jewelry shops. But these features are easy to replicate; what is special is the ethnic peace on Seventy-Fourth Street, where people whose origins are in India, Pakistan, Bangladesh, or Sri Lanka adjourn their homeland quarrels and mingle without fuss or fear in shared religious festivals, national days, or on cricket pitches and soccer fields.

Little India's birth was not planned, but adventitious. Its origins have been chronicled by the Queens College social scientist Madhulika Khandelwal, who tracked down Subhash Kapadia, proprietor of Sam & Raj, the electronics and appliance store that led the way for Indian business owners in 1976. "We had a sense that this area was an important one for Indian immigrants," he told her. "Queens was the favorite borough of Indians, and several subway routes intersected at Seventy-Fourth Street. But we had no conception that our business would pioneer such a large expansion of Indian businesses on this street." Now shoppers from all over America—not all of South Asian origin—daily converge elbow to elbow (or sari to *shalwar kameez*) in Little India.

We met with Professor Khandelwal, an animated woman whose alert eyes accent her fluent words. In her no-frills office, from which she directs Queens College's Asian/American Center, she spoke of growing up Hindu in North India and of her years studying history under a revered professor at Delhi University. In 1985, half on impulse, she successfully applied to pursue graduate studies at Carnegie Mellon University. ("I would look at the map and wonder, like, just where is Pittsburgh?") Once in America, she was intrigued by attitude changes among her recently resettled compatriots, and she asked, "How come there is so little scholarly work on Indian immigrants? There was virtually nothing, only some newspaper articles." With Carnegie Mellon's encouragement, she moved to New York; there she propitiously met the

Queens College anthropologist Roger Sanjek just as he was assembling a scholarly team to study the borough's proliferating, still-novel ethnic communities. The result was *Becoming American, Being Indian: An Immigrant Community in New York City*, published in 2002 by Cornell University Press, in which Khandelwal details the ways Indian-Americans have effectively leveraged upward their knowledge of English, their commercial savvy, and their kinship solidarity. For instance, at successful motels from coast to coast, guests are likely to find a proprietor named Patel who hails from Gujarat. As interesting was her finding, based on extensive oral histories, that mother-country taboos concerning caste, class, and gender weakened as Asian migrants and (especially) their offspring ingested American values. Not only did Indian Hindus, Muslims, Buddhists, and Sikhs discover their unifying common culture, but so did Pakistanis, Bangladeshis, Sri Lankans, Guyanese, and Trinidadians. All have come to celebrate Diwali, the Hindu festival of lights, in late autumn. She also encountered an awkward Asian family reunion within the patchwork Borough of Queens.

Two centuries ago, the British Raj encouraged and/or propelled the migration of thousands of able-bodied Indians to the lucrative sugar, fruit, and timber plantations in the West Indies and present-day Guyana. Contract laborers were routinely stripped of identifying documents, so descendants typically retained only the vaguest knowledge of their origins on the subcontinent. Over time, ethnic Indians evolved their own identity in the British West Indies and in Guyana (where, as a press cliché put it, a "leftwing dentist of Indian extraction" named Cheddi Jagan served as chief minister from 1961 to 1964, sending Cold War shudders through Washington). Post-1965, West Indians began arriving en masse at Kennedy Airport. As Madhulika Kandewal told us, "In Queens, you will not only find Gujaratis and Punjabis, but a large population of Indo-Caribbeans, especially in Richmond Hill. And it took some time for [earlier migrants] to say, 'Oh, you are also from India?' People from India, especially, do not know their own history." Soon younger South Asians and West Indians began to view each other with greater empathy, especially since non-Indian Americans could scarcely distinguish differences among them.

All this nurtured a tradition of broad tolerance in Jackson Heights, a tradition that currently transcends ethnicity and extends even to such vexing issues as gay rights.

———

IN 2010, a weathervane election occurred in the all-important Democratic primary for a New York City Council seat representing the twenty-fifth district in Queens, which includes Jackson Heights. The winner was Daniel Dromm, a former schoolteacher of Irish descent, who decisively defeated incumbent Councilwoman Helen Sears, the sole such upset in that season's primaries. "This is unbelievable!" Dromm exclaimed to his cheering supporters, and he then alluded to his own experience as a leader in the gay community: "Being a person who has faced discrimination, who has faced hatred and knows what it does to people, I promise to every single community—to our South Asian community, to our Latino community, and to our LGBT* community—I am going to be your fighter on the City Council."

When we met him at his City Council quarters in Manhattan, we began to understand why he disarms the ambivalent. Dromm's mien is cheerful and his manner low key when addressing the sticky issues of sexual identity. As in this specimen remark: "I had a reporter say to me recently, 'Some people say, Mr. Dromm, that you're more concerned about gay rights than Latino rights.' And I said, 'That's very interesting, because all the gay guys who come into my office are Latinos.'" Honesty in his case has proved effective policy, especially when spiced with humor. (A revealing joke we heard in Jackson Heights went like this: "What do you do if you're gay in Colombia?" Reply: "You move to Jackson Heights.")

Then what are the issues that crowd Dromm's docket? "The biggest problems are really about immigration," he told us. "I was there one Friday afternoon maybe four months ago, and thirteen people walked into my office—at ten minutes before five o'clock, that's how it always happens, right? They had been defrauded by an organization called the

———

*Lesbian, gay, bisexual, transgender community.

American Immigrants Federation, or AIF. These people were undocumented, poor, probably working as deliverymen, busboys, things like that. And they each put up three thousand to seven thousand dollars to speed up their immigration processing. But there's no speeding up. The law is what the law is. It takes minimally between five to seven years if you've got everything in order, and all goes right." A civil suit followed against AIF, and it developed that gullible immigrants were likely misled by a verbal trick: the foundation's agents identified themselves as "notaries," and in Spanish *notario* can also mean *abogado* or "lawyer." "In English, a notary is not a lawyer, and that's the trick there," Dromm pursued. "So immigrants were getting advice from people who really shouldn't be giving it to them. And we hear such stories all the time. But as a result of a civil suit, we were able to extract $1.2 million dollars from AIF to reimburse some of the people defrauded by them." (The suit was brought by Attorney General Andrew Cuomo, later elected governor of New York and himself the scion of a political dynasty bred in Jamaica, Queens.)

Further twists in the politics of diversity came to our attention in our encounter with the co-authors of an innovative oral history of ethnic Queens, *Crossing the Boulevard: Strangers, Neighbors, Aliens in a New America* (2003). In its pages, Warren Lehrer and Judith Sloan, versatile writers, designers, teachers, and performance artists, chronicle the lives of a dozen migrants who have figuratively crossed Queens Boulevard (its multi-lanes are notorious for pedestrian fatalities). Their book attaches a CD sampler of songs and voices of their interviewees. These include a Bombay philosopher, a Czech table tennis champion, a Congolese asylum seeker, several Bhutanese exiles, and a Filipino journalist named Ninotchka. We were especially struck by their encounter with Juan Carlos and Camilo (last names withheld), gay partners from Colombia, along with their beloved dog Carlotta (she flew executive class from Bogotá). The pair had been serially subjected to beatings in Colombia, and as soon as legally possible they sought asylum as refugees. An immigration official said to them, "Okay, we need to reconstruct your whole story into one file in less than a month. Ask everyone you know to send us affidavits, who you are and what happened." They had by then joined the gay community in Woodside, were selling jewelry at a flea market in Kew Gardens, and as with many new-comers, had already been approached by a tout offering fake Social Security cards for $200 (the going fee). In April 2000, Camilo was noti-fied that he had received asylum; three days later Juan Carlos was granted the same status. Lehrer and Sloan astringently comment, "All their lives they had to conceal their sexual identity to keep from being killed. From their rather unique vantage point, the United States is a place where you must prove you are gay—really truly gay, always were gay, and will be gay—in order to stay in the country."

We arranged to meet Judith Sloan and Warren Lehrer at a Starbucks in Sunnyside located (where else?) on Queens Boulevard. Their anec-dotes poured forth, invariably flavored by their own take as urban explorers rediscovering their origins (Lehrer grew up in Queens, Sloan in Brooklyn). What sets Queens apart, they told us, is that everybody has a story, and that the borough's very diversity continually poses novel prob-lems. Had we heard, for example, about the *shisha* crisis in Little Cairo? *Shisha* is the tobacco smoked in a water pipe or hookah (in Egypt the word *shisha* signifies the hookah). In what is now dubbed Little Cairo in Astoria, numerous patrons of cafés puff on *shishas* (we noticed one bearded young man who was simultaneously texting on his Blackberry while smoking a *shisha*). Shortly after New York City's Republican Mayor Michael R. Bloomberg assumed office, he urged the City Council to approve a smoking ban on all restaurants and cafés, which it did. "Now a lot of these places [in Astoria] were called cafés," Warren Lehrer told us, "and they weren't called smoke shops. So all of a sudden they were getting fined, and soon city councilmen heard complaints that 'this isn't fair, it's a discrimination against our culture.' So the City Council has now approved an exception," for Queens and its *shisha* cafés.

The incident illustrated, in Lehrer's view, a new emphasis on cul-tural identity. "I don't think it comes from politicians. I think politi-cians in the last ten years have had to embrace it, because it means survival. Ethnicity really comes from post-1965 identity politics. People can now come to the United States and hang on to their language—it wasn't like Jews and Italians, who had to meld into the culture. It came from the bottom up. After black power, feminism, gay rights, you had immigrant rights. . . . When my grandparents came, even though they never really assimilated, they knew they were not going to get on an air-plane and go back to Poland. They knew it was goodbye to all that, and hello to all this."

Judith Sloan broke in: "I remember the year there was an earth-quake in Mexico, and we were with Mexicans working in Chicago—and immediately the communication starts. Now airfare is cheap, long distance is cheap, people have Skype. Eighty years ago, it took three months for a letter to arrive. . . . It's a different way of communicat-ing." In short, thanks to the social media and jet airliners, human movement is global and immigrants can retain their roots even in alien soil.

This new pluralism is also abetted by an evolving global doctrine of dual citizenship—that is, a US citizen can lawfully hold a second pass-port, serve in a foreign army, and vote in another country's election—a practice tolerated if not welcomed by the US government and sustained by Supreme Court rulings in 1952 and 1964. Moreover, even as national flags proliferate, traditional frontiers have been eroded by the European Union, passport laws, environmental realities, free trade pacts, the information revolution, jet airliners, and satellite television. *Pace* Marshall McLuhan and Thomas Friedman, we may not yet live in a global village planted on a flat earth, but neither notion seems prepos-terous. Its outlines can be discerned in Queens, New York, which is why Roger Sanjek titled his 1998 analysis of the borough's race and neigh-borhood politics, *The Future of Us All.*

A useful image occurred to Warren Lehrer: "What's different here from Denmark, France, and Germany is that the United States is a country of immigrants. Of course, you still have Americans who have an ethnic and racial view of what an American is—but also many of us now understand that we are also a country of invaders and runaways from other countries. I think, gladly, that the metaphor of a melting pot is melting away to something more like a salad." And what seemed to us most propitious in Queens was the impressive degree to which the cul-tural infrastructure—libraries, public schools, and civic associations—have embraced this evolution and thereby enriched the salad.

———

AMONG AMERICA'S neglected marvels is the Queens Public Library, founded in 1858 and now comprising sixty-two branches administered from central offices in Jamaica. The borough's system ranks first in the country in terms of circulation, second to Manhattan among municipal libraries in the size of its collection (twenty million items), and is unique in terms of its outreach to non-English speakers. It shelves more books, DVDs, and videos in more languages (sixty at last count) than any public library in the world. Moreover, it helps users learn English, look for jobs, fill out tax forms, prepare for nationalization tests, compose a curriculum vitae, ponder healthcare choices, find homework help, join reading clubs in Korean, and plumb the software of Microsoft in Spanish (this being a short list of services). The borough's public library system is distinctive not only in its independence from the far better-known New York Public Library and its branches, but also in the variety of its multicultural offerings. It hosts concerts, lectures, open-mike rap and poetry readings, hip-hop galas, and an ecumenical menu of Christian, Jewish, Islamic, and Hindu fetes.

All this was elaborated in our meeting with Fred Gitner, director of the library's New Americans Program (NAP). A wiry, shirt-sleeved executive presiding over a handful of aides in a cluster of cubicles, Gitner explained that NAP grew out of a 1977 federal grant prompted by the influx of newcomers settling in Queens. "The library had a huge German collection, which was fine for earlier immigrants," he told us, "but with the new [1965] law, and with Kennedy Airport becoming our new Ellis Island, not only was there a big increase of immigrants from different places, but they could [legally] be joined by family members, cousins and so forth—a major reason for the surge." Initially funded for three years, NAP focused on three groups, "the Spanish-speaking community which hasn't changed; the Greek-speaking community—everybody seemed to be coming to Astoria from Athens, where there were no jobs—which has since diminished; and finally the Chinese, mainly from Taiwan, still with us." The nascent outreach staff pioneered a directory of immigrant-serving agencies, originally a relatively short list. As expanded and now available in print or online, the directory lists 250 agencies with staffs fluent in sixty-odd languages. When we visited, the library's full-time demographer was anxiously weighing results of the 2010 census in order to plan acquisitions for the system's threescore branches. No longer need officials, educators, or librarians fly blind; they can precisely numerate the identity of their constituents.

Go, as we did, to the Flushing branch, credibly said to be the single most heavily used library in the United States. It has evolved into what Gitner calls "an International Resource Center" since its debut in 1998 "in a beautiful, award-winning building." He went on, "But already we saw certain features or services that weren't there, so we just completed a renovation a couple of months ago. We added a new and enlarged area to bring all the media together on different floors, and a cyber center for the computer area. . . . I think we have, maybe, about sixty languages in Flushing." He added, "One of our jobs is to buy material for all community libraries—that's our word for branches—so we buy [system-wide] in twenty-six languages." (We were especially impressed in the Flushing branch by its extensive shelves featuring DVDs of films in four Indian languages.)

Gitner was equally enthusiastic about a program called BOOST, an acronym for "Best Out of School Time," a citywide, foundation-funded program to encourage literary curiosity among the young. "So every system in New York did it in a different way," he told us. "We have a program called the Youth Enrichment Service that runs the BOOST program, but the person in charge is not a librarian, but an educator. So there's a structured program, for example, a certain amount of time for homework, a certain amount for being on the computer, and we also bring in speakers to talk about different topics." His target list of patrons has expanded to include a budding Afghan community in Flushing, where there are also Korean, Chinese, and Vietnamese as well as Hispanic, Italian, and Greek communities; a Turkish community in Sunnyside; and Astoria's amalgam of Asians, Egyptians, Greeks, Romanians, Serbs, and Croatians. ("It's mostly uneventful," Gitner said of the ethnically diverse patronage, adding, "but a few years ago there was a complaint that Serbian books were placed higher up on the shelves than Croatian books.")

Perhaps nowhere did the system seek to serve its ethnic outliers more conscientiously than in its Bayside branch, where it catered to requests among the *otaku*—Asian, black, and Hispanic aficionados of the esoteric book-length comics known in Japanese as *manga*. With their mostly black-and-white drawings, these books evoke toothy monsters and spiky-haired heroes and heroines engaging in mythological battles (and encouraging some teenagers to learn Japanese). As one satisfied consumer, eleven-year-old Seung Koh, explained to *The New York Times*, "With books, like, you only see words. It's so dull."

Gitner stressed, "We're a *popular* library, not a research library. For example, I recently began reading articles about Nollywood, so I looked into it. Nollywood is the word for low-budget films made in Nigeria, in English for the most part, and hugely popular among African-Americans, Afro-Caribbeans, and of course Africans. Queens doesn't have a huge African population, though we do have some, particularly from Nigeria, Ghana, and French-speaking Africa. So we started buying Nollywood films, and I said let's test them out in a few libraries. My God, we got calls from one branch manager, saying, 'Where did you get these, they're screaming for them; we can't keep them on the shelves!'"

The same outreach animates the hiring of library personnel. "Everybody who works in the New Americans Program has to speak another language," Gitner said:

> It's a requirement to work here. So my language is French, and I actually took a course in Haitian Creole at City College. I can't speak it very well but I can read it. Actually, we have a Haitian librarian downstairs who helps with the translations. And I noticed we didn't have any Haitian movies—it's not something you can find at Blockbuster. So I went with our Haitian librarian to a local store in Queens Village, explained the rules of the library—everything had to have copyright protection, we can't have bootleg stuff. Initially, he was tentative, but now we spend five thousand a year at this little store for Haitian films—and again, they're really, really popular.

A story that generated media attention concerned two migrants from Central Asia who discovered their calling in the Queens Library. Tatyana Magazinnik and her husband, David, both skilled, conservatory-trained pianists, came to Queens in 1993 from Tashkent, capital of

Uzbekistan. "My daughter didn't know English well; I didn't know English. I was trying to teach her myself," she recalled to a reporter sixteen years later.

She pursued: "The library was my lifeline at the time. We took out children's books to recite their language. We learned thirty words a day. We memorized them, put them on the wall. The next day, another thirty words. After half a year, she didn't need English as a second language any more. She just graduated from Vassar, Phi Beta Kappa. The library was everything to us."

Tatyana and David decided to study library science at Pratt Institute, and after graduation both were employed by the Queens system, in her case first as manager of a minuscule branch in Maspeth and then of a big and bustling Broadway branch that serves Astoria and Long Island City. Currently she is assistant director of all community libraries.

By any reasonable measure, we concluded, the libraries in this remarkable borough have become a benevolent source of light, much in the tradition of the wondrous and vanished Pharos, whose sea-directed fires loomed above the great Alexandria Library in the classic era. And in different ways, the public schools of Queens have likewise improvised and experimented in tailoring their programs to a multiethnic enrollment, or so our explorations indicated.

———

LIKE MANY VISITORS to the Renaissance Charter School (TRCS) in Jackson Heights, we were initially puzzled by its facade. Its building, located on a tree-lined side street, previously housed a department store, and its erstwhile show windows are now blank brown walls. At first glance, it seems an architectural hash without a theme. Still, here in 1993, the old department store was converted into a K-12 public school, only to evolve seven years later into an experimental charter school for some five hundred students. In the words of its charter, the school's mission is to nurture "educated, responsible young leaders who, through their personal growth, will spark a renaissance in New York." Were these goals delusional? Our own sense is that the school is on course.

What first impressed us in walking through its hallways was the noise-level: rapid-fire student chatter mingled with tune-up sounds from music rooms. These were not repressed youngsters. As they flocked through corridors, they spanned the spectrum of the human species in all its tints. We politely asked if we could sit in on a classroom discussion, and were allowed to eavesdrop on a brisk back-and-forth about hemophilia and its implications for the inbred pharaohs of Old Kingdom Egypt and Queen Victoria's descendants, including the Romanovs of Tsarist Russia. At our next stop, students were assembling data on human trafficking, a global blight that they documented with charts and maps posted on walls. "We've had a problem," their teacher confided, "our classroom computers are programmed to block access to certain words, like 'prostitution,' so our students have had to work around that." Down the hall we came upon an oversize bulletin board filled with thumb-tacked papers on the theme of "Where I Am From." Some responses were matter-of-fact, some were poetic, some illustrated, some wittily allusive; all were spontaneous and original.

So who are these paragons? How are they admitted? We had pre-arranged an afternoon meeting with Stacey Gauthier, the school's co-principal, together with its director of development and partnerships, Rebekah Oakes. In their adjoining offices crowded with filing cases and with visitors of all ages, this is what we learned: it all started with an Annenberg Challenge grant in 1992, allowing them to create a school different from the typical model in which each unit had to be an elementary, middle, or high school. The new school would teach *all* these grades, "And so from 1993 until 2000, we were both a traditional and a not-so-traditional public school," Gauthier told us. "And so we had certain things in place," Oakes added. "Because we were an alternative school, for example, we were a lottery school back then [meaning all students were chosen by draw], but we were able to structure classes so that we had a racial mix." This flexibility meant that admission decisions could take account of gender, race, and ethnicity, with priority given to applicants whose siblings were already enrolled.

The creation of charters—demonstration schools in all five boroughs that can operate with greater autonomy—won New York legislative approval in 1998. But most early charters were secondary schools, not K-12s, and also unlike other charter schools, Renaissance was and remains fully unionized. From the outset, the new charter staff worked with parents, students, and its own board of trustees in devising innovative programs. On Wednesdays, the school conducts "global labs" on history and geography for tenth graders; on Tuesdays ninth graders are divided into three labs to discuss global arts and letters. Once a year, there is Rensizzle Week, when students and staff spend a week on mutually agreed extra-curricular subjects.

Gauthier explained how Rensizzle Week works: "I have a passion for teaching about world religions, so I'd go around and say, 'Do you want to be in my group?' There's a lot of marketing going on, which is kind of fun. . . . But there has to be an exit project—such as making a film about what you are doing. For example, we had a group of young women filming ads in Times Square and studying how women are portrayed in them, and why sex sells products, and whether they think the products could be sold differently. That was a great one."

Among these and other innovative ideas, none impressed us more than a bold and risky decision to frame a yearlong project around an extended field trip. "We decided that one thing we didn't like was a one-shot trip," Gauthier told us. "Yes, it's great to have fun going somewhere, but that should be tied to something more sustainable and longer lasting." The tryout expedition was to post–Katrina New Orleans, and the sequel in 2010 was a field trip to Maya sites and villages in Mexico. "Both trips involved year-long classes for which the students had to apply. It was open to anybody, so it wasn't just the smartest kids or a certain grade. They had to be willing to join in, and explain why in an essay. In addition, they had to agree to take part in a class lasting a year that took place after school or during lunch hours, because they would still be doing their regular schoolwork."

Thirty-nine students signed up for the New Orleans field trip, where for a week they helped out by mowing lawns and painting houses. They interviewed everybody, from bottom to top, asking hard questions, as for instance, why the affluent French Quarter was being rebuilt while the less affluent Ninth District was not. On returning home, they briefed the entire school, from kindergarten through the twelfth grade, discussing weather and hurricanes in lower grades and race and politics in upper grades. Gauthier: "It was a pretty emotional experience for them, talking with people of mixed ethnicity down there." Oakes: "It was interesting because our students were very multicultural, kids of all colors going down there, and they were surprised, actually, that the degree of darkness in your skin made a huge difference in New Orleans."

The succeeding Project Maya involved eleven students, bigger distances, and a wider sweep of themes, ranging from geography and archaeology to history and linguistics. Gauthier: "My daughter was one of the kids on this trip, and she was interested in the concept of beauty among the Maya, and how what's beautiful there isn't beautiful here." Oakes: "[The Maya] was an area of my own interest, since I was an anthropology graduate student. It's always, like, you hear the Mayans are gone. The Mayans aren't gone. There's still a lot of them down there, so how did their culture change?" The expenses for Project Maya were borne in part by bake sales organized by parents and by the school's partnership with the National Geographic Society's educational foundation.

Adding it up, it's hard to believe that the Renaissance Charter School could more imaginatively exploit its own diversity. As of 2011, its 537 students were 43.1 percent Hispanic, 19.8 percent African-American, 19 percent white, 17.29 percent Asian, 0.04 percent Native American, and 0.02 percent multiracial (using self-chosen designations). Fifty-nine percent of all students receive free or reduced-price meals. Class size had averaged twenty-five, but owing to a budget freeze it now hovers between twenty-six and twenty-seven. Roughly 60 percent of all students complete all thirteen grades (Gauthier: "We lose quite a few kids to moving; we have a pretty mobile population"). About 20 percent of the eighth graders are admitted to the city's high-performance high schools, Stuyvesant High, Bronx Science, Brooklyn Tech, Hunter High, and Townsend Harris (the latter adjoining the Queens College campus). Gauthier explained, "We always wonder if it's [students transferring to other high schools] a good thing or a bad thing. It's good because we've prepped them, it's bad because we'd love to keep them here. A lot of charter schools won't take new students into upper grades, because they feel they can't bring them into their culture, which to me is just baloney. If somebody leaves in the eleventh grade, we fill the slot with a kid from the waiting list. It's our job to Renaissance-ize them, or whatever you call it, and our mission for them is to graduate and be able to go to college."

In 2009 and 2010, every member of the graduating class did just that. And in an era when bullying (and cyber-bullying) by teenagers is a staple talk-show topic, it should be noted that in its first seventeen years, the school has yet to expel a student for violating its own explicitly nonpermissive disciplinary code.

To be sure, TRCS is but one drop in the borough's big bucket of pupils. Trying to rank schools in terms of quality is to blunder into a minefield; all grading systems are in different ways suspect. The consensual judgment among New York educators that the Queens system as a whole ranks above the citywide average recalls the radio wit Garrison Keillor's signature line that every pupil in his mythical Minnesota town is above average. Even so, throughout the borough many public schools have tailored their curriculum to the needs of a multiethnic populace. Notable among them is the International High School in Long Island City, located within LaGuardia Community College, which gives priority to students who have been in America for less than four years and are struggling with English. Especially innovative is the East-West School of International Studies (grades six through twelve) in Flushing, at which proficiency in both English and one of three Asian languages is required for graduation. More traditional are the nationally top-rated Benjamin Cardozo High School in Bayside, with its focus on law and political science, and Townsend Harris High School with its emphasis on classical studies.

———

YET WHAT OF COLLEGE? On this topic, we are indebted to our friend and colleague Andrew Hacker, who with co-author Claudia Dreifus wrote *Higher Education?* (2010), a critical survey (as its question mark implies). An emeritus professor of political science at Queens College, Hacker has spanned student generations, adding weight to his email comments on an early draft of this chapter. He underscored the borough's success in assimilating students who were either born here to foreign parents or who arrived as youngsters, then added:

A visit to one or two ordinary Queens College classes could have been enlightening. Here are the names of some of our students during the just-ended academic year: Ebenhaezer Alwi, Nunzia Delfino, Tricha Dindya, Danni Hu, Bilal Shaukat, Xiomara Vilchez, Qipeng Zhao, Farzana Amin, Rashid Chipantiza, Ghazal Hakhamjani, Dongsub Hong, Kenya Kipp, Steffi Matadial, Muhammad Mirza, Taddao Siri-amonthep, Israel Suero, and Kerim Tulun.

But now comes my point. If, while in my class, you had shut your eyes and toned out any inflections, you would not have been able to distinguish the comments of any of these students from those American-raised undergraduates named Smith, Jones, Johnson, Lefkowitz, Kelly, Costello and Meyer. So far as what happens in my class, which is in American politics, there is nothing "ethnic" about the students I've listed. It would be a grave factual error to "ethnicize" them. (Even if they are bilingual.) In fact, most of them want to be living somewhere other than Queens very soon after graduation. So one "purpose" of the Borough of Queens is to do a quick job of turning the next generation into generic Americans. Zangwill's "melting pot" which you quote at the beginning, is going on right now.

We should add that Hacker was among our guides on our initial forays in Queens. In Flushing, we were approached by one of his former students, now in his thirties who all but cried out, "Hello, Dr. Hacker. Do you remember me?" He indeed did. So taken as a whole, only a curmudgeon could credibly accuse the borough's educators of indifference to the challenges of a patchwork enrollment. Still, we also found that elsewhere in Queens, unexpected difficulties of assimilation had arisen within the most basic political unit: the family.

———

OF THE MANY communities hatched by the borough's property developers, arguably the oddest is Rego Park in central Queens. Its arable acres were tilled early in the nineteenth century by Chinese immigrants growing vegetables for sale in Manhattan's Chinatown. In the booming 1920s, their land was snapped up by the Real Good Construction Company, which proceeded to bestow its own name—Real

Good condensed into Rego Park—on a new village of 525 single-family row houses. These one-family homes were then encircled by apartment buildings while scores of stores sprouted along Woodhaven and Queens Boulevards. Rego Park acquired its own station on the Long Island Railroad in 1928, and within a decade it was linked to subway lines and expressways.

Who lived in Rego Park? Until the 1960s, its householders were mostly middle-income or blue-collar families of Irish, German, Italian, and East European descent. Starting in the 1970s, the mix changed. At first a trickle, then a stream, and finally a flood of immigrants arrived from Central Asia, and these newcomers were joined by smaller numbers from Iran, Israel, China, India, Colombia, South Korea, and Romania. Rego Park became "an alphabet soup of nationalities" according to Ellen Freudenheim's useful 2006 guide to the borough's many villages. "If you hear people jokingly refer to the neighborhood as 'Regostan,'" she notes, "it's because thousands of Central Asian Jews, that is immigrants from the Bukhara region (Uzbekistan) of Russia have settled here in the past decade." With these new arrivals came yeshivas, kosher delis, menorahs, and doorway mezuzahs, along with Russian nightclubs, jewelry shops, and dance studios. Further afield rose a dozen Bukharan restaurants, known for their dumplings, kebabs, and *plov,* a kind of pilaf blending rice, carrots and meat.

Development of the area continued in the 1960s when master builder Samuel J. LeFrak, whose organization produced more housing in metropolitan New York than any of its competitors, decided to create a monumental apartment complex that would bear his name. Completed in 1967, LeFrak City packed some five thousand apartments into twenty balconied towers on forty-two acres bounded by the expressway separating Rego Park from neighboring Corona. The huge project hewed to its creator's three "S" rule that "housing should be close to subways, schools and shopping." Thus tenants had access to four subway lines, three bus routes, and two airports; its eighteen-story towers overlooked the bumper-to-bumper traffic on the Long Island Expressway (where for years a billboard slyly reminded drivers, "If we lived here, Daddy, you'd be home by now"). As LeFrak stressed to a reporter, he also added a fourth "S," for "safe." From its inauguration, his city employed a sixty-person security force and subsequently installed surveillance cameras in its elevators.

An enthusiastic art collector, LeFrak claimed that one model apartment boasted kitchen and bathroom walls painted on commission by a young and struggling Andy Warhol: "You know, maybe he painted a couple of teakettles, something colorful like a can of Campbell's soup, and in the bathroom, a couple of little sailboats and swans. Some nuts painted them over! I can't find them!"

LeFrak City was built on lands once owned by President Martin Van Buren, which LeFrak purchased a century later from the Astor family (LeFrak spent $8 million for the land and $150 million for construction, making it the country's largest privately financed apartment project in its time). Its original tenants were predominantly middle class and Jewish. Without leaving their city, as many as twenty-five thousand residents could stroll to a supermarket, the post office, library, and cinema or swim in one of five outdoor pools. It seemed to incarnate the modernist Le Corbusier's ideal *ville radieuse* as realized by a canny American of Franco-Jewish descent whose utilitarian adage was "total facilities for total living." (LeFrak's parents left France in 1904, in the wake of the Dreyfus affair.)

Regrettably, as with other apartment complexes inspired by Le Corbusier, the angularities of class, politics, and human behavior complicated a tidily geometric Utopia. Congress in 1968 approved the Federal Fair Housing Act, which proscribed racial discrimination in renting. Two years later, the Justice Department sued the LeFrak Organization, claiming that prospective black tenants were being steered away from an overwhelmingly white apartment complex. LeFrak signed a consent decree; the government dropped the case. By 1976, African-Americans occupied some 70 percent of the LeFrak City apartments. White tenants fled, citing concern over crime, drug trafficking, and worsening maintenance. For his part, LeFrak told a *New York Times* reporter that the project's problems did not occur simply because more blacks became tenants. Rather, he said, the suit forced the company to lower its economic standards for admission.

In any case, the fortunes of LeFrak City declined, as did those of New York in the waning century. As drug gangs waged turf wars in its hallways and subterranean passages, the project was pejoratively dubbed "LeCrack City." A nadir was plumbed in 1997 when police, acting on tips from tenants, arrested members of four gangs known by their street names as Wise, Everlasting, Infinite, and Tonto. According to their intergang pacts, one mob specialized in marijuana, another in cocaine; one operated during daylight, another at night. After the arrests, Queens District Attorney Richard A. Brown summoned a news conference at which he displayed drugs, bulletproof jackets, assault rifles, and more than $100,000 gathered in this single bust.

Unfazed, Sam LeFrak persisted. After all, he remarked to a journalist in 2000, "I gave it my name, and I'd never thought of taking it off." By then, fresh tides of immigrants had flowed into his city. During the century's final decade, around 51,000 Jews from Central Asia had arrived in America; some 70 percent settled in Rego Park, Elmhurst, Corona, and Forest Hills. Simultaneously, a stream of brown- and dark-skinned Muslims from West Africa and the Maghreb converged in Queens. By the mid-1990s, a fifth of LeFrak City's tenants belonged to these outwardly incongruent groups; a mosque opened in the project, along with a refurbished synagogue and a Baptist church. Civility reigned. The Bukharan residents have historically lived peacefully alongside Muslims and like them share conservative family values. Crime diminished, morale improved, and an ethnic truce prevailed at LeFrak City (as its creator doubtless consoled himself before his death at eighty-five in 2003). Or were the demons still lurking? We decided to explore for ourselves.

———

CONSULT STANDARD references, and you are likely to find that Bukharan Jews are an unusual Hebraic community whose forebears somehow trekked via Persia into Central Asia many centuries ago, possibly during Israel's Babylonian Captivity, circa 700 to 500 BCE. The migratory tribe's life initially centered in the oasis city of Bukhara (also spelled Bokhara), long an autonomous Muslim emirate and once a sizable trophy in the Anglo-Russian rivalry known as the Great Game. Over time, "Bukharan" became the generic name for thousands of Jewish merchants, artisans, barbers, shoemakers, cooks, musicians, dancers, and scholars scattered among a dozen Silk Road cities in Central Asia. They survived as a (sometimes barely) tolerated minority under Persian, Mongol, Arab, Tsarist, and Soviet rule. Culturally and linguistically, Bukharans elude most templates; they speak Bukhori, a blend of Hebrew, Farsi, and Russian, and they are neither Sephardic nor Ashkenazi (although closer to the former). When Central Asian doors finally opened in the late 1980s, Bukharans emigrated en masse to Israel and the United States, although remnant communities still linger in Uzbekistan, Tajikistan, and Kyrgyzstan.

What standard references inadequately convey is the patriarchal stubbornness and the ready wit of this remarkable people. Having survived for centuries in their parallel universe, Bukharans cling to their identity as if to a lifeline; they are not promising candidates for rapid assimilation. To learn more, we initially sought meetings with community leaders, but we were frustrated by linguistic and telephonic barriers. We decided, finally, to strike out on our own, beginning at the Rego Park subway station at Queens Boulevard and 63rd Drive. The station arcade encloses a dance studio (conducted by Malika Kalontorava, formerly a leading dancer in Tajikistan), a shoe repair shop, and a busy jewelry shop. On impulse, we entered the jewelry shop to ask its owner if he knew how we might contact Aron Aronov, founder and director of Rego Park's Bukharan Heritage Museum. "I know him. Let me call him," the owner said, shortly adding, "He's on the phone." We explained our mission. "Wait on the boulevard outside the subway entrance," Aronov instructed. "I'll pick you up in five minutes."

Our preferred mentor's minivan arrived punctually, and we were welcomed by a spry and slender septuagenarian with curling grey eyebrows. "First," he said, "I want to show you where I live." He wheeled into nearby Wetherole Street, where cars were parked curbside before their owners' cottages. As Aronov explained, Bukharans typically demolish their on-site garages abutting rear alleys in order to widen backyard space for the barbecues, long benches, and round tables necessary for continuous celebratory parties or recurrent mourning rites. (Bukharan families not only sit shiva for Judaism's required seven days, but also conduct monthly memorials for a year, and then annually.) In front yards, where prior homeowners cultivated gardens and lawns,

Bukharans commonly pour cement—an ongoing source of neighbor-hood quarrels. Always there is a satellite dish so that new arrivals can receive Russian-language programs (Aronov said that his aging mother resisted learning English and was all but mated to the video screen).

Aronov added an intriguing biographical footnote. Richard Nixon, on the eve of his political comeback in 1967, toured Russia to burnish his foreign policy credentials. Nixon wished to see Tashkent, the capital of Uzbekistan, where it chanced his assigned translator was Aronov. (Aronov claimed fluency in ten languages and intermittently switched to French or Spanish for an elusive word as he spoke with us.) When Aronov received his assignment he checked with Moscow on what he was to do. "This was in Brezhnev times," he told us as he steered expertly through side streets, "and Moscow informed me that their ambassador in Washington had described Nixon as a 'political corpse'—but even so, I managed to get a decent, full-size limousine for him." Their encounter proved a success, and having tasted Bukharan *plov*, Nixon requested a recipe for his wife Pat; his twenty-something guide obliged by mail. Thereafter, Aronov told us, he remained in touch with the soon-to-be president.

Shortly after arriving in Rego Park in 1989, Aronov founded his Bukharan Heritage Museum, located originally in his own basement. Soon the press dubbed him "the unofficial mayor of Queensistan," and within a decade his museum acquired grander quarters in an upper-floor suite within the Queens Gymnasia, a flourishing yeshiva/private school on Woodhaven Boulevard. The museum's three rooms are crammed, floor to ceiling, with two thousand items, ranging from intri-cately embroidered robes, copper cooking utensils, Torah scrolls, Bukharan carpets, woven silk kaftans, hundreds of photos, and such esoteric instruments as the resonant *doyira* drums and the two-stringed guitar called a *rubob*. Admission to the museum is free, but by appoint-ment; visitors are likely to have its director as their guide.

Asked about his community's relations with Islam, Aronov com-mented that in Central Asia, Muslims and Jews were united in their loathing of Soviet rule, and that they had similar diets, dress codes, and music—and in fact, newly arrived Bukharans often had more trouble acculturating in Queens than in Muslim Central Asia. What proved especially troublesome were conflicting domestic norms. In the old country, adolescent celibacy was the rule, betrothals were always subject to parental approval, and a husband was invariably the breadwinner, his dominion unquestioned. These norms collided with modernity in Queens as children dated and wed and as wives obtained better-paid jobs than their professionally trained—but often jobless—mates. No issue proved more disruptive than spousal abuse, especially if a physically threatened wife dialed 911. "The marriage is ended if a wife calls the police," Aronov said, categorically.

These cultural disorders formed the dark subtext of a widely reported 2009 jury trial in Queens in which a Bukharan mother was charged with hiring an assassin to kill her estranged husband after losing a bitter dispute for custody of their four-year-old daughter (who witnessed the killing). Mazoltuv Borukhova, a thirty-five-year-old physician, was found guilty of telephoning her cousin to trigger the murder of her Bukharan husband, Daniel Malakov, a successful orthodontist. Borukhova's trial is detailed in the obliquely titled *Iphigenia in Forest Hills* (2011) by the astute controversialist and *New Yorker* writer Janet Malcolm. Malcolm describes the defendant as gentle, cultivated, and wronged, and yet "She couldn't have done it, and she must have done it." (The prosecution's case was bolstered by ninety-one cell phone calls from Dr. Borukhova to the killer.) Thus an otherwise good woman, feeling profoundly wronged by a frustrating custody process she could not really comprehend, may have struck back (so Malcolm suggests) very like Clytemnestra when her husband Agamemnon ordered the sacrifice of their daughter Iphigenia to secure divine favor for his Trojan expedition. (As of our writing, an appeal of Dr. Burokhova's conviction was pending.)

But our day's foray had a different, less problematic second act. Our tour with Aronov concluded when his minivan dropped us near the Long Island Expressway overpass joining Rego Park to LeFrak City. There we threaded through apartment towers bearing a potpourri of place names grouped by regions (e.g., Ceylon, Singapore, and Mandalay; Argentina, Peru, and Brazil) until we reached the LeFrak City Community Library, located below the main reception area on Fifty-Seventh Avenue. We had talked the previous day with branch manager Eric Howard, who told us there would be a swearing-in ceremony that afternoon for the newly named officers of the local Friends of the Library. Soon we were seated in a spacious auditorium near tables laden with snacks, mingling with fifty or more LeFrak tenants, their children and their guests, including Fior Rodriguez-Langumas, director of immigrant services for U.S. Congressman Gary Ackerman; New York State Senator José Peralta; City Councilman Daniel Dromm; plus a posse of local journalists. The library's spacious new quarters attested to LeFrak City's rebirth. On reopening in 2003, the branch doubled its original eight thousand square feet, added a stadium-style story room for children, and installed a bank of twenty computers, and thus could lend a record 160,000 items in 2010. (The renovation was underwritten by $600,000 from the Queens capital budget, plus a $50,000 grant from Richard LeFrak, son of the founder and third president of the LeFrak Organization.)

The meeting's galvanizing purpose was soon apparent. Library Day (April 6) was nearing, and the Queens Public Library and its sixty-two branches, having already suffered $5.6 million in budget cuts in 2010, now faced a further slash of $11.8 million in city and state funding. In swearing-in new officers of Friends of the Library, Councilman Dromm called out to youngsters seated in front rows, "What's a friend? Yes, that's right—someone who will stand up and fight!" Speaker after speaker detailed what the cuts meant to the library system (reduced opening hours, weekend closings, fewer new books, staff layoffs) and outlined a protest strategy: swelling rallies in Manhattan's City Hall Park, sending delegations to Albany, and showering politicians with letters and e-mails that emphasized the library's outreach, especially to immigrants. (Six months later in a rare about-face, the City Council *did* revoke the proposed cuts.)

What most struck us while attending this library rally was the primal significance of community associations and civic groups, whose potency and abundance struck us as the likely unifying explanation for the borough's creative, and peaceful, diversity.

———

"THERE IS ONLY ONE country in the world which, day in and day out, makes use of an unlimited freedom of political association." Thus Alexis de Tocqueville in *Democracy in America* (1835) distilled his impressions after visiting our young republic four years earlier. He continued, "And the citizens of this same nation, alone in the world, have thought of using the right of association continually in civil life, and by this means have come to enjoy all the advantages which civilization can offer." Allowing for his eagerness to influence Europeans with America's example, and noting that democracies everywhere have long since encouraged (or pretend to encourage) citizens associations, his tribute fits Queens. Day in and out, more associations proliferate in this county than probably anywhere in America—not just political associations, but ethnic, fraternal, professional, religious, burial, parental, cultural, feminist, sports, chess playing, historical, drinking, gay rights, literary, cinematic, theatrical, popular and classical music, and so forth. Their events are publicized in local newspapers and the foreign-language press that also flourishes. Again, Tocqueville was prescient: "I am far from denying that newspapers in democratic countries lead citizens to do very ill-considered things in common; but without newspapers, there would hardly be any common action at all."

A short list of the borough's English-language papers, most prefixed by "Queens" would include *Tribune, Chronicle, Light, Courier*, and *Times Ledger*, plus a score of neighborhood papers. Heading the class is *Newsday*, a Long Island–based tabloid and winner of nineteen Pulitzer Prizes, known for its thoughtful columnists and available throughout the metropolitan area. As to the foreign-language press, no reliable count exists. In Astoria, we passed a polyglot newsstand with an array of Greek and Arabic gazettes—plus three Romanian-language journals. When we expressed surprise at seeing so many of the latter for so fractional a minority, the grinning vendor reached within his kiosk, saying "Here are two more I keep for special customers." Newsprint, not the computer screen, remains (for the present) the medium of choice for newcomers wary of the mysteries of the Web; ditto for small businesses, whose advertisements pack the pages of the local and foreign language press.

A visitor senses that a productive plasma flows through the borough's civic associations, the press, and a thriving private sector, generating the synergy that helps explain the borough's recovery from its doldrums a half century ago. Two public careers illustrate the flow: Peter

A. Koo, an entrepreneur and philanthropist of Chinese origin, a Republican who represents Flushing and its environs in the New York City Council; and Helen M. Marshall, a former teacher and librarian, a Democrat who presides as the eighteenth borough president of Queens, becoming the first African-Caribbean-American and second woman to hold that office. A takeoff platform for both Koo and Marshall was an interesting, innovative institution known as the community board. It is worth pausing to describe the community board system, whose creation springs in part from the advocacy of the urban reformer Jane Jacobs, who was living in Manhattan's Greenwich Village when she wrote *Death and Life of Great American Cities* (1961).

In 1974, amid a season of reform, New York's political chiefs mandated the citywide formation of fifty-nine local community boards (CBs), each to be governed by unpaid board members empowered to choose a district manager, hire a staff, and rent offices. In the words of the city's website, board members are meant to be complaint takers, mediators, information sources, advisers, advocates, "and much more." CBs manage block parties, street fairs, interethnic holidays, parking problems, and cleanup programs, and their members offer views on everything from access to public schools to zoning for high-rise development. Board members serve two-year terms, half on recommendation of City Council members, and all formally chosen by borough presidents.

Queens has fourteen community boards. Among the most active is CB4, serving Elmhurst-Corona, a densely settled and highly diverse neighborhood. No outsider has tracked CB4's activities more closely than anthropologist Roger Sanjek. From 1983 to 1996, he attended sixty-two CB4 monthly meetings, and along with a team of field-workers, he monitored dozens of white, Asian, Latino, and Afro-American associations. In Sanjek's informed judgment, "Without a Community Board there would have been no public forum at which white, black, Latin American, and Asian leaders had a place to interact. Each racial and ethnic group in Elmhurst-Corona would have confronted mayoral and permanent government power without the power of numbers and expertise that CB4 made possible."

Impressed by Sanjek's words, we sought out Richard Italiano, CB4's current district manager, with whom we talked before his board's monthly meeting at Elks Lodge #878, a vintage stone and wood building perched on Queens Boulevard. Soon a hundred or so local residents filled the hall; each was handed minutes of the previous month's meeting, that night's agenda, and a list of the twenty-nine board members present and of the thirteen who were absent. (Italiano told us that regular attendance was a factor in deciding which members deserved an additional term.) As the meeting progressed, householders and shopkeepers sparred with the board members on the pros and cons of turning a two-way street one-way alongside a new shopping mall and on the request by a Hispanic-owned restaurant for permission to open a sidewalk café.

We noticed that no board member (judging by names) was recognizably Asian and that only nine of forty-three were obviously Hispanic. Earlier, we asked Richard Italiano, a forty-year CB4 veteran, calm in manner with a wry smile, to explain his board's ethnic balance. "Way back when I grew up here," he said, "it was a Jewish area, but then they moved out and the Italians came, and then *they* moved out as the Spanish came. We're always in transition. Now it's the Spanish, but a lot of Indians are also here, so it's all mixed up." A CB4 insider told us later that as each ethnic wave ebbs, a residue of seniors remains in place, and since board members are unpaid, retired householders are overrepresented.

Whatever its anomalies, the system works. "We're kind of, like, a little city hall," Italiano said. "We do everything here except marry people. If somebody has a complaint about the pickup of garbage trucks or about a streetlight that's out, they come to us. On a larger scale, we also do zoning. If somebody doesn't comply with zoning, we'll take that on." Community boards have mobilized effective opposition to high-density projects that menace the quality of life in single-family-home neighborhoods. In part if not in whole measure, Jane Jacobs's campaign against endless canyons of soulless concrete has borne real fruit in a greener Queens.

———

WE WERE TOLD frequently in Queens that Asian-Americans generally tended to avoid the political limelight. Was this true, and if so,
why? When we put the question to Professor Khandelwal at Queens
College, she responded, "I'm glad you asked, because I normally don't
talk about this to people who don't understand. First of all, Indians do
not go into politics very easily, because in their previous experience, it's
only good-for-nothings who go into politics." Moreover, newcomers
from South Asia had scant knowledge of America's civic structure or
about voluntarism, and thus only a handful initially took part in community boards. "But that was a dozen years ago, and now it's a very different landscape," Khandelwal said. Beginning in the 1990s, a younger
generation of Asian-Americans spawned an acronymic stew of associations in Queens: Youth Against Racism (YAR), South Asian AIDS
Action (SAAA), Concerned South Asians (CSA), and the South Asian
Lesbian and Gay Association (SALGA).

Women's issues and spousal abuse loomed high on the Asian-
American activist agenda, as they did in other immigrant communities.
In 1989, South Asian young professionals founded Sakhi (meaning a
woman's female friend) and established a hotline through which bat-
tered women could seek help. Moreover (as Khandelwal reported),
Sakhi organized awareness-raising demonstrations to the point of post-
ing this placard before an accused abuser's Jamaica residence: "Is It
Your Business If Your Neighbor Beats His Wife? You Bet Her Life It
Is!" Little of this conforms to the stereotype of supposedly passive Asian
immigrants.

On the mainstream political terrain, two Chinese-Americans from
Flushing have crossed critical political thresholds in New York. Leading
the way has been Taiwan-born John Chun Liu, a Democrat who in
2001 was elected to the City Council from northeast Queens, becoming the first Asian-American to be elected councilman. Two votes later,
Liu broke another barrier with his 2009 landslide win in the race for
comptroller, the first citywide victory for an Asian-American. (Liu drew
on his credentials as a local manager for PricewaterhouseCoopers, a
high-profile accounting firm.) As significant was the election of Peter A.
Koo to fill John Liu's council seat, in his case becoming the first Republican in a century to carry his district. How did *that* happen? We

requested an interview, and an hour was fixed at his legislative offices in downtown Manhattan.

Councilman Koo struck us as the obverse of the easy-smiley, baby-kissing, how's-the-wife stereotypical politician. He projects competence, courtesy, and authority, qualities that a stricken customer would seek in a pharmacist, Koo's own calling. He came to Queens from Hong Kong as a youngster in 1971. While working for minimum wages at Kentucky Fried Chicken and Dunkin' Donuts, Koo studied online at the University of New Mexico to qualify as a pharmacist. He then founded Starside Pharmacy, now comprising five stores in Flushing. Why did he succeed locally when competing with superstores like CVS and Duane Reade? James McClelland, Koo's chief of staff, weighed in: "The big chains don't do well because the smaller mom and pop shops are more capable of catering to the demographics. Walgreens doesn't have a Cantonese speaker, a Mandarin speaker, or a Korean speaker. Small businesses fill that void." Peter Koo amplified: "Our pharmacy from the beginning was very different. We set out to give full service, so we not only gave customers pharmaceuticals, but help with many problems— with their bills, or with Con Edison, or with a credit card company. Some are older people and they don't understand a lot of things they get in the mail, or why it takes so long to apply for a senior apartment." (The role of pharmacies in providing translation services was earlier underscored by our visit to the bustling Maram Pharmacy on Thirty-Seventh Avenue in Jackson Heights. Proprietor John Kranjac, of Slavic Balkan and Italian parentage, and his wife, Adriana, of Colombian origin, translate for customers, and a nearby Russian-speaking colleague and a Korean physician can be called on to help. A chronic source of confusion on prescriptions, we learned, is the word "once," as in "once a day," since as it is spelled in Spanish, once [*on-say*] means eleven, sometimes causing serious overdosing by Hispanic patients.)

The councilman's upward political path led from Flushing business associations, service clubs (Lions and Rotary), a host of charities, and especially from CB7. Concerning the paucity of Asians on CB7, in Koo's judgment the major problem has been lack of information: "They don't know how to be on a community board, that you have to know the borough president or the City Council person to be nominated."

Yet in Flushing, that is changing: "We sometimes have too many people who want to be candidates." As we departed, Chief of Staff McClelland detailed Councilman Koo's calendar for the preceding Saturday: "At noon, he went to a Chinese lady's eightieth birthday party, and after that to the Ebenezer Baptist Church's 140th anniversary celebration, and that night he went to a Chinese-American Association dinner honoring Kaity Tong [a popular, prize-winning, Chinese-born local news anchorwoman]. That was his day in Flushing. That was all in one day."

Of the constituency problems crowding Peter Koo's inbox—housing, immigrant rights, access to schools, and zoning for development—none is more basic than health care. In past decades, Queens has lost four insolvent hospitals, leaving only eleven to serve 2.3 million inhabitants. Private hospital emergency rooms are required simply to diagnose impoverished Medicaid or undocumented patients, who then are forwarded to city-operated hospitals, a process known pejoratively as "dumping." Hence the importance of the borough's major health care provider, the Elmhurst Hospital Center, a municipal institution known for its high standards and the fluency of its full-time and volunteer interpreters. As Jayne Maerker, the director of Elmhurst's volunteers, told us, the interpreting team overall annually averages one hundred thousand translations in eighty languages at a cost of $750,000 (for which the hospital is not compensated). In this and other ways, Elmhurst thrives on diversity. Its medical staff, for example, is supplemented by "shadow doctors," that is, immigrants with foreign medical degrees who gain experience that can hasten their accreditation in America. Residents relish diagnosing exotic diseases, immigrant nurses feel culturally comfortable, and an almost fiesta cheerfulness animates the corridors of its mini-Pentagon building. And one of its most important patrons and benefactors is Peter Koo, whose Community Charitable Organization has provided generous grants, including funds for Elmhurst's fleet of wheelchairs.

Yet the survival of this full-service municipal hospital came into question in February 1995. Former Mayor Rudolph Giuliani, in an act of budgetary and ideological "dumping," urged the instant privatizing of most municipal medical facilities, notably including the 624-bed Elmhurst Hospital. The year before, its multiethnic staff of four thousand had treated a half million patients in its emergency rooms, clinics, trauma centers, and inpatient and outpatient wards. In the uproar that ensued, CB4 played a pivotal role. Its board members wanted to know who would treat jobless and indigent patients if Elmhurst were privatized. Queries the board put to city hall were simply ignored. In April 1995 (as Roger Sanjek recounts), CB4 voted 28 to 3 to oppose privatization, and so notified the mayor. A year later, a rebellious City Council sued Giuliani for denying it a chance to vote on the sale of municipal hospitals. In 1997, a state supreme court judge ruled that the proposed "dumping" was illegal. Thus Elmhurst Hospital Center, now rated as a jewel in its class, survives as a municipal hospital thanks in good part to the campaign initiated by community boards. Among the leaders in that successful struggle was the future borough president of Queens, Helen Agnes Marie Marshall.

———

IF ANYBODY INCARNATES the recovery of Queens in the past half century it is Helen Marshall, a peppy octogenarian who has made the most of her roles as activist, conciliator, educator, publicist, and grandmother superior. She has played a part in all the principal quality-of-life controversies in her borough, and she has advised, comforted, and prodded the multiple ethnic communities in a patchwork realm. Following her election as borough president in 2005, she creatively expanded the influence of an office with a title grander than its actual powers. For example, she promptly established the Queens General Assembly, comprising twenty-eight delegates and their advisers from fourteen community districts who convene regularly so that citizens of different backgrounds can speak their minds to the president. In her words, the general assembly was "a core initiative of my Marshall Plan," meant to realize the promise of a society "that is a model of tolerance, pluralism, and mutual respect."

We met Ms. Marshall in her offices at Borough Hall, a WPA-vintage building facing Queens Boulevard in Kew Gardens. This bureaucratic setting only enhanced the contrasting vitality of its incumbent borough president, a tireless, fireball with blonde hair who delights in unpredictable digressions. We began by praising her general assembly's innovative Diversity Calendar, a detailed listing of major holidays observed by Christians, Jews, Muslims, Hindus, Sikhs, and Buddhists, along with key national days. Did she encounter any ethnic communities of which she was not familiar? Well, there was a Polish-American community located in an enclave "where Queens and Brooklyn attach to one another, and which is very much a Polish area." She recently helped celebrate Poland's national day in Queens, a fete also attended by Warsaw's consul general. "People are happy to hear about information from back home, and they serve their food and also dance. A guy with boots makes me do the polka with him. It's a wonderful event! You know, I used to dance and was very much into modern dance several years ago."

So it went for close to two hours. On a few occasions, Ms. Marshall's memory for names flagged, and she turned for assistance to Susie Tanenbaum, her community and cultural coordinator (and protégé of anthropologist Roger Sanjek). We learned that the president's father was Guyanese, who at sixteen "jumped on a Slavic boat" that circled the world, and thus learned seven languages. On returning to Guyana, "he saw this pretty lady (that was my mother) and decided he was not going on those boats any more. My mother said [to her father], 'I have done everything you asked. Now I want to go to America.'" And they did. Ms. Marshall's grandfather, already a U.S. resident, became her mother's sponsor: "He was from Barbados, but his children were born and raised in America. In those days, if you were sponsored, it was a big thing. It was much easier to become a citizen than it is today—so much red tape." Her mother never wanted to revisit Guyana, but "my sister and I went back two years ago, and I went as borough president!"

Marshall was born in the Bronx, where her father worked as a housepainter. After attending local public schools and marrying, she and her husband Donald moved to Corona. Their first son was in second grade and another boy was on the way; hence her concern with schools and her activist role in the Corona PTA. She enrolled in Queens College, earned a degree in education, and then managed a special education teacher assistant program (known as SETA) for training paraprofessionals. (As borough president, she has promoted construction of thirty new schools with more than 17,800 places.) In the 1970s, as a board member of CB3 representing Corona, Helen Marshall joined with CB4, representing East Elmhurst, to press for better schools, immigration rights, and upgraded health care. Having earned these battle stars, Ms. Marshall in 1974 became the first African-American to be chosen as Democratic leader in her district, followed by another such first in 1982 when she was elected to the State Assembly. As she acquired seniority, her skills as an interethnic mediator were tested by a possibly volatile conflict embroiling blacks, a Korean-owned store, and LeFrak City.

It was sparked by a murky incident on Monday afternoon, February 4, 1991, when a Korean-American produce manager named Yong Cha Kim was charged with injuriously beating Bobby Yates, an eleven-year-old African-American. The incident occurred in a C Town supermarket in Elmhurst, patronized mostly by tenants in adjoining LeFrak City. Kim claimed he saw Yates, whom he described as an unpaid bag packer working for tips, filch money from "the fish bucket," the jar at checkout counters where customers leave coins. In Roger Sanjek's meticulous reconstruction, Kim said he scolded Yates, who ran down an aisle, breaking a bottled fabric softener. Kim grabbed the boy and detained him, then called the youngster's mother and the police. Cynthia Yates disputed most of Kim's account, asserting that her son had been physically abused without cause and had been locked in a freezer. The police charged Kim with third-degree assault, but found no evidence for the freezer allegation.

It chanced that Mrs. Yates was a parishioner of the House of the Lord Pentecostal Church in Brooklyn. The church's pastor, the Reverand Herbert Daughtry, a well-regarded civil rights activist, had recently assisted a much-publicized, yearlong boycott of a Korean-American grocery in Flatbush on racist grounds. Rev. Daughtry introduced Mrs. Yates to the lawyer who represented leaders of the Brooklyn boycott and arranged for a busload of demonstrators to join her on a picket line the following Saturday at the C Town market, presumably to initiate a similar boycott in Elmhurst. However, only forty people demonstrated that day and a mere six the following day. The boycott never took place.

What happened? First and crucially, African-American community leaders in LeFrak City moved promptly to defuse the conflict. "We don't want this to be a Brooklyn-type situation," said Ruby Muhammad, a leader of the city's tenant association, whose acting president, James Brown, was more explicit, telling *The New York Times*, "We wash our own linen here. We don't need outsiders to come in." Assemblywoman Helen Marshall arrived immediately at LeFrak City and met with the supermarket's owner. She told the press, "We feel we don't have to do a massive demonstration. We can work with him." Second, and as important, a community task force (CTF) was established in partnership with the local police to establish what actually occurred on February 4. In a series of open meetings, Sanjek relates, "People reviewed their experiences with local merchants and voiced long-simmering frustrations over treatment of customers and the declining number of black employees. Complaint forms were distributed, and the assemblage formulated a list of 'demands' to present at a CTF meeting with merchants the following week. They included the 'hiring of a Black or Hispanic manager or supervisor to mediate future conflicts,' 'ceasing unwarranted surveillance of customers,' and 'hiring employees who speak fluent English' [particularly cashiers.]"

Looking back two decades later, Borough President Marshall recalled in detail the entire sequence, especially the urgent weekend call from the Reverend Daughtry: "He said, 'Sister Marshall, I'm coming in and I got to get permission to come in.' He said it in a joking way, 'cause he's really a good man. So he came, and we had a meeting that same night, the night before [Sunday] the boycott was to happen. We had everybody coming in, and one of the women from [Community] Board Four was a UN translator, so we knew what she'd say was accurate. We decided, huh uh, no, there's not going to be any Korean boycott here. It would have killed everything. It would be terrible if this happens."

Along with her local allies, Helen Marshall consulted with the borough police chief: "He said, 'Make sure you have sawhorses, and a place for them [the pickets] to walk, and it's got to be fifty-feet away from the entrance, okay?'" On the critical Sunday, only two mothers and five children came to picket, "and Daughtry came, and got up on a sawhorse, and he said, 'I am here because I was requested to come, and I want to tell you this community has great leaders, and I'll leave this in their hands.' And that was it. No more nonsense. That was a victory."

It *was* a victory. Nothing gets less media attention than a crisis averted. In this case, local activists and their political colleagues collaborated in quelling a conflict exacerbated by differing cultural traditions. As Yong Cha Kim (the market's produce manager) protested, in Korea all adults view themselves as surrogate parents if a youngster misbehaves; but not so with children in other cultures. These illusive nuances are vital, even among ostensibly kindred peoples, as for example Korean and Chinese-Americans. This was underscored in our interview with Joyce Moy, director of the Asian American/Asian Research Institute at CUNY (City University of New York). She told us that the press exaggerated disputes between Korean and Chinese-Americans. Actually, in Queens these disputes often reflected cultural differences: "Koreans are somewhat more mobile than the Chinese population, in terms of driving. That's the result of immigration policy in this country. When the critical mass of Koreans came over in the 1960s and the 1970s, the majority was more educated, and probably a bit more moneyed [than the Chinese], so they were more mobile—you'll see, they trek through Long Island. The Chinese, depending on where they came from, tend to be less mobile, partly because they had been here longer and they arrived when there was a great deal of immigration based on blood ties, as opposed to the newer criteria along lines of education, investments, and so on." Hence continuing arguments, as when parking spaces near Korean stores are threatened by development, which tends to pit more mobile Koreans against more stationary Chinese-Americans.

When we later spoke with Helen Marshall, she agreed that the two Asian communities were different:

> When the Koreans came here, they couldn't get mortgages. Their church is their bank. Everybody chips into it, and ultimately they build a church, and they pool their money—the West Indians also used to do this, and it was called *sou-sou* [a savings arrangement where a group of people pool an equal amount of money for a fixed period]. You paid into it, and could get a loan to get things started. And guess

what? Before you know it, they're on their feet, they've got a business, the business is doing well and they're outstanding citizens.

Owing in good part to her skills at massaging the sensibilities of a diverse electorate, Ms. Marshall has maximized the authority of an otherwise downsized office. For nearly a century, dating back to the amalgamation of New York City, the five elected borough presidents had an equal vote on the potent Board of Estimate in determining citywide budgetary and land-use policies. In 1989, the Supreme Court ruled that this violated the Fourteenth Amendment since less populous Staten Island had the same vote as far more populous Brooklyn and Queens. The board was abolished, its powers bestowed on the City Council; a savvy commentator likened the diminished borough presidents to "neutered beasts." But each has a vote on the citywide board of education, each can propose legislation and appoint special commissions, and each shares with the City Council the naming of increasingly relevant community boards. And Helen Marshall, for all her grandmotherly aura, has shown the cunning of a fox in working in and around the interstices of a local political structure, designed half by Rube Goldberg, half by Machiavelli. She has earned, deservedly, a reputation for getting things done.

Of all places, it was in a public library that she first learned about hardball politics. "I will do anything to get libraries built," Marshall told us. "It was the first thing I did when I came to Queens." There was no local library in Corona, so Ms. Marshall and her associates put together a funding proposal and hit upon a likely location in a defunct Woolworth's five-and-dime store on Northern Boulevard. The store had a resonance; it was the site of a local civil rights campaign to break the hiring color bar in Queens.

On being appointed its director, she helped organize the library board, learned how to select books for its shelves, and sponsored a high school contest to choose a name. The Langston Hughes Community Library and Cultural Center opened in 1969, two years after its namesake's death, and since then it has assembled 40,000 volumes of material related to African-American life and has become a major repository for documents on the civil rights era. In 1987, it became part of the

Queens Public Library system, and in 1999 it relocated in an attractive purpose-built facility, complete with auditorium, exhibition gallery, and a homework assistance program.

Yet in Ms. Marshall recounting, the branch's formative years had prickly moments. East Elmhurst and Corona had long been on the breakthrough frontier of race relations, and were once called the "black Beverly Hills" because of their array of jazz and sports star residents, notably Louis Armstrong, Ella Fitzgerald, Dizzy Gillespie, Harry Belafonte, and Baseball Hall of Famer Willy Mays. But the area also became a recruiting ground for Black Panthers and for disciples of Malcolm X, who in fact was living East Elmhurst prior to his assassination in Manhattan in 1965. This was much in the air when workmen began converting the dime store into a library. Among those watching were black militants headquartered in a storefront across the street. When the library opened, a confrontation ensued. In her words, "We called a meeting, a regular meeting. There was white stuff still on the windows, and the floors weren't covered, and I'm sitting in the front row with the lady I had appointed as assistant. The Panthers got hold of some kids, who marched in at a certain time and went around the room. Their leader said he thought a man was supposed to run this library—and I'll tell you one thing, that room was filled with guns. And I said, 'I don't have to be the director of this library, but you'll have to kill me to get me to stop working here.'"

Passions ebbed, and Marshall went on to be elected district Democratic leader, state assemblywoman, and the City Council member for Elmhurst and Corona. As borough president, she has not shied from hot-button issues. In March 2011, she published a 110-page directory titled *DV: Domestic Violence, Sexual Assault, Child Maltreatment, and Elder Abuse*. A typical listing is for Turning Point for Women and Families, headquartered in Flushing and expressly addressed to Muslim women affected by domestic violence, offering citywide counseling in six languages under the leadership of a Bangladeshi professional, Robina Niaz. The publication of the directory was followed by Marshall's appointment of a task force bringing together fifty relevant organizations to gather ideas and information on immigration policy.

In between, Marshall finds time to dedicate a new cricket pitch, to meet with the borough's poet laureate (an honor initiated by her immediate predecessor as borough president, Claire Shulman), and to join at the annual civic ceremony in observance of Ramadan held at the New York Hall of Science, one of many museums and landmark houses she has also assisted.

Not far from Borough Hall is the former residence of another African-American, Ralph Bunche, whose memory deserves wider celebration. Not only did Bunche provide crucial research to Sweden's Gunnar Myrdal's groundbreaking treatise on racism, *An American Dilemma* (1944), but he was awarded a Nobel Peace Prize for his peacemaking feats in the Middle East as a United Nations mediator. He lived in Kew Gardens for thirty years, until his death in 1970. We are confident that Bunche would have saluted a neighborhood peacemaker whose license plate on her official car condenses her message: "Visit Queens—See the World."

6

HYPHENS:
DIVERSITY AND ITS DISCONTENTS

E Pluribus Unum (Out of many, one)

—MOTTO OF THE UNITED STATES,
ADOPTED BY CONGRESS IN 1782;
PROPOSED BY PIERRE EUGÈNE DU
SIMITIÈRE, BORN IN GENEVA,
DIED IN PHILADELPHIA 1784

FOR TWO YEARS we voyaged through four continents in search of societies that had attained ethnic peace, or its proximate facsimile. Our quest was also doctrinal, entailing a passage through straits fiercely guarded on one shore by xenophobic pessimists, and on the other by feel-good optimists. We strove to steer a middle course, focusing on the benefits of diversity without ignoring the deficits. Nowhere did we find a glib phrase or magic formula that might dispel the disenchantment expressed by European leaders with "multiculturalism," a word saddled with as many ambiguities as it has letters. We concluded firstly, that there is no land without outsiders (save Iceland, perhaps); that the benefits conferred by immigrants weigh like feathers in the marketplace of opinion, unlike their perceived negative tonnage; and that (to vary the metaphor) a germ of fact about foreigners can grow into an epidemic of unreason. Throughout our travels and research, we sensed a reprise of commonly forgotten past disputes, as for example the political import of the hyphen. Does it connect, or separate?

From the onset of mass migration to the United States, as in other industrializing nations, concerns arose over the problems of assimilation. Among early targets were Irish Catholics, of whom roughly two million arrived between 1820 and 1860, an influx that provoked *The Texas State Times* to expostulate in 1855: "These minions of the Pope are boldly insulting our Senators; propagating the adulterous union of Church and state; abusing with foul calumny all governments but Catholic; and spewing out the bitterest execrations of all Protestantism." Worse, Roman Catholics allegedly received $200,000 annually from the Vatican to suborn American liberties. Moreover, the writer added, "We have the best reasons for believing that corruption has found its way into our Executive Chamber, and that our Executive head [President Franklin Pierce] is tainted with the infectious venom of Catholicism."

Nowadays this seems mildly comic. Most students of American history are familiar with similar tirades and their political promotion by the Native American Party, or Know-Nothings, whose popularity evaporated after the Civil War. Yet who today remembers Paul Blanshard? Born in Ohio in 1892, schooled at Harvard Divinity and Union Theological Seminary, by turns a Socialist, a Congregational minister, and a freethinker, Blanshard was author of the best-selling *American Freedom and Catholic Power* (1949), a sustained polemic drawn from his articles in *The Nation,* a quasi-official organ of the liberal establishment. Citing his own past experience as an investigative official in New York City, Blanshard excoriated the Roman Catholic Church as "an undemocratic system of alien control." His book was praised by Albert Einstein, Bertrand Russell, and John Dewey, scarcely know-nothing troglodytes. In 1950, *The Nation* announced with an irreverent wink that Blanshard would be its Vatican correspondent during that Holy Year. A decade later, anti-Papist nightmares seemingly materialized in the presidential bid of Senator John F. Kennedy. A Catholic for *President?* As the candidate's counselor and speechwriter, Ted Sorensen wrote years later, "Strange as it seems today, the chief obstacle to [JFK's] nomination and election in 1960 was based not on doubts about his age or experience, or his controversial family, or his voting record in the Senate, or even his health. It was based largely on his Roman Catholic faith."

Fittingly, the decisive round in the 1960 election was fought in Texas. Because religious doubts figured so prominently in JFK's primary campaign, Sorensen urged the senator to tackle the question directly at a September 1960 meeting of the Houston Ministerial Association. Kennedy by then had consulted with key Protestant theologians, and care was taken to invite influential critics of the Catholic Church to Houston. In arguably his most critical campaign speech, Kennedy eloquently avowed that in the United States, separation of church and state "is absolute." With a bow to his audience, he added a Texas turn in celebrating American diversity: "At the Alamo, side by side with Bowie and Crockett, died Fuentes and McCafferty and Bailey, Badillo and Carey—but no one knew whether they were Catholic or not. For there was no religious test there." Overall, even Blanshard was impressed. Following his election, President Kennedy participated in prayer breakfasts with a then friendly Reverend Billy Graham. As Sorensen relates, he also "met privately—in my office, so that even visitors in the White House could not know—with anti-Catholic pamphleteer Paul Blanshard, seeking his agreement to the inclusion of private colleges in the higher education bill, and [the President] kept me in touch with Blanshard generally." Thus a Roman Catholic finally presided in the Oval Office. And the republic did not totter.

———

HISTORY MAY NOT REPEAT, Mark Twain is said to have remarked, but on occasion it rhymes. There is indeed a repetitious assonance in the alarms voiced during the past two centuries about the perils of multicultural immigration. Who *are* these newcomers flooding into North America, Europe, and Australia? Don't their true loyalties really lie with a foreign flag or faith? Doesn't that weaken the social cohesion vital to any democracy? Aren't foreigners robbing jobs from native-born workers and farmers? Don't they live in separatist enclaves, walling themselves apart from our common culture? And why, oh why, do so many resist learning their host country's ways and languages?

On the eve of American Revolution, such questions were already being aired concerning German speakers from Middle Europe arriving with their strange religions and alien tongues. After the devout Amish and Mennonites came French speakers suspected of being godless Jacobins or Napoleonic spies. Their presence became a divisive party issue, and in part to ensure their deportation the dominant Federalists pushed for passage in 1798 of the Alien and Sedition Acts. As Abigail Adams reported to her husband, then the Chief Executive, extremists known as Ultra-Federalists were offering this Fourth of July toast: "John Adams. May he, like *Samson* slay thousands of Frenchmen with the *jaw-bone* of Jefferson." (Thomas Jefferson was then being denounced by the Ultras as "the Grandest of All Villains" and as a covert ally of the "frenchified faction in this country.") Yielding to this xenophobic clamor, Adams signed the four different Alien and Sedition Acts. It was, he later acknowledged, the biggest blunder of his presidency, which he attributed to relentless pressure from the Ultras.

This became the template for the American response to agitation about immigrants: radicals define the vocabulary, jittery centrists surrender reluctantly and years later, apologize. Still, the Founders committed a graver offense: at no point before, during or after the struggle for independence, did any of them seriously address a profounder moral issue: how to deal with unwilling immigrants from Africa. Before and after the American Revolution, an estimated 645,000 blacks survived the brutal Middle Passage to America, where slaves remained legally chattel until their formal emancipation in 1865. By then, millions of Irish Papists also had arrived, followed by sizable intakes of Italian Catholics, Orthodox Slavs, and observant Jews from Southern and Eastern Europe, each bearing suspect baggage. In a special category were Chinese immigrants, many of them contract laborers, who were accused of working too hard for too little, precipitating the racist 1882 Chinese Exclusion Act. Next followed thousands of Japanese farmers, artisans, and shopkeepers, at first welcomed in Hawaii and California, but later perceived as pawns in Tokyo's imperial games.

Few tracked popular stereotyping more astutely than Chicago's Finley Peter Dunne (1867–1936), whose ear for political blarney was pitch perfect. Dunne was an Irish-American who came to America by way of Canada. In his widely read newspaper columns, Dunne invented a saloonkeeper named Mr. Dooley who regularly discussed topical events with his admiring foil, Mr. Hennessey. (Dooley liked to parody extremist views, much in the mode of television's Stephen Colbert.) When upstart Japan's armed forces unexpectedly humbled Tsarist Russia in 1905, Mr. Dooley thus reflected on what that meant for Americans:

> I'm in a state of alarum all th' time. In th' good old days we wudden't have thought life was worth livin' if we cuddent insult a foreigner. That's what they were f'r. Whin I was sthrong, before old age deprived me iv me pathritism, an' other infantile disordhers, I niver saw a Swede, a Hun, an Eyetalian, a Boohlgaryan, a German, a Fr-rinchman, that I didn't give him th' shoulder. If 'twas an Englishman, I give him th' foot too. Threaty rights, says ye? We give him th' same threaty rights he'd give us, a dhrink an' a whack on th' head. It seemed proper to us. If 'twas right to belong to wan naytionality, 'twas wrong to belong to another. If 'twas a man's boast to be an American, it was disgrace to be a German, an' a joke to be a Fr-rinchman. An' that goes now. Ye can bump any foreigner ye meet but a Jap. He's a live wire. . . . Why, be Hivens, it won't be long till we'll have to be threatin' th' Chinese dacint. Think of that, will ye!

Granted, there were sensible reasons for American unease about an ever-expanding, emperor-worshipping, stridently militarist Japanese Empire. Pearl Harbor seemed to confirm extreme xenophobic fears of a global Yellow Peril. Overnight, nearly everyone in America deemed to be Japanese shriveled into a "Jap." Responding more to popular outrage than military imperatives, President Roosevelt early in 1942 approved the West Coast internment of 110,000 persons of Japanese origin into so-called relocation camps. Those herded into makeshift quarters included tens of thousands of US-born citizens, with their children, aged parents, and others possessing a fraction of Japanese blood. Recently, following the 9/11 terror attacks, some American revisionists have sought to justify this past internment on national security grounds, but their evidence is at best exiguous. The consensus among military and legal historians remains that Japanese-Americans did not pose a significant threat either on the West Coast or in Hawaii (home to 150,000 Japanese-Americans, a third of its population, where no mass detention was attempted). Moreover, the all-Japanese-American 434th Regimental

Combat Team (motto: "Go for Broke") while fighting in Italy became the most decorated unit in US Army history. Seen in calmer retrospect, it was not just the hope of economic gain that proved as potent a magnet for Japanese immigrants; it was also American values.

There occurred an absolving symmetry when President Ronald Reagan, a conservative former governor of California, expressed contrition in 1988 while signing legislation awarding reparations to internees and their descendants. Even more resonant was a White House ceremony four years later when George Herbert Walker Bush signed a supplementary bill to the same effect. As a boarding school student, young George was so shaken by Pearl Harbor, that on turning eighteen he enlisted in the US Navy, becoming its youngest pilot. He engaged in fifty-eight combat missions in the Pacific and earned a Distinguished Flying Cross and three Air Medals. His public service literally dated from the infamous day. Hence the healing echo in the Oval Office in 1992 when President George H. W. Bush approved further financial compensation and apologized anew for the internment of Japanese-Americans, an unjust act atoned in part by $1.6 billion in restitution awards. Score one for Mark Twain; in this instance, history rhymed.

––––––

RHYMING ALSO HAS a global dimension. The peopling of the world's three outsize English-speaking countries—Canada, Australia, and America—has followed a broadly familiar dynamic. First, European conquest and dispossession of indigenous nonwhites, then white colonization. Next, having wrested genuine self-rule, leaders of each nation by and large welcomed white Europeans and more selectively Asians and Hispanics. Post–World War I, the welcome chilled; when refugees fleeing Fascism pleaded for visas, only a fraction of Europe's tired and tempest tossed were able to squeeze through America's Golden Door. Then, in the 1960s, a radical shift occurred. Driven primarily by a shared need for substantial numbers of young, skilled, semi-skilled, and unskilled workers, all three countries lowered racial barriers. The 1965 US Immigration and Nationality Act abolished a racist "national origins" quota that had been in place since 1924. A year later, Australia formally abandoned its "White Australia" policy, and by 1973 eliminated race as a justifiable criterion for selecting immigrants. In 1971, having previously liberalized its immigration laws, Canada became the first country to espouse "multiculturalism" as national policy, as implemented by a federal ministry bearing that name. Finally, on humanitarian or economic grounds, all three Anglophone nations detailed exceptions for asylum seekers, college students, immigrants with high-value skills, and for those seeking family unification.

Within this broad dynamic, there were obvious differences:

Australia: In the eighty years between the first British landing at Botany Bay in 1788 and a final boatload of convicts in 1868, Australia was settled largely by male and female felons, evolving into what the Aussie-born author Robert Hughes called "the Noah's Ark of small time criminality." This past still colors Australia's ongoing debate on atoning for past abuse of Aboriginals—most especially the kidnapping of their children, a practice that persisted until 1969—plus the early and ongoing sequestering of Aboriginal lands, and in Tasmania, the elimination of its native peoples (the last full-blooded Tasmanian Aboriginal died in 1876, at the age of seventy-six).

Canada: The French explored, named, and colonized Canada, beginning with the arrival of Gallic fur traders at Port Royal in 1605 and at Quebec City three years later. Subsequently, having won the French and Indian War (known in Canada as the Seven Years' War), Britain in 1763 annexed the entire huge dominion to its empire. This had two consequences, the first commonly overlooked: no longer needing British military help to fend off encroaching Franco-Catholics, Anglo-Protestants in the thirteen colonies resented, and then rebelled against, the new taxes imposed by a faraway British Parliament to finance an arguably superfluous garrison. The second and more obvious consequence, a bipolar struggle arose within Canada between a growing English-speaking majority and the stubbornly French-speaking minority centered in Quebec Province, a conflict partially mitigated in 1968 when French and English were both designated as Canada's official languages. (A spillover effect occurred in the United States. The 1803 Louisiana Purchase marooned a French-speaking community in Louisiana, to this day the only state where France's legal code is honored in courts.) As in Australia, Canadians still debate the moral and material amends owed to indigenous peoples (the "First Nation") whose lands were seized and whose children were also taken into custody to instruct them in the benefits of European civilization.

America: Beginning with a Dutch captain's offloading in 1619 of "twenty Negars" in Jamestown, human bondage flourished in British America. The lucrative slave trade generated New England fortunes, notably in Boston and Providence, an unholy traffic defended by eminent Protestant divines (and vainly opposed by early-day Quaker abolitionists). At the outbreak of the Revolution, slaves accounted for roughly one-fifth of the 2.5 million colonists and around 40 percent of Virginia's inhabitants. Hence Samuel Johnson's warranted rebuke in *Taxation Not Tyranny* (1775): "How is it that we hear the loudest yelps for liberty among the drivers of negroes?"

Jefferson's first draft of the Declaration of Independence did condemn King George III's tolerance of the slave trade as a "cruel war against human nature itself." But his words were deleted at the vociferous insistence of delegates to the Continental Congress from South Carolina and Georgia. Writing years later, Jefferson added a footnote: "Our northern brethren also, I believe, felt a little tender under those censures for, though their people had very few slaves themselves, yet they had been pretty considerable carriers of them to others." In other words, slavery in America was never peculiar to the South; the North was as complicit in slavery's origins.

Our purpose in exhuming this dirty linen is simply to note that on the matter of oppressing nonwhites, Australia, Canada, and the United States have no cause to lecture one another. All were implicated in the sin of racism. Still, in fairness, we wonder which of the world's principal nations has not dispossessed its original inhabitants, tolerated forced labor, and dealt roughly with minorities speaking an alien tongue? On this moral matter, every nation inhabits the same glass house. The contours of our world were determined by Europe's imperious expansion, by the warrior states in South Asia and in pre-Columbian America, by the vying tribes of Africa, and the quarreling believers of the Holy Land. History itself thus too often ends in a sterile and endless debate between winners transfixed by the present and losers trapped stubbornly in the past.

SIFTING THROUGH our notes, we were struck by another theme common to the politics of diversity in the United States, Canada, and Australia. In all three countries, the benefits of immigration are tangible but diffuse, cumulative rather than short term. Aggregate gains arising from pluralism tend to pass unnoticed, whereas every bump in the road is promptly trumpeted. In short, diversity's upside is macro, its downside micro. This dichotomy became especially apparent to us in Australia.

It is November, or late spring in the Antipodes. At first glance, Sydney is much as advertised: a cheery modernist metropolis, branded by its perky opera house whose scalloped topsails catch the harbor breezes. Merely to walk along serpentine George Street, chatting with shopkeepers and youngsters of every hue, is to echo the agreeable surprise of prior travelers. As Jan Morris, the Welsh chronicler of Pax Britannica, commented in 1992, Sydneysiders are friendly, polite, and disarmingly candid: "The supra-national, supra-ethnic fraternity of kind, educated, open-minded people which exists like a freemasonry in every city of the world, is powerfully represented here."

On the surface, Australia generally and Sydney in particular seem like posters for diversity. Few democracies have been more welcoming to every creed, with Melbourne vying with Sydney in the diversity department (since the 1990s, *The Melbourne Age* has published daily prayer times for Muslims, as transliterated from the Arabic). The current pacesetter is Sydney, Australia's most populous city and the capital of New South Wales. Roughly one in four of Sydney's 4.2 million inhabitants is foreign born; an estimated 10 percent are Muslims who worship at twenty major mosques. No one ethnic group predominates in Sydney or Melbourne, the result of a carefully calibrated national immigration policy that balances countries of origin, awards bonus points for needed skills, offers special visas to students, and provides sanctuary for some asylum seekers.

Moreover, diversity's overall benefits could scarcely seem more positive, as described in a 2011 special report in *The Economist* titled "No Worries?" Not only has Australia kept jobless rates down while maintaining steady growth rates, but according to the weekly's twelve-page supplement, the principal engine of prosperity has been immigration. In *The Economist's* summation: "Immigration is good for the economy. Over the past forty years population growth has been responsible for about two-fifths of the growth in real GDP. . . . Without it, Australia would have slipped into recession in 2008. Increasingly, the people admitted through its managed-migration program bring skills that are in short supply in Australia."

Of some three hundred thousand immigrants admitted nationwide in 2008, two-thirds were classed as temporary workers; some were granted permanent residency, along with selective students and asylum seekers. This stream of newcomers proved essential to Australia's swelling commodity exports, especially to China, currently the principal purchaser of the country's coal and key minerals.

And yet the benefits of this influx have failed to register on popular consciousness, whereas political reputations and headlines billow whenever a boat packed with asylum seekers is said to threaten national security. By common account, the defining episode occurred in August 2001 when the *Tampa*, a Norwegian cargo vessel, rescued 438 Indonesian asylum seekers trapped in a sinking fishing boat. At that time, Australia's Liberal Prime Minister John Howard was trailing in key polls as his party braced for oncoming federal elections. The Howard government barred the captain of the *Tampa* from Australian waters, so the bereft passengers offloaded in Nauru, a quasi-bankrupt island state. Only one was granted asylum rights by Canberra; the rest scattered, with New Zealand accepting 186. This incident exemplified Howard's "Pacific Solution" of repelling successive waves of boat people, most of them asylum-seeking Muslims. His hard line fortuitously intersected with the 9/11 attack on America; in the wake of both events, his party posters portrayed a resolute John Howard, flanked by flags and his fists clenched, above this message: "*We* Decide Who Comes to This Country and the Circumstances in Which They Come." Pamphlets carrying the same slogan were deposited nationally in mailboxes. Newspaper ads informed voters, "A vote for your local Liberal team protects our borders and supports the Prime Minister's team." Vote they did; the opposition Labor Party conceded defeat two hours after the polls closed in November; its overall showing of 38.45 percent was its worst since 1933, when the party was routed during the Great Depression.

In a postelection epilogue, it developed that the vaunted "Pacific Solution" had at a cost of a half-billion dollars blocked the arrival of a less-than-awesome armada of 2,390 boat people, mostly Indonesian Muslims, plus a scattering of Iranians, Iraqis, and Afghans. Why then were so many Australians so alarmed by so few? A plausible explanation is offered in *Australia's Immigration Revolution* (2009), edited by three scholars, Andrew Marcus, James Jupp, and Peter McDonald. In Jupp's article he writes, "Essentially, as in many other democracies, opposition to sudden and uncontrolled [immigrant] flows created a political backlash. But there is also something distinctive in the extreme Australian response, a function of its small population and historic sense of being a British outpost in a hostile Asian region." In statistical reality, Australia ranked a distant tenth among major democracies coping with asylum applications; from 1995 to 2001, its six-year total was 69,750, compared to Germany's 709,260 and Great Britain's 473,690. Hence *The Economist's* judgment that Australia's least impressive feature is its political leadership: "Instead of pointing to the great political benefits of immigration, [the] two parties pander shamelessly to xenophobic fears about asylum seekers washing up in boats."

As in other democracies, pandering flourishes in Australia whenever officeholders fear a critical loss of votes to the aggressively expanding anti-immigrant movements such as those that have sprung up across Europe and in North America. In Australia, the specter haunting officeholders has been Pauline Hanson, former leader of the One Nation party, which for two decades has targeted nonwhite newcomers as a menace. Unknown until her election in 1996 from Queensland to the federal parliament, Hanson in her first speech anticipated the rhetoric of most anti-immigrant populists. She began by insisting that she only voiced commonsense wisdom, rooted in her own experience as a mother of four and proprietor of a fish and chips shop in a suburb of Brisbane. Nevertheless, she believed she spoke for the silent mass of Australians whose views were patronizingly ignored by mainstream parties. In her words,

I and most Australians want our immigration policy radically reviewed and that of multiculturalism abolished. I believe we are in danger of being swamped by Asians. Between 1984 and 1995, forty percent of all migrants coming to this country were of Asian origin. They have their own culture and religion, form ghettos and do not assimilate. Of course, I will be called a racist, but if I can invite whom I want into my home, then I should have the same right to have a say in who comes into my country. A truly multicultural country can never be strong or united. The world is full of failed and tragic examples, ranging from Ireland to Bosnia to Africa and closer to home, Papua New Guinea.

She reminded opposition Laborites of the words of a former leader, Arthur Calwell, a champion of White Australia, whom she thus quoted: "Japan, India, Burma, Ceylon and every new African nation are fiercely anti-white and anti-one another. Do we want or need any of these people here? I am one red-blooded Australian who says no, and who speaks for ninety percent of Australians." Hanson said those were exactly her views.

In 1998, Canberra's mainstream officeholders were stunned by a Queensland state election in which Hanson's newborn One Nation party rolled up one-fourth of the popular vote, securing eleven of eighty-nine seats in the Legislative Assembly. It was then that Prime Minister Howard—who until then had pointedly declined to criticize Pauline Hanson's views—unveiled his "Pacific Solution." Hanson protested, "John Howard sailed home on our One Nation policies. In short, if we were not around, he would not have made the decisions he did." Thereafter, her party's fortunes declined as centrist politicians echoed its platform. Hanson herself, having survived bitter political and legal disputes, dwindled into a media celebrity, at once admired and mocked. Her stardom peaked in 2004 when television viewers chose her as a losing finalist in Australia's version of *Dancing with the Stars*, her ballroom partner being Salvatore Vecchio (his Internet tag: "Contract estimator by day, Latin dancer by night!"). Pauline Hanson's devotees could not care less what pointy-headed intellectuals said about her. They love her for the enemies she has made.

———

INTRIGUED BY THE arguments over diversity in Australia scarcely known to most Americans, we sought out Geoffrey Brahm Levey, a lecturer on political theory at the University of New South Wales. Levey is Australia's entry in the select cadre of scholars now exploring the varied mutations of multiculturalism. Among the cadre's luminaries are Canada's Will Kymlicka (*Multicultural Citizenship: A Liberal Theory of Minority Rights*), Charles Taylor (*Reconciling the Solitudes: Essays on Canadian Federalism and Nationalism*), and France's Patrick Weil (*How to Be French: Nationality in the Making Since 1789*). Like his associates in a budding discipline, Levey has studied and taught abroad (in America, Britain, and Israel in his case) hence his breadth of focus in *Political Theory and Australian Multiculturalism* (2008), a symposium he edited, introduced and summed up. Returning to Sydney from America in 1996, Levey founded his university's Program of Jewish Studies, serving as director until 2005. He has co-edited *Secularism, Religion, and Multicultural Citizenship* (with Tariq Madood).

The hallmarks of this emerging field are seriousness, erudition, and complexity, the obverse of the pugilistic formulas that typically resound among fiercer critics of multiculturalism. By contrast, academic theorists apply the solvent of reason to the muddled history of "identity," "citizenship," "nationality," and specifically "multiculturalism," a neologism of the 1970s. (*Webster's Unabridged Dictionary*, Third Edition [1971], lists sixty words prefixed by "multi," none affixed to "culture.") So what does multiculturalism signify? Levey distinguishes three levels: *ethnic nationalism,* meaning a community of shared culture and common descent; *liberal nationalism,* positing a single community with a shared culture and language, but without a common ethnic descent; and *post nationalism,* which rejects the need of a national culture altogether, but divides over its replacement. Moreover, within each definition lie subsidiary distinctions.

Add to the semantic jigsaw the long-established concepts jus soli, whereby citizenship is determined by the land of one's birth (hence the "birther" controversy), and jus sanguinis, whereby the citizenship of the parents determines that of their children. In America, both doctrines have long prevailed, and recent court decisions affirm the right of US citizens to obtain and use foreign passports. Thanks to the European Union, old frontiers have eroded and a single visa suffices for travel in most member states.

All this has nurtured two divergent views of citizenship within this academic coterie: one called "thick" citizenship, implying strong support for common values, the other "thin" citizenship, which accepts plural loyalties and prefers as its metaphor an "ethnic salad" in place of a "melting pot." In Levey's view, thick citizenship in theory is supposed to be about assimilating democratic norms, but in practice it implicitly privileges a dominant Anglo-Australian community. Hence its advocates "tend to do what they accuse Australian multicultural policy of doing—namely, essentialize ethnic group identity and membership, rather than allowing for their internal diversity, dynamism and hybridity." And what of the "thin" approach to citizenship? In Levey's view, its proponents too quickly discount the significance of national character and civil society: "As everyone knows, the French are really different from the Germans, Canadians are different from Americans, and Australians are different from the Brits and the New Zealanders." Adherents of the "thin" school ignore "the many ways in which liberal democratic states already and inevitably endorse particular ethnocultural traditions, from the language spoken to state symbols."

For American readers, the essays of Geoffrey Levey and his colleagues are unexpectedly rewarding in their asides. For example, despite their sunny "hey, mate" egalitarianism, we learned that "Old Australians" tend to be formally hierarchical in defining who qualifies as a "New Australian." Hyphens, in particular, are not acceptable in a policy that values "integration" more than "assimilation." As Levey explains, "We have Indigenous Australians and Greek Australians and Vietnamese Australians and so on—all without a hyphen. There are exceptions, and they too are significant: Anglo-Australians or Anglo-Celtic Australians. The hyphen is reserved for the dominant ethnic grouping that first defined the core culture of the nation."

On this matter, Australia has simply reversed American usage in a way that thrusts to the essence of multiculturalism. Few linguistic symbols have a more curious history than the hyphen. The term "hyphenated American" first became current in the 1890s. Its original associations were derogatory, especially after the outbreak of World War I. During the national debate over US neutrality, German-Americans were commonly derided as apologists for Kaiser Wilhelm II and his savage Huns; following America's 1917 entry on the Allied side, everything Teutonic became suspect (sauerkraut famously morphed into "liberty cabbage"). For their part, Irish-American Catholics generally favored neutrality since their homeland was mired in a struggle against British Protestant rule that crested in the abortive 1916 Easter Rising. (Eamon de Valera, later to become president of the future Irish Republic, was among the Rising's leaders, but because he was born in New York, he was spared the firing squad—a placatory British gesture to a still-neutral United States.)

In the arguments that preceded America's entry, former President Theodore Roosevelt led the attack on hyphens. "There is no room in this country for hyphenated Americanism," he pointedly told a Knights of Columbus audience in New York City on Columbus Day, 1915. "I do not refer to naturalized Americans. Some of the very best Americans I have ever known were naturalized. . . . But a hyphenated American is not an American at all." He ominously feared that America would cease to be a nation if it became "a tangle of squabbling nationalities, an intricate knot of German-Americans, Irish-Americans, English-Americans, French-Americans, Scandinavian-Americans or Italian-Americans, each preserving its separate nationality." So prevalent was this allergy that even the less histrionic Woodrow Wilson also inveighed against hyphens following his return in 1919 from the Paris Peace Conference. "Any man who carries a hyphen about with him," he informed a cheering crowd, "carries a dagger that he is ready to plunge into the vitals of this republic whenever he gets ready."

The antipathy to hyphens contributed to the so-called Palmer raids of 1919 and 1920, the deportation of foreign-born radicals, the 1927 execution of the Italian-born anarchists Nicola Sacco and Bartolomeo Vanzetti (found guilty of murder after a suspect trial that was sustained by the president of Harvard), and the headline-grabbing ascent in the 1930s of the House Committee on Un-American Activities, chaired by Rep. Martin Dies (D-Texas).

Nevertheless, post–World War II, a sea change in American atti-
tudes occurred. There are various possible reasons: To returning GIs,
abroad may no longer have seemed so alien. Additionally, the horror of
the Holocaust quelled long-socially acceptable anti-Semitic remarks.
Meanwhile, New York's status as a global metropolis magnified after it
became host to the United Nations, while the Reverand Martin Luther
King, Jr. and the 1960s civil rights movement broke a long silence on
racism, North and South; and tardy embarrassment was widely
expressed about earlier dispossession of Native Americans. Whatever the
causes, the hyphen ceased to threaten. Negroes sought and won recognition as African-Americans. As for other ethnic communities, *The
New York Times's Manual of Style and Usage* (1999 edition) was explicit:
"Use the hyphen in a compound denoting national origin: i.e., *Italian-
American; Japanese-American.*" Across the border, Canadians followed a
broadly similar path. Thus the dagger was sheathed.

Reflecting on all this, in order to learn more about diversity,
Australian-style, we met with Geoffrey Levey. Our encounter took place
at the main campus in Sydney of the University of New South Wales,
known in Australia simply as UNSW.

———

UNSW IS AN internationalist, science-oriented, liberal arts conglom-
erate, broadly comparable to CUNY in New York or to Britain's Sussex
University. Established in 1949, UNSW today comprises seventy-six
schools, sixty-nine research centers, six institutes, and four residential
colleges; its enrollment totals more than 50,000, of whom 14,000 students are from 130 other nations. Its growth has paralleled Australia's
post–World War II emergence as an economic and cultural power.
UNSW's main campus in eastern Sydney is a glass and steel beehive, a
gleaming example of mainstream modernism, clean if soulless, efficient
yet impersonal. It was here, over coffee we met with Levey, forty something, casual in dress and manner, lightly bearded but with a glint of
mischief in his eyes.

Don't judge simply by facades, Levey cautioned as we looked
around. He was interested in our quest for successful examples of diversity, and outwardly Australia would seem an admirable candidate.

In 1947, including around 87,000 Aborigines, its population was 7.6 million—the overall majority being of British descent. By 2011, its total topped 21 million, a rate of national increase without global parallel (save for Israel). As of 2006, Australia's newcomers arrived from some two hundred countries, the main sources being Great Britain (24 percent) and New Zealand (19.5 percent), the rest by deliberate policy divided into smaller parcels.

Even so, "Old Australians" viewed with apprehension the "New Australians," and the former's unguarded remarks were often a good measure of their sense of siege. Had we heard, for instance, about Tony Abbott, a former federal health minister? During a 2006 debate in Parliament over what he viewed as ethnic juggling, or "branch stacking," within the opposition party, Abbott rhetorically asked, "Are there any Australians left in the so-called Australian Labor Party today?" The invidious implication, in Levey's view, was that if you're an immigrant, you cannot be truly Australian. (Abbott later apologized for his wording.) A related issue in Sydney concerned the pretexts for opposing mosques and synagogues. Concerning mosques,

> It's typically framed in two ways. There is the noise of the mullahs calling the congregation to prayer—and that's not the Christian way. But mind you, I've lived in Oxford for years, where you always have the eternal ringing of bells. The other objection, regarding synagogues, concerns traffic, which upsets a lot of communities. In Bondi Junction in [Sydney's] eastern suburbs, where the Jewish community is concentrated, there have been complaints by non-Jews about synagogues on the same grounds. You know what I mean: noise, traffic, people spilling out of synagogues.

Far more significant, Levey stressed, were the mob riots in December 2005 at Cronulla Beach on Sydney's southern shore. By global standards, interethnic relations in Australia have been comparatively peaceful, "We've had our flare-ups, but they're nothing compared to most parts of the world. Cronulla is the single glaring exception." It began with a confusing scuffle between Lebanese immigrants and off-duty lifeguards; within a week inflammatory words on talk radio

inspired this text message to local youths: "Come to Cronulla this weekend to take revenge. This Sunday every Aussie in the Shire go down to
North Cronulla to support Leb and wog bashing day." On the
appointed day, some five thousand would-be bashers gathered at the
beach, their shirts sporting these slogans: "We Grew Here, You Flew
Here," "Wog Free Zone," and "Ethnic Cleansing Unit." While crowds
chanted "Lebs go home" and "Fuck off, Lebs," leaflets were circulated
by members of the Australia First Party and the Patriotic Youth League.
By day's end, sixteen rioters were arrested and charged with 512
offences; twenty-five persons were reported injured, including two
ambulance officers.

"These were extremely ugly scenes, the likes of which had never
been seen in Australia," Levey elaborated. "Here were these angry,
alcohol-crazed Anglo-Australians bashing and kicking anybody who
looked different, even lots of Indians." One of the rioters was filmed
repeatedly kicking his victim on the ground. "It turned out that this guy
was a classical pianist from a Christian family who lived in the Cronulla
area." For his part, the kicker remarked in stunned surprise, "I just don't
know what possessed me." Yes, there were instances of Lebanese misbe-
havior, such as scuffing sand in the faces of beachgoers while playing
soccer. But there was no rational warrant for the mob assault. Still, in
Levey's judgment, the national response was "very Australian, and it
worked. People were genuinely shocked. Various programs were initiated; social workers sought to bring the two communities together (and
this is very Australian) by training young Muslim men and women as
surf lifesavers, and so integrate them into the lifesaving subculture. And
it's been four years without any repeat—touch wood."

Here he paused, drew a breath and added: "But if one were to ask
whether Australia has been a successful multicultural country [in terms
of] the initiatives it has taken to promote, celebrate, and accommodate
cultural differences, I think the answer would be more mixed." For all
the talk about multiculturalism, he continued, "There has never been in
this country ready acceptance by the policymakers—and certainly not
by the population—of multiple cultural identities." There were exceptions here and there, as for example in Melbourne where the police
academy went out of its way to design a hijab headdress for its first

Muslim female graduate. "It was designed in a way so that it was secure against attempts to strangle her while she was doing her work as a police officer." Also in Melbourne, an immigration museum was opened in 1998 in a handsome Victorian building known as the Old Custom House. But outreach was the exception, Levey went on, more typical was the controversy under way in Sydney over a request by the Muslim community to open a school in the suburb of Camden, which planning authorities rejected on environmental grounds. "And in these disputes, you always get the usual comment, 'We're not racists, we just don't want them here.'"

Overall, we were struck by Geoffrey Levey's favorable estimate of the United States and Canada as exemplars of enlightened diversity. Two North Americans countries with different histories have emerged as global pacesetters in accommodating immigrant cultures. Both countries have learned to live with the hyphen, and to accept the demographic reality that their founding ethnic groups are already in the minority in key cities and states, as they will be nationally if current demographic rates continue. This shift in demographics surely, is the acid test for diversity. Levey likes to cite an observation by the philosopher Michael Walzer, the noted American theorist of just wars: "What has always struck me as the most remarkable feature of American history, impossible to imagine in any 'old world' nation state, is that the Anglo-Americans allowed themselves to become a minority in—what they must have imagined to be—*their* country." (This was written in 2001; seven years later, American voters chose a Hawaii-born hybrid as *their* Chief Executive.)

With so many voices deploring or applauding America's real or alleged decline as a superpower, it strikes us as odd that so little is made of the country's successes (along with Canada's) in creatively harnessing immigrant energy. It is to this theme that we finally turn.

———

WHAT, REALLY, IS AMERICAN history about? In 1949, a young Harvard professor named Oscar Handlin offered an interesting answer: "Once I thought to write a history of the immigrants in America. Then I discovered that the immigrants *were* American history." Handlin himself was born in 1925 in Brooklyn of Russian Jewish parents; after graduating from Brooklyn College, he earned his graduate degree in history at Harvard before commencing research on *The Uprooted: The Epic Story of the Great Migrations That Made the American People.* Drawing on novels, folklore, and newspapers, Handlin's book won a Pulitzer Prize and established its subject as worthy of academic concern.

It retrospect, he concluded, of the great forces shaping the new continent, the most important was the movement of peoples:

> The arrival of a labor force that permitted the expansion of industry without pauperization of the native workers; the fact that costs of production could fall while the capacity to consume continued to grow; the remarkable fluidity of a social system in which each new group pushed upward the level of its predecessors—these were the phenomena that gave immigration a prominent role in the development of the United States.

Study after study has sustained his reckoning. It is routinely alleged, for example, that immigrants cost jobs of native-born workers, that they tend to become freeloading wards of a welfare state, and that they thus are doubly an economic liability. All such assertions are either demonstrably false or misleading. In the United States, Canada, and Australia, there is a consistent association between economic growth and peak years of immigration. By spurring consumption, newcomers create more jobs than they displace, and immigrants often seek employment in occupations for which native-born workers commonly lack the training or interest. Foreign-born workers, whether legal or not, pay more in taxes collectively than welfare benefits they receive.

This is borne out by successive government and academic studies. The U.S. Census Bureau found that between 1990 and 2001, America's civilian labor force grew by 16 million to 141.8 million, half the increase owing to immigrant workers who energized the economy in these high-growth years. The thirty-member Organization for Economic Cooperation and Development (OECD) regularly monitors trends in global migration, and its reports confirm the same multiplying effect. As to being a drain on welfare benefits, a 1997 study by the

National Research Council of the National Academy of Sciences found that newcomers over their lifetime pay roughly $80,000 more per person than the federal benefits they receive. In the long run, writes Michele Wucker, director of the World Policy Institute, in her 2006 study of immigration policy, "New legal immigrants will provide a net benefit of $407 billion to Social Security alone over the course of fifty years, according to calculations by the Office of the Chief Actuary of the Social Security Administration."

Finally, and counterintuitively, in America's one hundred largest metropolitan areas, especially in neighborhoods where foreign-born and nonwhite families mostly live, crime rates in fact *decreased* between 1990 and 2008. "Violent crime rates dropped by almost thirty percent in cities, while property crime fell by forty-six percent," according to a 2011 Brookings Institution report. Using data from the FBI and the Census Bureau, the report's authors found that the relationship between crime and demography (i.e., the degree to which a neighborhood is black, Hispanic, poor, and foreign-born) "diminished considerably over time." In short, it is safer to live among immigrants and nonwhites than in more affluent neighborhoods—a phenomenon rarely mentioned, much less celebrated, in the mainstream media.

Going further, the two North American nations have repeatedly pioneered innovations that contain the risks and/or absorb the shocks of ethnic diversity. It is worth considering the ways.

PROMOTING AUTONOMY TO COUNTER SEPARATISM

The United States and Canada, having led the way as supersized federations, have pragmatically adapted federal principles to defuse separatism. An outstanding and underappreciated U.S. example is the special commonwealth status attained in 1952 by Puerto Rico by mutual agreement among Spanish-speaking islanders, the White House, and Congress. Ceded to the United States by Spain as a spoil of war in 1898, the island remained a virtual colony until its first elected governor, Luis Muñoz Marin, proposed a novel status: Puerto Ricans would be granted linguistic autonomy, U.S. citizenship, and home rule, but no votes in Congress or for president. Propelled in part by selective exemptions from federal taxes—a key element in the bargain—the islanders then energized a slumbering economy under "Operation Bootstrap." In successive plebiscites, Puerto Ricans (current population, 3.7 million) have consistently favored commonwealth status instead of seeking statehood or independence. In a landmark decision, the UN General Assembly voted in 1953 to remove Puerto Rico from its list of non-self-governing colonies, thereby legitimizing agreed-upon autonomy arrangements. Whatever its surviving flaws, an unambiguous benefit of the island's status as an Associated Free State (*Esatado Libre Asociado*) is the eclipse of the sanguinary Nationalist Party, whose gunmen once sprayed bullets at the U.S. Congress and in 1950 came close to assassinating President Harry Truman.

No less relevant has been Canada's success in defusing a similarly feral separatist movement in French-speaking Quebec. First, some history. Canadian federalism dates to the British North America Act of July 1, 1867 (once feted annually as Dominion Day, now reborn as Canada Day). The act delineated four provinces (now grown to ten), Quebec, Ontario, New Brunswick, and Nova Scotia, each with specified powers under a central Parliament comprising an elected House of Commons and Senate. From its inception, the act deferred to Quebec's majority of French speakers by enshrining use of their language as well as English in courts and legislative bodies. But this failed to appease Quebec nationalists, who with some reason protested that French-Canadians were treated like helots, even in Montreal, since Anglo-Canadians held the reins of economic power. In 1967, the centenary of dominion status, separatists formed the Parti Québécois, polarizing both province and country. A year later, a Liberal MP named Pierre Elliott Trudeau (1919–2000), a lawyer schooled in Montreal, London, and Cambridge, Massachusetts, was elected as Canada's fifteenth prime minister. Trudeau outdueled the separatists in 1970, firmly quelling civil disorder in Quebec while securing passage of an Official Languages Act that accorded French and English equal status nationally. His triumph was sealed when in successive plebiscites, in 1980 and 1995, Quebecers rejected secession. It came almost as an anticlimax in May 2011 when in federal elections a separatist party, the Bloc Québécois, verged on near extinction in its provincial showing, losing all but four of the forty-seven seats it contested.

As with the case of Puerto Rico, Canada's sea change regarding cultural autonomy rested on a principle that validated the result. In both cases, consent of the governed was required, as expressed in plebiscites. All this provided a robust and frequently cited legal precedent for similar arrangements elsewhere. Moreover, in 1971, at Trudeau's impetus, Canada became the first country to legislatively endorse multiculturalism and establish a ministry so named. Thus the long-enshrined primacy of Anglophone Canada faded away in a country that became multilingual as well as bilingual (as Trudeau himself hoped). The change is mirrored in the origins of Canada's governors-generals, once the British Crown's exalted surrogates and presently the symbolic head of state. The first seventeen incumbents included five earls, four barons, three marquesses, two viscounts, and two dukes. Since 1978, Canadian-chosen incumbents include the Haitian-born Michaëlle Jean, Hong Kong–born Adrienne Clarkson, and various males of French and Ukrainian descent.

Moreover, as the Canadian political philosopher Will Kymlicka points out, Canada more than a century ago began granting territorial autonomy and language rights to substate national groups. Ever since, other democracies with sizable minorities have moved in the same direction. In his reckoning, "The list includes the adoption of autonomy for the Swedish-speaking Aaland Islands in Finland after World War I, autonomy for South Tyrol and Puerto Rico after World War II, federal autonomy for Catalonia and the Basque Country in the 1970's, for Flanders in the 1980's, and most recently devolution for Scotland and Wales in the 1990's." Yet little of this commonly known.

LIFTING THE LAMP ON IMMIGRATION

Not only does peaceful autonomy fail to register on the world's consciousness, the same is true regarding the benefits of immigration. Every burst of violence linked directly or indirectly to minority ethnic communities, registers instantly on television news or in the blogosphere.

Yet there is both a hunger and a need for recognizing the role of immigrants in North America. The hunger is confirmed by the popular response to the Ellis Island Immigration Museum; since its doors opened in 1990, 700,000 names of arriving ancestors have been recorded on a Wall of Honor, said to be the world's longest list. Spurred by its success, Canada has opened three similar museums, and France recently inaugurated its own controversial version, as described in an earlier chapter.

There is also a need to counter the stereotype of newcomers as underclass wastrels seeking welfare benefits. How many Canadians, for example, realize that nearly one-third of their country's wealthiest citizens are foreign born? According to a 2011 Harris survey of affluent Canadians, defined as those possessing more than $1 million in investable assets, 30 percent were born elsewhere. "These findings speak to the Canadian spirit of multiculturalism," according to Andrew Auerbach, head of Harris Private Banking. For that matter, Americans could repair their own ignorance about a neighbor normally as invisible as the undefended frontier, some 5,525 miles long, that famously divides the two countries. As with autonomous entities, it would be useful to organize a meeting of directors and senior curators of immigration museums to establish global standards of potential value in contending with external lobbying by patrons, officials, and ethnic communities.

GIVING REASON A CHANCE

The world also owes to Canada the valuable doctrine of "reasonable accommodation," devised in 2005 by a Quebec commission cochaired by the philosopher Charles Taylor and the sociologist Gérard Bouchard. Their task was to find ways of resolving potentially divisive interethnic issues without litigation. For example, a question arose in Montreal's secondary schools on permitting Sikh boys to wear a *kirpan* or dagger, as prescribed by their faith, in class. Mediators proposed a reasonable accommodation—that teenagers could bring a *kirpan* measuring a few inches if securely sewn within their trousers. With similar flexibility, the Royal Canadian Mounted Police modified rules to allow Sikhs to wear a turban rather than the traditional trademark headgear. However, when such issues go to court, resistance hardens. Canada's Supreme Court ruled in 2006 that the Sikh *kirpan* was a religious symbol, not a weapon. This did not persuade security workers at the Quebec National Assembly, and in 2011 their ban on *kirpans* was upheld in a 113–0 vote. Speaking for the assembly was Louise Beaudoin of Parti Québécois, who explained that multiculturalism was a Canadian and not a Quebec value, while her colleagues cited local polls showing 95 percent support for the ban. All the more reason to anticipate by mediation rather than by legislation disputes involving dress codes and religious holidays.

THE POWER OF MULTIPLES

Cities throughout North America have found that binary ethnic quarrels fester more readily than disputes involving multiple minority communities, for a practical reason. Multiples encourage forming coalitions, which in its nature requires compromise. With exceptions, the most persistent civil conflicts occur when two ethnic groups contest the same land: Israelis and Palestinians, Northern Ireland's Protestants and Catholics, Sri Lankan Buddhists and Hindus, Cypriot Greeks and Turks, and so forth. But these disputes tend to fade when antagonists merge into a more diverse setting; hence the paradox that otherwise quarreling Indians, Pakistanis, Sri Lankans, and Bengalis coexist civilly along with a dozen other immigrant communities in Queens, New York. Hence as well the benefits of Canada's Multiculturalism Day, celebrated on June 27. On that day in 2011, the Vancouver Public Library hosted a festival that featured Brazilian samba, First Nation (i.e., Native American) storytelling, Cantonese opera, Japanese theater, and Persian music. Where multiples seemingly cannot live peacefully together (as in Lebanon, former Yugoslavia, and Afghanistan) there is usually a good reason, namely that neighboring states intervene to support allied groups, thereby fueling a protracted proxy conflict.

———

TAKEN TOGETHER, these are some of the reasons why President Barack Obama spoke not just for the United States but for all North America in this passage of his 2009 inaugural address:

For we know that our patchwork heritage is a strength, not a weakness. We are a nation of Christians and Muslims, Jews and Hindus—and non-believers. We are shaped by every language and culture, drawn from every end of the Earth; and because we have tasted the bitter swill of civil war and segregation, and emerged from that dark chapter stronger and more united, we cannot help but believe that the old hatreds shall someday pass; that lines of the tribe shall soon dissolve; that as the world grows smaller, our common humanity shall reveal itself, and that America must play its role in ushering in a new era of peace.

Wise and healing words, worth remembering when one is told that one or another immigrant group is somehow different and more sinister than all its once-demonized predecessors. Or on being informed that instead of providing a path to legal citizenship for undocumented Hispanics, they should be kept in purgatory until their deserved expulsion. We prefer the contrary spirit of the popular historian David McCullough, who replied in a July 2011 television interview when asked about the tempest-tossed who have resettled on these shores: "That's who we are—thank goodness!"

EPILOGUE

THE FUTURE OF US ALL

Opening, as we do, an asylum for strangers from every portion of the earth, we should receive all with impartiality. It should be our pride to exhibit an example of one nation, at least, destitute of national antipathies and exercising not merely overt acts of hospitality, but those more rare and noble courtesies which spring from liberality of opinion.

—WASHINGTON IRVING, *THE SKETCH BOOK* (1819)

NOW IMAGINE THAT in 1819 Washington Irving had fallen into a deep sleep (like his invented character, Rip Van Winkle) only to awaken in 2012. What might he make of today's disordered world? It's an interesting conjecture. Irving was America's original all-purpose, stand-alone author of international repute. Haphazardly schooled, he became fluent in many genres: fiction, history, biography, travel sketches, essays, and parodies (e.g., his *History of New York*, purportedly written by a nonexistent Diedrich Knickerbocker). In the term's best sense, Irving was worldly. On a frugal budget, he explored much of Europe; visited Walter Scott at Abbotsford; flirted with recently widowed Mary Shelley; and befriended John Murray II, his and England's leading publisher. Prior to his death at seventy-six in 1859, he fittingly served as US envoy in Madrid. It was an apt posting since Irving was not only the biographer of Columbus, he was also the first American writer to recover the glories of Moorish Spain. His *Tales of the Alhambra*

(1829) put Granada's then-crumbling palace on the map, and energized its restoration. (Granada would return the favor in 2009 with an elaborate exhibition in his honor.)

From today's perspective, Washington Irving is of unexpected relevance to our subject, for three reasons. First, unusual in his time, Irving delved seriously into the history of Islam, and in doing so countered the cartoon stereotypes of murderous Muslims. Second, long before Madison Avenue existed, he confirmed the power of branding as a mortar of civic pride, notably in New York City. Third, Irving's own character illustrates the salient role of *attitude* as contrasted with specific policy measures in fostering interethnic civility; he continuously showed a decent respect, salted with humor, for opinions and cultures that differed from his own. In that sense, were he to awaken in 2012, Washington Irving could justly claim to be America's half-forgotten prophet of today's pluralist nation.

———

IRVING'S DECENT RESPECT is evident in his path-breaking, almost wholly unread, two-volume *Mahomet and His Successors*, published in 1848 to 1849, a work notable for its judicious tone concerning Islam. For example, he pairs the Koran's perplexing "maze of controversial doctrines" concerning the divinity of Jesus with comparable disputes among early Christians. Irving (whose father was a Scots-born Presbyterian) carefully details the "jarring sects" that embroiled his own religion in its formative centuries, viz., the Arians, Sabellians, Monophysites, Eutychians, Jacobites, Mariamites, Collyridians, Nazarenes, Ebionites, Gnostics, Maronites, Corinthians, Docetes, Carpocrastians, Basilidians, and Valentinians. "It is sufficient to glance at these dissensions," Irving comments, "which we have not arranged in chronological order, but which convulsed the early Christian church, and continued to prevail in the era of Mahomet, to acquit him of any charge of conscious blasphemy in the opinions he inculcated concerning the nature and mission of our Saviour."

In the same spirit, he rejects as an "important mistake" the belief that Islam denies souls to the female sex and excludes them from paradise. This error arises, he writes, from the Prophet's omitting the enjoyment of sex by females in paradise "while he details those of his own sex with the minuteness of a voluptuary." Irving cites the beatification of virtuous females in the Koran's 56th Sura to acquit Mohammed of vulgar chauvinism. Moreover, Irving finds no basis in the Koran for its supposed prohibition of "making likenesses of any living thing." Instead, the words regarding image making "seem merely an echo of the second commandment, held sacred by Jews and Christians."

As fair-mindedly, he finds that the Prophet, though not "a gross and impious imposter that some have represented him," was very much "a creature of impulse and excitement, and very much at the mercy of circumstances." Or, in another characterization, he attributes to Mohammed "a quick apprehension, a retentive memory, a vivid imagination, and inventive genius." Irving's portrait of the Prophet as spiritual leader and secular warlord was mainly drawn from German-language accounts, which he acknowledges.

By contrast, Irving's description of Moorish Spain glows with the immediacy of his own direct encounter with its surviving monuments. "It is impossible," he writes in *Tales of the Alhambra,* "to travel about Andalusia and not imbibe a friendly feeling for these Moors. They deserved this beautiful country. They won it bravely; they enjoyed it generously and kindly. No lover delighted more to cherish and adorn a mistress, to heighten and illustrate her charms, and to vindicate and defend her, than did the Moors to embellish, enrich, elevate and defend their beloved Spain."

Indeed, Irving continues, the Islamic conquest "brought a higher civilization, and a nobler style of thinking, into Gothic Spain." Wherever Arabs secured a seat of power, he writes, "it became a rallying place for the learned and ingenious; and they softened and refined the people whom they conquered." Hence, "The original ground for hostility, a difference of faith, gradually lost its rancor. Even in temporary truces of sanguinary wars, the warriors who had recently striven together in the deadly conflicts of the field, laid aside their animosity, met at tournaments, jousts, and other military festivities, and exchanged the courtesies of gentle and generous spirits. Thus the opposite races became frequently mingled together in peaceful intercourse."

Too romantic? So claim later critics, who note that this supposed idyll ended with the expulsion or enforced conversion of Muslims and Jews, as policed in the sixteenth century by the implacable Spanish Inquisition. Indeed, as the Yale legal scholar Amy Chua points out, even in more tolerant times both Muslims and Jews were required to wear identifying badges, and intermarriage with Christians was punishable by imprisonment, torture, and, by law, even execution. Nonetheless, Chua writes in *Day of Empire* (2007), what matters is *relative* tolerance, since "Spain was for most of the fourteenth and fifteenth century the best place—sometimes the only place—for non-Christians to live and prosper in western Europe. Many of Spain's Muslims benefited from special treaties, granting them the right to practice their own religion and to be governed by their own laws." As for Spanish Jews, prior to their expulsion in 1492, many flourished as skilled artisans, others were landowners and financiers, and some became court scholars and physicians.

Moreover, Chua continues in her incisive survey of global empires, "The benefits Spain reaped from relative tolerance were vital to its territorial expansion and imperial rise. Besides the intangible rewards of cultural and intellectual invigoration, Spain gained two essential advantages from its non-Christian populations: manpower and money." Spain's subsequent turn to intolerance, in her view, inflicted catastrophic costs on its sprawling empire, so much so that by 1640 it had become a declining power on the brink of collapse. While it is by no means clear that a tolerant Spain could have become a "hyperpower," Chua writes, "there is no question that imperial Spain's intolerance stymied its ascent and precipitated its downward spiral."

This is surely a relevant page of history for today's hyperpower (a term signifying global dominance applied, half admiringly, to the United States by Hubert Vedrine, a former French foreign minister). In Chua's view, the master key to America's ascent has been its history as a nation of immigrants. "Inside its borders," in her synthesis, "the United States has been uniquely successful in creating an ethnically and religiously neutral political identity capable of uniting as Americans individuals of all backgrounds from every corner of the world."

Chua's own biography mirrors this hypothesis. Her ethnically Chinese parents migrated to America from the Philippines (formerly a

Spanish colony prior to its annexation by the United States). Growing up Roman Catholic in the Midwest (where she carried Chinese food in a thermos to school), she later attended Harvard and married Jed Rubenfeld, also a professor at Yale Law School, who is Jewish. Still, her mind-opening books on diversity were barely known to the general public until her provocative, *Battle Hymn of a Tiger Mother* (2011) became a best seller and talk-show topic. That, too, is the American way.

While our rediscovery of Irving was under way in summer 2011, a self-described Norwegian "Christian crusader" slaughtered nearly eighty civilians in Oslo, having just posted online a garrulous manifesto notable for its paranoid ignorance about Islam. The massacre occurred as Western diplomats, spy services, and academic specialists struggled to make sense of popular uprisings in the Middle East, whose contagious spread hardly any of them anticipated. After the "Arab Spring" had gathered momentum, US Navy Seals tracked down and then executed Osama bin Laden in his hideaway at Abbottabad, site of Pakistan's equivalent of West Point. The supposedly devout soldier of Islam who provoked a "war on terror" proved to be a disheveled old man gazing at a television screen, the essence of Hannah Arendt's banality of evil. When later that year, Britain reeled as riots in London spread to outlying cities, officials and media analysts were at a loss to detect a unifying motive, especially any linked to Islamic minorities. It was a bad season for ethnic clichés.

———

IN ANOTHER RESPECT, Irving also opened doors. He anticipated the potency of branding; that is, the notion that a word or an image can provide the intangible glue that binds citizens and/or consumers together. In 1807, Irving introduced "Gotham," ever since a byword for New York, inspired by a proverbial village in Robin Hood country known for the cleverness of its inhabitants (its residents feigned insanity to avoid taxes). Far more penetrating was the word "Knickerbocker," inspired by Irving's imagined author of his breeches-down history of Dutch New York.

In prefacing a new edition of his supposed history in 1848, the flesh-and-blood author found that his phantom double had become "a household word" that gave "the home stamp to everything recommended for popular acceptation." He listed a score of Knickerbocker societies, insurance companies, steamboats, omnibuses, pickles, and bread. Moreover, he added, "when I find New Yorkers of Dutch descent priding themselves on being 'genuine Knickerbockers,' I please myself with the persuasion that I have struck the right chord." A century later, the Manhattan telephone directory posted no fewer than a hundred entries under "Knickerbocker," including an elite club, a broadcasting company, a hat shop, a tearoom, and the Knickerbocker Demolition Company. Topping up the pudding, in 1950 the city's just-formed professional basketball team adopted the same name, shortened to "Knicks," as inscribed on the uniforms of its visibly multiracial players. The "K" word has thus added authenticity and local pride to whatever Gothamites are doing, saying, or selling.

Still, it was during the 1966 to 1973 mayoralty of John Vliet Lindsay, a liberal Republican turned Democrat, that branding escalated. In those years, New York was beset by transit strikes, hard-hat riots, feminist sit-ins, public school turmoil, and power blackouts. To burnish the city's image, the city's Convention and Visitors Bureau in 1971 hit upon a fresh symbol: the Big Apple. Originating as racetrack slang, the phrase had its print debut during the 1920s in columns by a sportswriter, John FitzGerald, and was later taken up by migratory jazz musicians. Nowadays the phrase is universally recognized (a 2011 query on Google generated 69 million results) and has inspired a host of copycats (Big Apricot, Peach, Orange, Lime, Mango, etc.). FitzGerald himself was memorialized in 1997, when the New York City Council designated 54th Street and Broadway, his home base, as "Big Apple Corner."

As we found in our travels, multicultural societies everywhere benefit from such branding. Thus India's State of Kerala was reborn in the 1990s as "God's Own Country;" Sydney is visually wedded to its emblematic opera house; and Kazan, the capital of the Russian Republic of Tatarstan, has its iconic twinned cathedral and mosque in its Kremlin to serve as a matrix. Contrariwise, after riots broke out in Paris suburbs in 2005, surveys determined that immigrant families in the *banlieues* did not consider themselves Parisians, whereas their nonviolent, mostly Islamic counterparts in Marseille identified strongly with their city; its neighborhoods; and its soccer team, Olympique de Marseille. In New York, not only does the borough of Queens "embrace diversity" in subway posters, but Helen Marshall, its elected president and an Afro-Caribbean American, routinely presents visitors with a button reading "Visit Queens—See the World." Branding is useful, cost free, and as venerable as Cross, Crescent, and Star of David.

Washington Irving proved prescient in a related urban respect: as an advocate of free public libraries. America's earliest libraries were membership only, such as the New York Society Library, founded in 1754 (and still thriving) on New York's upper East Side, of which Irving was a trustee. He was also a friend and counselor of America's richest entrepreneur, the German-born fur-trader turned financier John Jacob Astor. When Astor died in 1848, his will earmarked $400,000 for the establishment of a free reference library, and Irving was named as executor. Irving thus oversaw the creation of the Astor Library, was elected as its president, and presided in 1854 when its new building and 80,000 books were opened to the public. (The structure still stands on Lafayette Street near Astor Place, and nowadays is home of the Joseph Papp Public Theater.) Astor's bequest was followed by the projected creation of another free library, funded by a $2.1 million trust bequeathed by former New York Governor Samuel J. Tilden, and by the donation to the city of James Lennox's rare book collection. In 1895, via an inspired bargain, the Astor and Lennox libraries were merged with the Tilden Trust to create the New York Public Library. As important, in 1901 the Scottish-born industrialist Andrew Carnegie sowed $5.2 million to seed branch libraries in all five New York boroughs (Queens and Brooklyn benefited, but chose to operate their own already independent library systems).

No benefaction proved more beneficial in a city filled with dazed immigrants than providing foreign-language books and English-language instruction, without charge. When the New York Public Library's Beaux Arts palace had its debut on Fifth Avenue in 1911, the first request posted by curious patrons thronging opening day was for an obscure Russian-language book by one N. I. Grot, a critique of the ethical ideas of Tolstoy and Nietzsche. The slip was filed at 9:08, and the book delivered within six minutes (or so the NYPL website states).

Indeed, regarding libraries, Americans can with justice claim bragging rights. Those of us who have grappled with European central and academic libraries (especially in France and Germany) can attest to the user-friendly virtues of their counterparts in the United States. (In Berlin, tellingly, no library is more popular among Germans than the Amerika-Gedenk-Bibliothek with its open shelves, made possible by a US gift during the Cold War.) During our own travels, we made a point of visiting public libraries, and found none with an outreach program comparable to those in Queens. The borough's branches shelve more foreign-language books than any library system in America, or probably anywhere—not just printed books, but videos, DVDs, and even foreign comics, plus a staff competent to offer advice on learning English, deciphering computer software, filing tax forms, writing résumés, and seeking US citizenship.

In America's straitened times, two bits of good news: (1) the various Queens libraries are establishing links with diverse communities across the world, and (2) the New York City Council in 2011 restored $23 million in budget cuts originally proposed for all public libraries; this followed a deluge of petitions and postcards from users, especially in Queens. It was said to be the largest budget restoration in memory, and it meant that all the city's libraries could avoid disabling cutbacks in staff and opening hours—at least until the next budget crunch.

———

STILL, SEEN FROM today's vantage, Washington Irving's most compelling trait was his *attitude* toward peoples his contemporaries scorned as savages, heretics, and zealots. In this he proved a true American disciple of the Enlightenment. Take, for example, his discussion of Native Americans. In two extended essays in *The Sketch Book*, Irving dissented from prevailing prejudices. "It has been the lot of the unfortunate aborigines of America," he wrote in the first essay,

> to be doubly wronged by the white men. They have been dispossessed
> of their hereditary possessions by mercenary and frequently wanton
> warfare; and their characters have been traduced by bigoted and inter-
> ested writers. The colonist has often treated them like beasts of the

forest; and the author has endeavored to justify him in his outrages. The former found it easier to exterminate than to civilize; the latter to vilify than discriminate. The appellation of savage and pagan were deemed sufficient to sanction the hostilities of both; and thus the poor wanderers of the forest were persecuted and defamed, not because they were guilty, but because they were ignorant.

Irving's next paragraph deserves full quotation:

The rights of the savage have seldom been properly appreciated or respected by the white man. In peace he has often been the dupe of artful traffic; in war he has been regarded as a ferocious animal, whose life or death was a question of mere precaution and convenience. Man is cruelly wasteful of life when his own safety is endangered, and he is sheltered by impunity; and little mercy is to be expected from him when he feels the sting of the reptile and is conscious of the power to destroy. *The same prejudices which were indulged thus early, exists in common circulation today.* (Our italics.)

———

IN ALL THESE ACCOUNTS, America's first literary lion disclosed a willingness to study, listen, and empathize before handing down indictments of suspect Muslims in Moorish Andalusia, or of heathen aborigines wandering in New England forests. Always he avoided strident polemics and when possible, added a self-mocking satiric dig. His merits in the latter department were evident in the mock letters purportedly written from New York in 1807 by Mustapha Rub-a-Dub Keli Khan to his friend Asem, chief slave driver to the Bashaw of Tripoli. All nine letters appeared in *Salmagundi,* an irregular Gotham periodical consisting of "whim-whams" concocted by Irving and his friends, whose aim was to "instruct the young, reform the old, correct the town, and castigate the age." The journal was a precursor of *The New Yorker* with a splash of *Mad* magazine; it survived for thirteen months until its demise in early 1808.

Mustapha was said to be the captain of an Arab ketch taken prisoner in New York during hostilities between the United States and the

Barbary pirates, America's first collision with the Islamic Middle East, indelibly recalled as "the shores of Tripoli." In Irving's telling, Mustapha is astonished to discover that Americans deem themselves the world's most pacific nation. "The simple truth of the matter," he writes to his slave driver friend Asem, "is that these people are totally ignorant of their true character; for according to the best of my observation, they are the most warlike." And how so? "To let thee know at once into a secret, which is unknown to these people themselves, their government is pure unadulterated LOGOCRACY or *government of words.* The whole nation does everything *viva voce,* or by word of mouth, and in this manner is one of the most military nations in existence. Every man who has, what is called here, the *gift of gab,* that is a plentiful stock of verbosity, becomes a soldier outright."

And who in particular foments these brawls? Mustapha claims they are "editors or SLANG-WHANGERS" who exist in every town and village, and fire an unceasing barrage of words. Not content with advising President Thomas Jefferson, "Every now and then, a slang-whanger, who has a longer head, or rather a *longer tongue* than the rest, will discharge a shot quite across the ocean, leveled at the head of the Emperor of France, the King of England; or (wouldst thou believe it, oh, Asem!) even at his sublime highness the Bashaw of Tripoli! These long pieces are loaded with a single ball or language, [such] as tyrant! usurper! robber! tyger! monster!" Then the slam-whanger, having fired his shot, "struts about with great self-congratulation, chuckling at the prodigious bustle he must have occasioned, and seems to ask every stranger, 'Well, sir, what do they think of me in Europe?'"

Mustapha also thus reports on America's newborn capital, Washington, DC:

> But in nothing is the verbose nature of this government more evident, than in its grand national divan, or congress, where the laws are framed; this is a blustering, windy assembly where everything is carried by noise, tumult and debate; for thou must know, that the members of this assembly do not meet together to find out wisdom in the multitude of counselors, but to wrangle, call each other hard names and hear *themselves talk.* When the congress opens, the Bashaw first

sends them a long message (i.e., a huge mass of words—*vox et preterra nihi*) all meaning nothing; because it only tells them what they perfectly know already.

Next follows "all talk and no cider," signifying that "This vast empire, therefore, may be compared to nothing more or less than a mighty windmill, and the orators, and the chatterers, and the slang-whangers, are the breezes that put it in motion."

Himself a moderate Federalist, Irving then takes aim at President Jefferson: "As to his highness, the present Bashaw, who is at the very top of the logocracy, never was a dignitary better qualified for his station. He is a man of superlative ventosity, and comparable to nothing but a huge bladder of *wind*. He talks of vanquishing all opposition by the force of reason and philosophy; throws his gauntlet at all the nations of the earth, and defies them to meet him—on the field of argument!"

Mustapha thus sums up the Western world as he saw it: "The infidel nations have each a special characteristic trait, by which they may be distinguished from each other—the Spaniards, for instance, may be said to *sleep* upon every affair of importance—the Italians to *fiddle* upon everything—the French to *dance* upon everything—the Germans to *smoke* upon everything—the British islanders to *eat* upon everything—and the *windy* subjects of the American logocracy to *talk* upon everything." Or so it seemed to Mustapha Rub-a-Dub Keli Khan, formerly of Tripoli, as transcribed by Irving in 1807.

Speaking in his own voice in another essay, this neglected prophet of American pluralism threw out a timeless challenge to his own fellow citizens:

What have we to do with national prejudices? They are the inveterate disease of old countries, contracted in rude and ignorant ages, when nations knew little of each other, and looked beyond their own boundaries with distrust and hostility. We, on the contrary, have sprung into national existence in an enlightened and philosophic age; when the different parts of the habitable world, and the various branches of the human family, have been indefatigably studied and made known to each other; and we forgo the advantages of our birth, if we do not shake off the national prejudices, as we would the local superstitions of the old world.

———

INSPIRED BY IRVING'S example, we conclude our survey by offering eleven guidelines for promoting civility in diverse societies. Each is distilled from our own explorations, with the preliminary caution that every society has its peculiarities and our guidelines are all subject to local circumstances.

One. Wherever feasible, choose peace rather than land, since the pains of partition and/or occupation invariably exceed the gains. Our example is Flensburg, once the epicenter of the immemorial Schleswig-Holstein dispute pitting Germany against Denmark. After World War II, having been offered the chance to retake contested territory, the Danes opted for peace—providing that the newborn German Federal Republic would fully honor the cultural rights of Danish speakers within its borderlands. Bonn agreed, and the arrangement succeeded. It formed a precedent for other pragmatic arrangements, such as ensuring linguistic rights for majority German speakers in Alto Adige, the former Austrian province awarded to Italy after World War I. If ever an Israeli-Palestinian accord is agreed upon, these precedents could prove relevant for protecting minority rights on both sides of a hopefully agreed upon frontier.

Two. Take time to make the case—economic, cultural, political—for diversity and do not leave unanswered stereotyped caricatures of currently unpopular minorities. Yes, Islam has its violent fringe, as does Christianity (vide the 2011 massacre in Oslo), and Judaism (recall the fundamentalist assassin of Israel's peace-seeking Prime Minister Yitzhak Rabin). Why is so little said about Muslim peace seekers? A case in point is Ghaffar Khan (1890–1988), a devout Muslim and pacifist whose nonviolent followers humbled the British Raj on the Northwest Frontier. Or what about Swami Vivekananda (1863–1902), the apostle of inclusive Hinduism? His memory remains fresh in India, if not in Chicago, where his 1893 address to a Parliament of Religions evoked an ovation and astonished press comments, coast to coast.

Three. Do not abjure the second passport or demonize hyphenated citizenship. In today's global village, plural citizenship is less a menace than a recognition of a new reality shaped by jet airliners, the Internet, and social media. Most migrant workers are eager to legalize their status, and to characterize opening their path to citizenship as some kind of "amnesty" makes neither legal nor moral sense. In this regard, America's successful integration of its immigrant communities surely deserves greater recognition, respect, and emulation. No better showcase exists than Queens, where for more than two centuries newcomers have arrived, thrived, and multiplied, with negligible negative results. All the world's diplomats should be given a free pass to Ellis Island, along with supporting literature on long-term benefits of diversity.

Four. Fear not the persistence of minority tongues. Different languages pose practical problems, especially in schools, but more often than not these are bogus issues puffed up by pseudo-populists. To lower the rhetorical heat, emphasize the benefits of multilingualism in a globalized economy. Given its dominance in diplomacy, commerce, science, air travel, and information technology, English in particular needs no legislative crutches. Indeed in countries like India, the prevalence of English as a subsidiary language has opened doors and minds, and it helps account for a consistently robust growth rate. Moreover, all the world's nations are in varying degrees "imagined communities," in the useful phrase of Cornell University's British-born Benedict Anderson. None of the four "commons" once deemed essential to nationhood—common ethnicity, language, territory, and religion—have in fact proved essential. The Christian West has long coped with minority languages.

As Patrick Geary writes in *The Myth of Nations* (2002), only half the population of France spoke standard French in 1900; the rest spoke Celtic, Germanic, and Romance dialects. In fact, it is arguable whether the volunteers who in 1792 marched from polyglot Marseille singing "La Marseillaise" (turning a battle song into an anthem) spoke French, a debate wittily dissected by the UCLA scholar Eugen Weber in *My France: Politics, Culture, Myth* (1991). Similarly, the Holy Roman Empire, the cradle of a reborn Germany, was three-fourths non-

German speaking, and in Bismarck's Prussia at least five other languages were spoken: Polish, Lithuanian, Estonian, Sorbish, and Dutch. As William Pfaff reminds us in *The Wrath of Nations* (1993), there has been no *English* monarch since the twelfth century; the current royal incumbents are by blood German, before that Dutch, Scottish, Welsh, and Gallic. Today's language debates are only novel to those who are ignorant or indifferent to this history.

Five. In constructing homes for new immigrants, *horizontal* appears to be more successful than *vertical*. Few modernist dogmas seem to us more problematic than the Swiss-born architect Le Corbusier's enthusiasm for high-rise apartments to shelter (among others) immigrant families. In France as elsewhere, these "projects" (as they are known everywhere) turned into hives of ethnic alienation, especially in the featureless *banlieues* that encircle Paris. By contrast, most neighborhoods in Queens consist of one-family homes amid relatively low-rise brick apartment houses, nurturing street life and identification with neighborhoods; as Andrew Hacker told us, "Nobody lives in Queens." Not surprisingly, ethnic strife and organized crime have recurrently troubled LeFrak City, a huge "project" much in the Corbusier mode. For the moment, as we have described, peace prevails in LeFrak City, partly thanks to the next item on our list.

Six. Do not underestimate the power of professional, parental, and civic associations. In Kerala, Hindus, Muslims, and Christians regularly address common problems across the same table; this proved a key ingredient in preserving social peace in a highly diverse state. Marseille Espérance is one example, the network of community boards in New York is another, of forums that bring together diverse neighbors, sometimes to the exasperation of property developers seeking approval for shopping malls, high-rise apartments, and parking lots. And public schools in Queens wisely engage parents in their PTAs, one of the springboards for Borough President Helen Marshall's political ascent— along with her service in a local community board and in public libraries (to which we now turn).

Seven. Use public libraries to give immigrant newcomers a welcoming space where not only books but DVDs are available in their mother tongue. We have showcased the libraries of Queens, where free help is available on the everyday perplexities of living in a new country with its strange ways. Let it be added that libraries can (and should) provide assistance in using computers, the devices most calculated to penetrate cultural walls. And not least, periodic book sales offer librarians the chance to weed their shelves, seek contributions, and recycle the essential building blocks of cultural literacy.

Eight. Make empowerment of women a priority, the better to erode barriers between ethnic communities, promote economic growth and smaller families, combat spousal abuse, raise health standards, and provide role models for students. We were struck by this correlation in the Indian state of Kerala, where amicable relations among Hindus, Muslims, and Christians had a solid basis in near-universal literacy but also in the recognition of gender equity. In every community we visited, we found activist feminist organizations. Yes, as Dr. Praveena Kodoth told us at the Center for Development Studies in Trivandrum, women are still underrepresented in senior political posts, but there is now a grassroots movement agitating for gender equality—and it crosses religious, caste, and political lines.

Nine. Celebrate difference of creed and culture with a calendar that records the major religious festivals and national holidays of diverse minorities. This makes educational and political sense; every office-holder knows the value of a friendly reference to a constituent's ancestral homeland or a special feast day. As to dress codes, let policymakers strive to reasonably accommodate cultural differences through consensual negotiations, in hopes of averting a noisy and sterile legislative debate on the wearing of headscarves, skullcaps, turbans, and crucifixes. Canada, for example, has led the way in "reasonable accommodation," and thus provides space in schools in which Muslim students can take part in Friday prayers. As to dress codes, agreeing to disagree may well be the only civilized approach to an admittedly fraught policy issue.

Ten. Recognize, celebrate, and elect the political leaders who actively promote diversity, be they presidents (like Tatarstan's Shaimiev), mayors (like Marseille's Gaudin), borough presidents (like Queens's Marshall), or governors (like Puerto Rico's Luis Muñoz Marin, who invented commonwealth status without ever winning his due). Human agency is an essential element in attaining Pax Ethnica.

Eleven. Do not underestimate the allure of popular culture, rap music, or sports to diminish class differences and foster a society in which someone named Barack Hussein Obama can rise to the political summit. Barring an explosion of unreason, the unleashing of our worst impulses, a true Pax Ethnica could be in every sense the future of us all.

ACKNOWLEDGMENTS

These are lean times for trade books on political subjects lacking head-line appeal. Along with other independent scholars (our preferred self-description) we could not have researched our theme without funding. Our first debt therefore is to PublicAffairs and its founder, Peter Osnos, who at the genesis encouraged us to stake out our unfamiliar terrain. Having a prospective publisher, we sought grants to help cover costs. Three foundations made our travel and research possible: the Carnegie Corporation of New York, the Gould Family Foundation and the Pulitzer Center on Crisis Reporting. We owe special thanks at the Carnegie to President Vartan Gregorian and his colleagues Patricia Rosenfield and Stephen J. DelRosso; at the Gould to its board of trustees; and at the Pulitzer Center on Crisis Reporting to Director Jon Sawyer and his associates Nathtalie Applewhite and Janeen Heath (who initiated us into the world of blogging).

As always, our researches were assisted by a pride of libraries and their staffs, notably the Butler and Lehman academic collections at Columbia University, and the New York Society Library, with its bor-rowable collection of rare nonfiction. In Connecticut, we owe thanks to the full-service Westport Public Library (which assisted us with interli-brary loans), and to its partners in Weston, Fairfield, and the Pequot Library in Southport.

Also important was the special assistance of the World Policy Insti-tute, whose director, Michele Wucker; her associate Kate Maloff; and David Andelman, editor of the *World Policy Journal,* provided not only ideas but the assistance of these versatile interns: Eleanor Morgan Albert, Elizabeth Dovell, and Melissa Bardhi. It was our practice to tape all interviews, and then to check every quotation. This trio wrestled with various tongues and accents with admirable patience and efficiency.

Seminars, conferences, and lectures at Columbia University, Barnard College, the World Policy Institute, the Carnegie Council of Ethics and International Affairs, New York University, and CUNY Graduate Center were fertile sources of ideas, as were the annual Wellfleet Conferences in Cape Cod, hosted by Robert and B. J. Lifton, where we learned much from Edwin and Patricia Matthews, Jim Skelly, Hillel Levine, and Charles Strozier (among others). Beyond this, we had the counsel of friends, among them Ted Smyth and Mary Breasted, Bruce Mazlish, Brian Urquhart, Michael Meyer and Suzanne Seggerman, Tadeusz Swietochowski, Colin Campbell and Deborah Scroggins, and Robert and Hannah Kaiser.

In all of our key destinations, we had the advice and assistance of "fixers" (journalistic argot for knowledgeable local assistants) and of friends, diplomats, and colleagues. In Flensburg, our way was opened by the German mission at the United Nations, with the help of the Bundestag veteran Karsten D. Voigt. In the city itself, our path was lit by Danish diplomats Henrik Becker-Christensen and Dr. Tove Malloy; Ewa Chylinski at the European Centre on Minority Issues; Anke Spoorendonk, the Danish representative in the Schleswig-Holstein Landtag; and her colleague Lars Erik Bethge, the party's press spokesman.

In Kerala, three seasoned observers offered vital counsel: Barbara Crossette, former *New York Times* bureau chief in India; and authors Mira Kamdar in New York and Ramachandra Guha in Bangalore. Others who helped include Kerala's Congress MP Shashi Tharoor, his assistants Praveen Ram and Jacob Joseph; Abraham George of the Shanti Bhavan Foundation; Alessandro Isola of the Global Exchange; and Suresh Kumar, who has long served as their cicerone and was our guru. Thanks also to Ajith Gopala Krishnan and our driver Prem Nidi. A special debt is owed to Roberto Toscano, then Italian ambassador to India, and his wife Francesca, for their counsel and hospitality in New Delhi. Those we met in Kerala are identified in the text.

In Tatarstan, our thanks first to Gulnara Khasanova, who helped us make our appointments, and to Vladimir Makarov, our local expeditor. Others who gave us essential advice and opened doors include Colette Shulman, Alsu Feiskhanova, Ravil and Irat Feiskhanov, and Rasik Sagitov of the World Organization of United Cities and Local

Governments. Professor Uli Schamiloglu of the University of Wisconsin-Madison led us to Professor Kate Graney of Skidmore College. We had welcome help from Ildar Agish of the US Capitallinvet Bancorp. Our American mentors included Professor Seymour Becker and his Russian-born wife Alla Zeide; both encouraged the creation of the multilingual journal *Ab Imperio,* whose editors we met in Kazan (with special thanks to Marina Mogilner). Our visit to Naberezhnye Chelny and its branch of Kazan State University was facilitated by Eduard Nazmeev and Anatoly Makarov. We valued our meetings with Culture Minister Zila Valeeva; with Rozaliya Mirgalimovna Nurgaleeva, director of Tatarstan's State Museum of Fine Arts; with Father Pitirim at the Bogoroditskii Monastery; and with Rafik M. Mukhametshin, rector of the Russian Islamic University. Our thanks also to Mariya Masyukova, the intern obtained through Columbia University's Harriman Institute, who checked our Russian-language transcripts.

In France, we owe special thanks to Deputy Loïc Bouvard, the doyen of the National Assembly, and his wife Elisabeth, who helped us find our way in the labyrinth of French politics. (Bouvard and Meyer were graduate schoolmates at Princeton.) Not only did Steven Erlanger and Nadim Audi of *The New York Times* Paris bureau furnish advice, but Scott Sayre accompanied us on a key interview. Charles Onians of Agence France-Presse was our essential partner in visiting the opaque *banlieues.* In Marseille, our guide and tutor was Sebastian Carayol, a writer and authority on popular culture. We owe thanks to Alice Hodgson for introducing us to Grégoire Georges-Picot, author and filmmaker in Marseille and to Andrew Purvis, whose *Smithsonian* article pointed the way.

In Queens, our initial obligation is to Professors Roger Sanjek and Andrew Hacker, who opened the doors. Essential advice was provided by Susie Tanenbaum, Community and Cultural Coordinator for the Queens Borough President, who mapped the political byways of the world's most diverse society. At the Elmhurst Hospital, we were assisted by Atiya N. Butler on the public relations staff. Authors and journalists who counseled us include Anne Barnard and Sam Roberts of *The New York Times*, James Michael Lisbon of *The Queens Light*, and Judith Sloan and Warren Lehrer. At the Queens Community House in Jackson

Heights we obtained useful leads from K. C. Williams, the director of adult education, and her colleague Anna Dioguardia. Thanks also to Sgt. Lizbeth Villafane, commanding officer, New Immigrant Outreach Unit, New York Police Department.

In our Manhattan neighborhood, informal supplementary sources included Alex (of Rego Park) at the Solomon Barber Shop; the corner food store managed by Paul Sing, a Punjabi; the diverse staff at Simche Cleaners; our Bangladeshi fruit seller and Jordanian news agent; and our apartment building staff (Montenegrin, Croatian, and Hispanic) and finally, to several score taxi and bus drivers, shopkeepers, druggists, waiters, and clerks who put up with our questions.

In Australia, we were welcomed and instructed by our hosts, James and Valerie Levy; obtained insights from our old friends Neville and Evelyn Maxwell; and benefited from a lengthy conversation with James Jupp, a three-star authority on immigration policies. Regarding Canada, Director of Communications Alain Olivier at the Quebec Government Office in New York supplied valuable links.

Our text was efficiently shepherded into print at PublicAffairs by Brandon Proia and Lindsay Jones, and by Peter Osnos and Susan Weinberg. But the authors alone are responsible for any surviving errors of facts or misjudgments in the foregoing pages.

—Karl E. Meyer and *Shareen Blair Brysac*

NOTES ON SOURCES

Our book could not have been attempted save for the landfill of books, papers, and articles dealing with its chosen theme. Elsewhere we acknowledge our debt to the many individuals who assisted our quest, to our online allies and the various conferences that enabled us to hear and meet academic specialists. What follows therefore is solely a record of published sources that we have gratefully mined. Where feasible, we have sought in our chapters to identify the works and authors we cite; we here append the full titles and comments on our principal sources. Some works are so specialized they may be hard find even in major libraries. We thus append, where appropriate, key Internet sites. We hope that our citations will prompt curious readers to excavate deeper into a rich seam of pertinent scholarship.

PROLOGUE: SANE OASES IN A RABID WORLD

In the first paragraph, the "exasperated observer" we quote was Oxford's witty connoisseur of human follies, Sir Isaiah Berlin. Concerning ongoing civil strife, a good overview is *Ethnic Groups in Conflict* (Berkeley: University of California Press, 2000), the revised edition of a seminal analytic survey by the Duke University political scientist, Donald L. Horowitz. See also Monica Duffy Toft, *The Geography of Ethnic Violence* (Princeton: University Press, 2003); Edwin N. Wilmsen and Patrick McAllister, eds., *The Politics of Difference* (Chicago: University Press, 1996), and for the views of a seasoned observer, William R. Polk, *Violent Politics: A History of Insurgency, Terrorism and Guerrilla War* (New York: HarperCollins, 2007).

In re the Arab Spring, the prescient report in *The Economist*, "The Autumn of the Patriarchs," appeared in its issue dated February 17,

2011. For a consensual academic account of Arab nationalism, pre-Spring, see the essays collected in *Rethinking Nationalism in the Arab Middle East* (New York: Columbia University Press, 1997), edited by James Jankowski and Israel Gershoni. On Islam in Europe, for views from the dark side, see (from a long list) Bruce Bawer, *While Europe Slept: How Radical Islam Is Destroying the West from Within* (New York: Doubleday, 2006); Efraim Karsh, *Islamic Imperialism* (New Haven: Yale University Press, 2006); and for a nuanced view, Jocelyn Cesari, *When Islam and Democracy Meet: Muslims in Europe and the United States* (New York: Global Publishing/St. Martin's Press, 2004).

For an influential early study of nationalism, see Hans Kohn, *The Idea of Nationalism* (New York: Macmillan, 1948), which staked out a field tilled thereafter by many successors, notably Ernest Gellner, *Nations and Nationalism* (Oxford: Blackwell, 1983); E. J. Hobsbawm, *Nations and Nationalism Since 1780* (Cambridge, UK: University Press, rev. ed., 1990); Anthony D. Smith, *National Identity* (Reno: University of Nevada Press, 1993); and for a longer view, Patrick J. Geary, *The Myth of Nations: The Medieval Origins of Europe* (Princeton: University Press, 2002). A recent and useful symposium is *The Nation-State Question* (Princeton: University Press, 2003), edited by T.V. Paul, G. John Ikenberry, and John A. Hall.

A past observer deserving more attention is Walter Lippmann, whose *The Stakes of Diplomacy* (New York: Holt, 1915) we quote. George Kennan's reflections on nationalism appear in *Around the Cragged Hill: A Personal and Political Philosophy* (New York: Norton, 1993). Daniel Patrick Moynihan's *Pandaemonium: Ethnicity in International Politics* (New York: Oxford University Press, 1993) is as timely as the morning news. Michael Mandelbaum's analysis of nationalism is from *The Ideas That Conquered the World* (New York: PublicAffairs, 2002). For a detailed examination of alternative paths, see Tufts University's Hurst Hannum, *Autonomy, Sovereignty and Self-Determination* (Philadelphia: University of Pennsylvania Press, 1992). See also Seamus Dunn and T. G. Fraser, eds., *Europe and Ethnicity: World War I and Contemporary Ethnic Conflict* (London: Rutledge, 1996). We owe the Bakunin quotation to the veteran British correspondent David Hirst's *Beware of Small States* (New York: Nation Books, 2010). A learned synthesis to which we are indebted in many chapters is A. J. P. Taylor's

The Struggle for Mastery in Europe 1848–1918 (Oxford: University Press, 1954). On the frustrations of partition, a basic text is Robert Schaeffer's *Warpaths: The Politics of Partition* (New York: Hill and Wang, 1990). Our quotation by Andrew Dickson White is from *Seven Great Statesman: In the Warfare of Humanity with Unreason* (New York: The Century Company, 1910), in his chapter on Bismarck. (Not just a diplomat, White was also founding president of Cornell University.)

CHAPTER 1
FLENSBURG: LAND OR PEACE?

Standard guidebooks are readily available that detail places of interest in Schleswig. For German readers, Horst-Dieter Landeck's *Flensburg: Ein Reisebegeleiter* (Boyens Buchverlag, 2006) provides an illustrated, feature-by-feature guide to Flensburg and its environs. The major source for the contemporary backstory (in English) is *Living Together: The Minorities in the German-Danish Border Regions,* published by the European Centre for Minority Issues in Flensburg (2001), edited by Andrea Teebken and Eva Maria Christiansen. Its appendix reprints the texts of the Bonn-Copenhagen Declarations of April 1, 1955, with its key clauses relating to the Danish minority inhabiting the German state of Schleswig. The literature on "The Duchies" is immense. Columbia University's library catalogue has 774 entries as of July 2011. For the Schleswig-Holstein Question, as viewed by contemporaries, see the *Encyclopedia Britannica* (1910), 11th ed., vol. 24, p. 335ff.

On Bismarck and the rise of German nationalism, our sources include A. J. P. Taylor's *The Struggle for Mastery of Europe*, cited above, and his *Bismarck: The Man and Statesman* (New York: Knopf, 1955). Theodor Herzl's comment on nationalism is quoted in Amos Elon, *Herzl* (New York: Holt, Rinehart, 1975). For a panoramic view, we are indebted to Princeton's Gordon Craig's *Germany: 1866–1945* (New York: Oxford University Press, 1978) and *The Germans* (New York: Putnam, 1982). For an influential German biography of the chancellor, see Emil Ludwig, *Bismarck: The Story of a Fighter* (New York: Blue Ribbon Books, 1931). An essential supplement is Fritz Stern's path-breaking *Gold and Iron: Bismarck, Bleichröder and the Building of the German*

Empire (New York: Knopf, 1977). As we were going to press, Jonathan Streinberg's *Bismarck: A Life* (New York: Oxford University Press, 2011) appeared, which we have now read with appreciation, especially since Steinberg has also written *Why Switzerland?* (Cambridge, UK: University Press, 1996), the best book we know of on Swiss exceptionalism.

For the events of 1848, we are indebted to Raymond Postgate, *Story of a Year: 1848* (New York: Oxford University Press, 1956) and Franz Mehring, *Karl Marx: The Story of His Life* (New York: Covici, Friede, 1935), plus the new and lively *Karl Marx: A Life* (New York: Norton, 2001) by Francis Wheen. On Bismarck's encounter with Disraeli, see the standard biography: W. F. Monypenny and G. E. Buckle, *The Life of Benjamin Disraeli* (London: John Murray, 1929), vol.2. On early-day war correspondents and the 1864 Danish-Prussian War, see *The History of The Times: The Tradition Established 1841–1884* (London: Printing House Square, 1939); and Philip Knightley, *The First Casualty* (New York: Harcourt, Brace, 1975). The frontline accounts we quote are from Edward V. Dicey, *The Battle of 1864* (London: Tinsley, 1866) and Antonio Gallenga, *The Invasion of Denmark* (London: Bentley 1866). On Queen Victoria and Palmerston, we consulted (among others) Jasper Ridley, *Lord Palmerston* (New York: Dutton, 1971) and Brian Connell, *Regina vs. Palmerston* (New York: Doubleday, 1961). Cobden's comment on the Danish-Prussian War is in John Morley, *Life of Richard Cobden* (London: T. F. Unwin, 1910). Walter Bagehot's verdict on Bismarck is in Ruth Dudley Edwards, ed., *The Best of Bagehot* (London: Hamish Hamilton, 1993). For a pro-Danish overview, see Charles Gosch, *Denmark and Germany since 1815* (London: John Murray, 1862). On the American dimension, see Jacob A. Riis's memoir, *The Old Town* (New York: Macmillan, 1909) and the insider reflections of the diplomat Maurice Francis Egan in *Ten Years Near the German Frontier* (New York: George H. Doran, 1919).

Lord Salisbury's reflections on language rights can be found in Salisbury, Robert Cecil, *Essays by the Late Marquess of Salisbury* (London: John Murray, 1905). Egon Friedell's engrossing and too-little-known insights span three volumes: *A Cultural History of the Modern Age: The Crisis of the European Soul from the Black Death to the World War* (New York: Knopf, 1953–1954; translated by Charles Francis Atkinson); his description of Kaiser Wilhelm is in volume three. Of the many books on the Paris Peace Conference, Margaret MacMillan's stands out: *Paris 1919: Six Months That Changed the World* (New York: Random House, 2001). The map-making postcards are from Harold Nicolson, *Peacemaking 1919* (London: Constable, 1933) and Charles Seymour, *Letters from the Paris Peace Conference* (New Haven: Yale University Press, 1965), letter dated May 31, 1919. See also Robert Lansing, *Peace Negotiations: A Personal Narrative* (Boston: Houghton Mifflin, 1921). Finally, for more information on the peripatetic Flensburg Lion, consult: http://en.wikipedia.org/wiki/Flensburg_Lion.

CHAPTER 2
KERALA: GODS' OWN COUNTRY

Two basic books from which we have drawn extensively are B. N. Ghosh and Padmaja D. Namboodiri, eds., *The Economy of Kerala: Yesterday, Today and Tomorrow* (New Delhi: Serials Publication, 2009), a warehouse of current social and economic data by a dozen Indian scholars; and Robin Jeffrey, *Politics, Women and Well-Being: How Kerala Became a "Model"* (New Delhi: Oxford University Press, 1993), by an Australian political scientist, especially valuable on political history. Two long-standing American students of Kerala, Richard Franke and Barbara H. Chasin, summarize their findings in *Radical Reform as Development in an Indian State* (Oakland, CA: Institute for Food and Development Policy, 1994). To these, an invaluable fourth work places Kerala's experience in a broader Indian context: Ashutosh Varshney, *Ethnic Conflict and Civic Life: Hindus and Muslims in India* (New Haven: Yale University Press, 2002). On Kerala's climatology, an interesting firsthand account is by the Scottish traveler Alexander Frater, whose title describes his strenuous feat: *Chasing the Monsoon* (London: Penguin Books, 1991). Concerning the particular question of migrant workers, see *Migration, Remittances and Employment: Short-Term Trends and Long-Term Implications* (Kerala: Centre for Development Studies, 2007), by K. C. Zachariah and S. Irudaya Rajan.

On Vasco Da Gama's explosive encounter with the Spice Coast, we turned for an overview to Richard Hall, *Empires of the Monsoon: A*

History of the Indian Ocean and Its Invaders (London: HarperCollins, 1996), then to Francois Belloc, *Unknown Lands: Log Books of the Great Explorers* (Woodstock, NY: Overlook Press, 2000). The quoted lines from *The Lusiads* are from Landeg White's translation of canto two, verse fifty (New York: Oxford University Press, 1997). Charles Boxer's *The Portuguese Seaborne Empire: 1415–1825* (New York: Knopf, 1969) is a fine standard account by a seasoned British Asia hand. For an interesting current Indian interpretation, see Sanjay Subrahmayam, *The Legend of Vasco Da Gama* (Cambridge, UK: University Press, 1997).

We especially benefited from *India After Gandhi: The History of the World's Largest Democracy* (New York: Ecco/Harper Collins, 2007) by Ramachandra Guha, an independent-minded Bangalore-based author who judicially revisits most major past disputes. Suketu Mehta's *Maximum City: Bombay Lost and Found* (New York: Knopf, 2004) can be bracketed with William Dalrymple, *The Age of Kali: Indian Travels and Encounters* (London: Harper Collins, 1998) as enlightening travel companions (see especially Dalrymple's description of the migratory forest masques of Kannur). Works expressly relevant to our theme include the French scholar Christophe Jaffrelot's *The Hindu Nationalist Movement in India* (New York: Columbia University Press, 1996); and by the same author, *Religion, Caste and Politics in India* (New Delhi: Primus Books, 2020); and (co-edited with Thomas B. Hansen), *The BJP and the Compulsions of Politics in India* (New York: Oxford University Press, 2001); the Mumbai academic Ram Puniyani's *Communal Politics: Facts Versus Myths* (New Delhi: Sage Publications, 2003), and the novelist Arundhati Roy's *The God of Small Things* (New York: Random House, 1997), based on her Kerala childhood; on the genesis of Hindu nationalism, see also *Rashtriva Swayamsewak Sangh*, by D. R. Goyal (New Delhi: Rādhā Krishna [Prakashan], 2000).

On Kerala's Muslim past, we serendipitously acquired in Calicut *The Ali Rajas of Cannanore* (Calicut: University of Calicut Press, 2002), with its appended key documents and invaluable glossary. Shashi Tharoor, now a Kerala Congress MP after an eventful career at the United Nations, assesses India's rise as an Asian power in *The Elephant, the Tiger and the Cellphone* (New York: Arcade Publishers, 2007). See also Mira Kamdar's *Planet India: The Turbulent Rise of the Largest Democracy and the Future of Our World* (New York: Scribners, 2007). New York–based Gita Mehta's witty reportage affords a welcome leaven to heavier works, an example being *Snakes and Ladders: Glimpses of Modern India* (New York: Doubleday, 1997).

Treatises on Hinduism are as multifaceted as the gods they describe. The polymath American academic Wendy Doniger's *The Hindus: An Alternative History* (New York: Penguin Press, 2009), a friendly scholarly appreciation, was unfairly attacked as blasphemous, notably by expatriate Indians who flooded the Internet with hate e-mails whenever her book was favorably reviewed (while speaking at a forum in London, an egg was heaved at her by an agitated non-admirer). Also controversial is *The Clash Within: Democracy, Religious Violence and India's Future* (Cambridge, MA: Harvard University Press, 2007) by Martha C. Nussbaum, an astute legal ethicist at the University of Chicago. Hence our relief in rediscovering in Kerala the welcome and inclusive spirit of Swami Vivekananda, an abiding influence in South India and an early expositor of Vedanta in the United States as recorded by Nevedita Raghunath Bide in *Swami Vivekananda in America* (Chennai: Vivekananda Kendra Prakashan Trust, 2002). Hinduism confounds clichés. Its complexities baffled Arthur Koestler, the surgical anatomist of all ideologies; his visit to Kerala is recorded in *The Lotus and the Robot* (New York: Macmillan, 1961) and reexamined in *Arthur Koestler: The Homeless Mind* (New York: The Free Press, 1998) by David Cesarani, a British professor of modern Jewish history.

CHAPTER 3
TATARSTAN: THE CAVE OF THE CLAN BEARS

For a good overview, we commend Harvard University's Dmitry G. Gorenburg, *Minority Ethnic Mobilization in the Russian Federation* (Cambridge, UK: University Press, 2003), with its succinct analysis of post-Soviet policies on ethnicity. The pivotal role of former President Shaimiev in negotiating Tatarstan's autonomy is detailed in *The Model of Tatarstan: Under President Mintimer Shaimiev* (New York: St. Martin's Press, 1999) by Ravil Bukharaev, a veteran of the BBC Russian Service. An insider view from Kazan is provided by Raphael Khakimov, a historian and senior adviser to Shaimiev, in *Russia and Tatarstan at a Crossroads of History* (Kazan: Institute of History, 2006). Under Khakimov's editorship, his own institute and the Kazan Institute of Federalism jointly sponsored *Federalism in Russia* (Kazan: Institute of History, 2002), published with the support of the MacArthur Foundation, a fertile symposium of twenty-plus scholars—all carrying the prestigious imprimatur of the Tatarstan Academy of Sciences. A similar academic coalition produced *Tatars* (Kazan: Institute of History, 2007), edited by Marjorie Mandelstam Balzer, comprising eight learned and readable essays on the history of an endlessly interesting people.

On Tatarstan's role in the Bolshevik Revolution, we are indebted to Victor Serge, *Year One of the Russian Revolution* (New York: Holt, Rinehart, and Winston, 1972) and to William Henry Chamberlain, *The Russian Revolution* (New York: Macmillan, 1935), being a meticulous, undeservedly forgotten account by a right-wing journalist. On the final days of the Soviet Union, among many sources, we quote from David Remnick, *Resurrection: The Struggle for a New Russia* (New York: Random House, 1997) and Jack F. Matlock, *Autopsy on an Empire* (New York: Random House, 1995). On language issues in Tatarstan, see Suzanne Wertheim, *Linguistic Purism and Language Shift in Tatar* (PhD dissertation, University of California–Berkeley, 2003) and "Language Ideologies and 'Purification' of Post-Soviet Years," in *Ab Imperio* (January 2003). On sovereignty, among our principal sources are Uli Schamiloglu, "Whither Tatarstan?" in *Perspectives on Change* (Center for Post-Soviet Studies, 1992); Gulnaz Sharafutdinova, "Paradiplomacy in the Russian Region: Tartarstan's Search for Statehood," in *Europe-Asia Studies*, vol. 55, no. 4 (November–December 2007); Raphael Khakimov, "Prospects for Federalism in Russia: The View from Tatarstan," and Katherine E. Graney, "Making Russia Multicultural: Kazan at Its Millennium and Beyond," in *Problems of Post-Communism*, vol. 54, no.6 (November–December, 2007). Graney has also authored an indispensible account of Tatarstan's pursuit of sovereignty, *Of Khans and Kremlins: Tatarstan and the Future of Ethno-Federalism in Russia* (Lanham, MD: Lexington Books, 2009).

On the Murtazin trial, see Global Voices Online, http://global voicesonline.org, titled "Russia: Tatarstan Blogger Sentenced to Almost

2 years in Penal Colony." On the internal politics of Tatarstan, see Midkhat Farukshin, "The Ruling Elite of Tatarstan," in *The New Elite in Post-Communist Eastern Europe* (College Station, TX: Texas A & M University Press, 1998). For Shamiev's statement on Islam, see *Arab News* (October 29, 2008), posted at http://arabnews.com/services. On the millennium celebration at Kazan, our details are based on BBC monitoring, Channel One TV, Moscow in Russian, August 25, 2005. On Chechnya vs. Tatarstan, among our many sources we wish to cite Stephen D. Shenfield, "Tataria and Chechnya: A Comparative Study," and Timur Aliev, "Grozny 2005," by the *Chechen Society* newspaper, at http://halldor2.blogspot.com/2005/03/grozn-2005.htmly.

Like many others interested in Russia's periphery, we mourn the demise of Paul Goble's blog, *Window on Eurasia.* Finally, for thoughts on all the above, consult the quarterly journal *Ab Imperio,* published in Kazan, passim; whose founding owed much to Professor Seymour Becker of Rutgers University, a leading historian of Russia's prerevolutionary empire.

CHAPTER 4
MARSEILLE: BLACK, BLANC, *BEUR*

We are indebted first of all to Andrew Purvis, whose essay, "Marseille's Ethnic Bouillabaisse" in *Smithsonian* (December 2007) first alerted us to the city's comity and led us to key sources. Oddly, there is no English-language portrait of Marseille comparable to Robert Hughes's *Barcelona* (New York: Knopf, 1992) or to other books on kindred Mediterranean cities, such as Alexandria, Smyrna, Salonica, and Trieste. It is a gap yearning to be filled. For the most part, interviews aside, we relied on French-language accounts, specialized studies, newspaper and periodical articles, and on two invaluable reports published in 2011 by the Open Society Foundations: *Unveiling the Truth: Why 32 Muslim Women Wear the Full-Face Veil in France* (Open Society Foundations) and *Muslims in Marseille* is available online at http://www.soros.org.

Jean-Claude Izzo's Marseille trilogy (*Solea, Chourmo, Total Chaos*) has been published in lively English by Europa Editions (New York, 2005–2007). On the Vichy era, we turned (among other sources) to

Robert O. Paxton, *Vichy France: Old Guard and New Order* (New York: Columbia University Press, 1972). On various World Cups and their reverberations, we relied on numerous press accounts, including those by Anne Rehou in *Le Monde* (August 29, 2010); Marcot Gabriele in *The Times* (London: March 1, 2010); and Craig Whitney in *New York Times* (July 13, 1998). Concerning the 2005 riots, our sources included the BBC News, "Timeline: The French Riots," published at http://news.bbc.co.uk/2/hi/europe/4413964.stm, which provides a detailed chronology; and for foreign views, see Andrew Hussey, "The Paris Intifada," *Granta* (Spring 2008, issue 101); John R. Bowen, "France's Revolt," *Boston Review of Books* (January–February 2006); and Graham Robb, *Parisiens* (New York: Norton, 2010). To this we add Molly Moore's perceptive account in *The Washington Post* (November 8, 2005).

On Marseille itself, we benefited from A. J. Liebling, "The Soul of Bouillabaise Town," *The New Yorker* (October 27, 1962) and from Alain Moreau, "The Importance of Local Identity Among Teenagers of Marseille," in *Savoir Faire* (No. 5, December 2005). On World War II, our sources included *The Complete War Memoirs of Charles de Gaulle 1940–1946* (New York: Simon and Schuster, 1964); Rosemary Sullivan's spirited *Villa Air-Bel: World War II Escape and a House in Marseille* (New York: HarperCollins, 2006); and Paul Jankowski, *Communism and Collaboration: Simon Sabiani and Politics in Marseille, 1919–1944* (New Haven and London: Yale University Press, 1989). On the role of Corsica, besides the entry in the *Encylopedia Britannica* (11th edition, 1910), see *The Politics of Heroin in Southeast Asia: CIA Complicity in the Global Drug Trade*, by Alfred W. McCoy, Catherine Read, and Leonard P. Adams (New York: Harper & Row, 1972); Tim Weiner, *Legacy of Ashes: The History of the CIA* (New York: Doubleday, 2007), and Ted Morgan's revealing *A Covert Life: Jay Lovestone: Communist, Anti-Communist and Spymaster* (New York: Random House, 1999).

A basic text on Marseille's postwar politics is Cesare Mattina's, "The Politics of Clientism as a Factor in the Social and Ethnic Reconstitution of Marseille," in *Savoir Faire* (No. 5, December 2005). For the city's slang, see Philippe Blanchet and Médéric Gasquet, *Le Marseillais de Poche* (Assimil, 2004). Mayor Defferre's dueling prowess was reported by Joseph Carroll in *The Guardian* (London), April 22, 1967, and the mayor's political position as defined by Jean Lacouture is from his *De Gaulle: The Ruler 1945–1970* (New York: Norton, 1992). On France's postwar politics, among the many works from which we benefited, we single out Francis de Tarr, *The French Radical Party: From Herriot to Méndes-France* (Oxford: University Press, 1961), with an appreciative preface by Méndes-France.

Anent today's France and its complexities, we quote "The Melting Pot That Isn't," in *The Economist* (July 26, 2001); Edward Cody, "In Marseille, Unease Over the Mosque Project," *The Washington Post* (November 26, 2009); and Andre J. M. Prevos, "Postcolonial Popular Music in France: Rap Music and Hip-Hop Culture in the 1980's and 1990's," in *Global Noise: Rap and Hip-Hop Outside the USA* (Middletown CT: Wesleyan University Press, 2011). IAM's song is from the album *De la Planete Mars*, translated in Izzo, *Total Chaos,* op. cit. See also Michael Kimmelman, "In Marseille, Rap Helps Keep the Peace," *New York Times* (December 19, 2007). Concerning urbanism, we consulted (among others) Andrew Hussey, *The Secret History of Paris* (New York: Bloomsbury, 2006); and Nicholas Fox Weber, *Le Corbusier* (Cambridge MA: Harvard University Press, 2007).

On France's Algerian wars, an essential work is Alistair Horne, *A Savage War of Peace: Algeria 1954–1962* (London: Penguin Books, 1979) to which can be added Ted Morgan's *My Battle of Algiers* (New York: HarperCollins, 2005). (Morgan excavated the telling quotation from *The Times*.) See also Martin Evans and John Phillips, *Anger of the Dispossessed* (New Haven: Yale University Press, 2007). We also drew from Steve Erlanger, "Films Open French Wounds from Algeria," *New York Times* (January 4, 2011), and a Reuters report, "Sarkozy Tells Algeria: No Apology for the Past" (July 10, 2007). Regarding the immigration museum, see Michael Kimmelman, "Ready or Not, France Opens Museum on Immigration," *New York Times* (October 17, 2007) and *Guide de l'exposition permanente* (lacking an author, publisher and date.)

On the headscarf and Muslim debate, our sources include John R. Bowen, *Why the French Don't Like Headscarves* (Princeton NJ: University Press, 2007); Malise Ruthven, "The Big Muslim Problem," *New York Review of Books* (December 17, 2009); and Simon Kuper, "The

Myth of Eurabia," *Financial Times* (October 4, 2009). A basic text on the whole identity debate remains Patrick Weil, *How to be French: Nationality in the Making Since 1789* (Durham NC: Duke University Press, 2008), along with other works by the same scholar. The quotation from Joseph Roth is from *Report from a Parisian Paradise* (New York: Norton, 1990). Once again, we advise persons seeking a comprehensive account of Muslims in Marseille to consult the Open Society reports, already cited.

CHAPTER 5
QUEENS: EMBRACING DIVERSITY

For an authoritative overview of Queens, past and present, a good place to begin is Claudia Gryvatz Copquin, *Queens* (New Haven: Yale University Press, 2007), the second volume in a series describing the neighborhoods of New York, under the general editorship of Kenneth T. Jackson. It describes the borough's ninety-nine neighborhoods, complete with census data. Its compact companion is Ellen Freudenheim's *Queens* (New York: St. Martin's Griffin, 2006), a practical Baedeker complete with restaurant tips. And the borough's inhabitants spring to life in the pages of Warren Lehrer and Judith Sloan's *Crossing the Boulevard* (New York: Norton, 2003) and in Joseph Berger's *The World in a City: Traveling the Globe Through the Neighborhoods of New York* (New York: Ballantine Books, 2007). A shrewd supplement to the many volumes on Gotham's politics is Sam Roberts, *Only in New York* (New York: St. Martin's Press, 2009).

For a closer look at ethnic politics in Queens, the invaluable in-depth analysis is Roger Sanjek, *The Future of Us All* (Ithaca, NY: Cornell University Press, 1998), which launched a series edited by Sanjek that includes the invaluable *Becoming American, Being India: An Immigrant Community in New York City* (Ithaca, NY: Cornell University Press, 2002) by Madhulika S. Khandewahl. See also the useful articles by Nancy Beth Jackson, "Living in Jackson Heights" in *The New York Times* (July 17, 2005), and by Sanjek, "Color-Full Before Color Blind: The Emergence of Multiracial Neighborhood Politics in Queens, New York City," *American Anthropologist* (2001: 762–772). New York City's

Office of Immigrant Affairs publishes a useful *Directory of Services for Immigrants* (2007), listing organizations serving newcomers.

Apropos "the Bystander Syndrome," the long-accepted version is detailed in *Thirty-Eight Witnesses* (Berkeley, CA: University of California Press, 1999), by A. M. Rosenthal, metropolitan editor of the *The New York Times* in 1964; a dissenting view is provided by the leading challenger, Joseph DeMay, accessible on his website. The impact of highways and Robert Moses on the borough is described by Robert A. Caro in "The City Shaper," *The New Yorker* (January 5, 1998). On libraries, we found useful data in Anne Barnard, "At Queens Libraries, a Passion for Japanese Comics Endures," *The New York Times* (May 16, 2010); and Ralph Blumenthal, "From Uzbekistan to a Desk at the Library," *The New York Times* (June 9, 2009). On LeFrak City, see "Troubled Lefrak City Turning the Corner," by Lee Daniels, *The New York Times* (March 4, 1984). On the 1991 fracas over a Korean-owned grocery, we found key quotations in James McKinley Jr., "Assault Charges Send Pickets to Queens Grocery" in *The New York Times* (February 10, 1991) and in Joseph Fried, "Brooklyn Clash Spurred Queens to End Boycott," also in the *Times* (February 12, 1991). The ambiguities in the trial of Mazoltuv Borukhova, charged with killing her Bohkaran husband, are clinically examined in Janet Malcolm's *Iphigenia in Forest Hills* (New Haven: Yale University Press, 2011). The quotations from Alexis de Tocqueville are from *Democracy in America* (New York: Harper & Row, 1966), translated by George Lawrence.

Regrettably, space does permit detailed listing of all the Queens newspapers whose many articles (and advertisements) gave us a surer sense of the borough's vibrant Pax Ethnica.

CHAPTER 6
HYPHENS: DIVERSITY AND ITS DISCONTENTS

The voluble Texas editor is cited in Richard Hofstadter, *The Paranoid Style of American Politics* (New York: Knopf, 1965). All details on Kennedy's Houston speech are from Theodore Sorensen, *Kennedy* (New York: Harper & Row, 1965) and his *Counselor: Life at the Edge of History* (New York: HarperCollins, 2008). On the early period of American democracy we have gratefully trolled (among many sources) Joseph J. Ellis's *Founding Fathers* (New York: Knopf, 2000) and *His Excellency: George Washington* (New York: Knopf, 2004), along with John Ferling, *Adams vs. Jefferson* (New York: Oxford University Press, 2004). The cunning anti-foreign monologue is from *Mr. Dooley Says* (New York: Scribners, 1910) by Finley Peter Dunne.

How Canada and slavery influenced the American Revolution has been explored by Theodore Draper, *A Struggle for Power* (New York: Times Books, 1996); by Hugh Thomas, *The Slave Trade* (New York: Simon & Schuster, 1997); by Larry E. Tise, *Proslavery: A History of Defense of Slavery in America, 1701–1840* (Athens, GA: University Press, 1987); by Adam Hochschild, *Bury the Chains: Prophets and Rebels in the Fight to Free the Empire's Slaves* (New York: Houghton Mifflin, 2005); and by Orlando Patterson, *Rituals of Blood: Consequence of Slavery in Two American Centuries* (Washington, DC: Counterpoint, 1998).

On Australia, a work notable for its fluent detail is *The Fatal Shore: The Epic of Australia's Founding* (New York: Knopf, 1987) by the Australian-born Robert Hughes, a silence-breaking account that helped inspire an entire corpus of similar studies. We also quote Jan Morris's *Sydney* (New York: Random House, 1992); David Marr and Marian Wilkinson's *Dark Victory* (Crows Nest, Australia: Allen & Unwin, 2009); a special report entitled "No Worries?" in *The Economist* (May 28, 2011) and an editorial in the same issue, "The Next Golden State." Key works for anyone researching diversity as seen Down Under include Andrew Marcus, James Jupp, and Peter McDonald, *Australia's Immigration Revolution* (Crows Nest, Australia: Allen & Unwin, 2009); and Geoffrey Brahm Levey, *Political Theory and Australian Multiculturalism* (New York/Oxford: Beghahn Books, 2008).

The literature on Canadian diversity is by now copious and contentious. We commend the following titles, which span the political spectrum: Will Kymlicka's *Multicultural Odysseys: Navigating the New International Politics of Diversity* (Oxford: University Press, 2007) *Multicultural Citizenship: A Liberal Theory of Minority Rights* (Oxford: University Press, 1995), and *Politics in the Vernacular: Nationalism, Multiculturalism, and Citizenship* (Oxford: University Press, 2001);

Charles Taylor, *Reconciling the Solitudes: Essays on Canadian Federalism and Nationalism* (Montreal: McGill-Queen's University Press, 1993); Blair Fraser, *The Search for Identity: Canada Postwar to the Present* (Garden City, NY: Doubleday, 1967); and Neil Bissoondath, *Selling Illusions: The Cult of Multiculturalism in Canada* (Toronto: Penguin Books, 1994).

Even more copious is the literature on immigration in the United States. For a survey of all immigrant cultures, see the quirky, fascinating *The Ethnic Almanac* (New York: Doubleday, 1981), by Stephanie Bernardo, a freelance writer of mixed Lebanese and Italian ancestry, who grew up in an Arabic enclave of Brooklyn, NY. Laura Fermi's *Illustrious Immigrants: The Intellectual Migration from Europe 1930–1941* (Chicago: University Press, 1971) is representative of many similar affirmative works (a genre pioneered in the 1930s by the Yugoslav-born Louis Adamic). The genre received its academic seal of approval with Oscar Handlin's *The Uprooted: The Epic Story of the Great Migrations That Made the American People* (Boston: Little, Brown, 1951). But for a very different view see *Diversity: The Invention of a Concept* (San Francisco: Encounter Books, 2003), by Peter Wood, a professor of anthropology at Boston University. Or, from a critical liberal vantage, see Arthur M. Schlesinger Jr., *The Disuniting of America: Reflections on a Multicultural Society* (Knoxville, TN: Whittle Communications: The Larger Agenda Series, 1991). On the current politics of immigration, an astute summary of pros and cons can be found in Michele Wucker, *Lockout: Why America Keeps Getting Immigration Wrong When Our Prosperity Depends on Getting It Right* (New York: PublicAffairs, 2006). In an innovative approach to a much-chewed-over topic, one can read, listen to, and view *The Authentic Voice: The Best Reporting on Race and Ethnicity* (New York: Columbia University Press, 2006), edited by Arlene Notoro Morgan, Alice Irene Pifer, and Keith Woods, an anthology of reportage with a DVD in its jacket. Finally, we perused and can commend the full text of the Canadian report, "Building the Future: A Time for Reconciliation," by the philosopher Charles Taylor and the sociologist Gérard Bouchard, accessible online at http://www.accommodements.qc.ca/documentation/rapports/rapport-final-integral-en.pdf.

EPILOGUE: THE FUTURE OF US ALL

For the works of Washington Irving, we have relied gratefully on three authoritative volumes in the Library of America, especially *History, Tales and Sketches* (1985), as well as on the handsome 1939 Heritage Press edition of *The Sketch Book.* The more complete Library of America text includes all his essays on the wars against Native Americans, as well as on the perils of chauvinism, and the risible "whim-whams" of a supposedly visiting Muslim. Strangely, a full-court search in major New York–area lending libraries failed to turn up a single copy of Irving's *Mahomet and His Successors* (two volumes, published in the 1850s). Nor could we locate a copy of this pioneering biography in the celebrated "twelve miles of bookshelves" in The Strand, New York's principal used bookseller. Finally, we came upon a stray paperback of volume one, in the bookshop at Sunnyside, the author's stylistically eclectic home near Tarrytown, New York. Published in Britain by Wordsworth Classics of World Literature, *Mohammed* (2007), is edited with an introduction by Hugh Griffith, and it appears to be the only currently in-print edition of the first volume of the first biography of the Prophet written by an American, *pace* the War on Terror. We benefited from Amy Chua's groundbreaking books, *World on Fire* (New York: Doubleday, 2003) and *Day of Empire* (New York: Doubleday, 2007). On Irving's life, we drew gratefully on two recent and lively biographies: Brian Jay Jones, *Washington Irving: An American Original* (New York: Arcade Publishers, 2008); and Andrew Burstein, *The Original Knickerbocker: The Life of Washington Irving* (New York: Basic Books, 2007). All other sources are indicated in the text.

INDEX

Karl E. Meyer, served on *The New York Times* editorial board and previously was a foreign correspondent and editorial writer on *The Washington Post*. Meyer has been the McGraw Professor of Writing at Princeton, and has taught at Yale and Tuft's Fletcher School. He is author of a dozen books and is emeritus editor of the *World Policy Journal*. He holds a PhD in politics from Princeton University.

Shareen Blair Brysac was a prize-winning documentary producer for CBS News and is author of *Resisting Hitler: Mildred Fish Harnack and the Red Orchestra*. She is the co-author, with her husband, Karl Meyer, of *Tournament of Shadows and Kingmakers: The Invention of the Modern Middle East*.

Meyer and Brysac live in New York City and Weston, Connecticut.

PublicAffairs is a publishing house founded in 1997. It is a tribute to the standards, values, and flair of three persons who have served as mentors to countless reporters, writers, editors, and book people of all kinds, including me.

I. F. STONE, proprietor of *I. F. Stone's Weekly*, combined a commitment to the First Amendment with entrepreneurial zeal and reporting skill and became one of the great independent journalists in American history. At the age of eighty, Izzy published *The Trial of Socrates*, which was a national bestseller. He wrote the book after he taught himself ancient Greek.

BENJAMIN C. BRADLEE was for nearly thirty years the charismatic editorial leader of *The Washington Post*. It was Ben who gave the *Post* the range and courage to pursue such historic issues as Watergate. He supported his reporters with a tenacity that made them fearless and it is no accident that so many became authors of influential, best-selling books.

ROBERT L. BERNSTEIN, the chief executive of Random House for more than a quarter century, guided one of the nation's premier publishing houses. Bob was personally responsible for many books of political dissent and argument that challenged tyranny around the globe. He is also the founder and longtime chair of Human Rights Watch, one of the most respected human rights organizations in the world.

·   ·   ·

For fifty years, the banner of Public Affairs Press was carried by its owner Morris B. Schnapper, who published Gandhi, Nasser, Toynbee, Truman, and about 1,500 other authors. In 1983, Schnapper was described by *The Washington Post* as "a redoubtable gadfly." His legacy will endure in the books to come.

Peter Osnos, *Founder and Editor-at-Large*